India's Global Powerhouses

Also by the Author

Nirmalya Kumar,
*Marketing as Strategy: Understanding the CEO's
Agenda for Driving Growth and Innovation*
(Boston: Harvard Business School Press, 2004).

Nirmalya Kumar,
Global Marketing
(New Delhi, India: BusinessWorld, 2006).

Nirmalya Kumar and Jan-Benedict E. M. Steenkamp,
Private Label Strategy: How to Meet the Store Brand Challenge
(Boston: Harvard Business School Press, 2007).

James C. Anderson, Nirmalya Kumar,
and James A. Narus,
*Value Merchants: Demonstrating and Documenting
Superior Value in Business Markets*
(Boston: Harvard Business School Press, 2007).

India's Global Powerhouses

How They Are Taking On the World

Nirmalya Kumar

with

Pradipta K. Mohapatra
Suj Chandrasekhar

HARVARD BUSINESS PRESS

Boston, Massachusetts

ISBN-13 (U.S. edition) 978-1-4221-4762-7
ISBN-13 (India edition) 978-1-4221-4078-9

Library of Congress Cataloging-in-Publication Data

Kumar, Nirmalya.
   India's global powerhouses : how they are taking on the world / Nirmalya
Kumar; with Pradipta K. Mohapatra, Suj Chandrasekhar.
      p. cm.
   Includes bibliographical references and index.
   ISBN 978-1-4221-4762-7 (hbk. : alk. paper)
      1. International business enterprises—India.   I. Mohapatra, Pradipta K.
II. Chandrasekhar, Suj.   III. Title.
   HD2899.K86 2009
   338.8'8954—dc22
                                                          2008041934

To Maya, my Made in India Multinational.
Being fluent in English, French, and Swedish is
wonderful, but do not forget Hindi, my dear.

To all my Indian friends and relatives—
too numerous to list, with affection.
—Nirmalya Kumar

To R. P. Goenka,
my lifetime of indebtedness, which I cannot pay back.
—Pradipta K. Mohapatra

To my late mother, my first and best teacher.
—Suj Chandrasekhar

CONTENTS

PREFACE

This book is the outcome of a very personal journey that began twenty-five years ago. Growing up in India during the "License Raj" as the son of two professional managers, like many ambitious young Indian students at that time, I dreamed of going to the United States. In 1983, I got the opportunity to pursue an MBA at the University of Illinois at Chicago. This was followed by a PhD in marketing at Northwestern University.

In the United States, I had the powerful immigrant experience of boundless opportunities that concluded in adopting U.S. citizenship. The United States has a remarkable integration process, the most salient aspect of which is the desire it creates in its new immigrants to become "American." My first decade in the States was all about deep cultural conflict, trying to escape my "Indianness" to become "American." At some stage, realizing it was an impossible transformation given my obvious Indian looks and observing the substantial changes taking place in India in the early 1990s, I felt a tug back to India. But India was not yet a place for anyone with an ambition to be a world-class business academic. As a compromise, twelve years after moving to the United States, I left for IMD—the International Institute for Management Development—on the shores of Lake Geneva. IMD provided a world-class business school and Switzerland, a relatively short flight to India. It was a central location between the American academic research community and my country of birth.

In 1996, I made my first business trip to India to write a case on a new supermarket chain called Foodworld that was being set up by the RPG Group. Pradipta Mohapatra was then the CEO of this exciting venture to become India's first modern supermarket chain. The case development led to a wonderful friendship, and Pradipta has helped me learn about Indian business. Pradipta is one of those rare managers who combine analytical with emotional intelligence and have the ability to think about business in a conceptual manner. He was also instrumental in helping obtain my first Indian board of directors appointment, with Zensar Technologies, in 2001. At that time I decided to move to London, from where it seemed there was a direct flight to India every half hour.

Since then, I have eagerly looked forward each year to eight or so trips to India for board meetings, consulting opportunities, and conference presentations. As a result, I have had the privilege of interacting with many executives, both Indian and non-Indian, who have educated me on what is happening in the country. In early 2006, I was invited to run a workshop for Essel Propack, a company unknown to me. Essel Propack, led by Ashok Goel, turned out to be a world leader in laminated tubes and a supplier to companies like Procter & Gamble and Unilever. I was intrigued as to whether there were other Indian companies like Essel. It was then and there that the idea of a book on India's global companies was born.

The stories of how Indian companies have gone global are presented in this book. The research for the book has convinced me that we are currently observing only the tip of the iceberg. Yes, there will be challenges along the way, but combined with the rise of China, there is little doubt that the advice to any youth in the coming years should be "Go East!" Most of the billionaires and great multinational companies are going to be made there over the next decades. A remarkable transformation in the location of opportunity has taken place in one generation since my youth. The world is back to where it was five hundred years ago, when, inspired by Marco Polo, explorers such as Christopher Columbus, Ferdinand Magellan, and Vasco da Gama left Europe seeking fortunes in the East. And yes, I have peacefully accepted that while I may aspire to be a global citizen, I will always be an Indian—or more specifically, a Calcuttan! It is my pleasure, through this book, to return home after twenty-five years.

ACKNOWLEDGMENTS

Our first and deepest gratitude is to all the managers who took time from their busy schedules to meet with us. Without their openness, insights, and, most important, their success in leading the transformation of Indian companies to global powerhouses, this book would not have been possible. Therefore, we start by thanking those who shared their stories with us:

Adi Godrej, Godrej Group

Aditya Mittal, ArcelorMittal

Ajay Piramal, Piramal Enterprises

Alan Rosling, Tata Sons

Anand Mahindra, Mahindra & Mahindra

Ashok Goel, Essel Propack

Azim Premji, Wipro

Baba N. Kalyani, Bharat Forge

Debu Bhattacharya, Hindalco

Dilip Kapur, Hidesign

Dilip G. Piramal, VIP Industries

Ganesh Natarajan, NASSCOM and Zensar

Harsh Goenka, RPG Group

Harsh Mariwala, Marico

J. J. Irani, Tata Sons

Kumar Mangalam Birla, Aditya Birla Group

N. Chandrasekaran, Tata Consultancy Services

Nandan Nilekani, Infosys Technologies

P. V. Kannan, 24/7

R. Chandrasekhar, Essel Propack

R. Gopalakrishnan, Tata Sons

R. K. Krishna Kumar, Tata Sons

Rajesh Hukku, i-flex solutions

Ravi Kant, Tata Motors

S. Mahalingam, Tata Consultancy Services

S. Padmanabhan, Tata Consultancy Services

S. Ramadorai, Tata Consultancy Services

Santrupt Misra, Aditya Birla Group

Satish Reddy, Dr. Reddy's Laboratories

Somesh Sharma, Piramal Enterprises

Sudhir Jatia, VIP Industries

Sundip Nandy, Wipro

Suresh Menon, VIP Industries

Tulsi Tanti, Suzlon

The research costs for this book were supported by the Aditya Birla India Centre at the London Business School. The school and I are grateful to Kumar Mangalam Birla for funding the center in his father's memory. Aditya Birla was a true pioneer, and it is only appropriate that this book is funded by a center in his name. Frustrated by the constraints on growth that the Indian government placed on business, Aditya Birla looked overseas for opportunities and was the first modern Indian businessman to go global.

One of the primary triggers for my India trips has been attending quarterly board meetings. Over the years, it has been a privilege to serve on the boards of ACC (Narotam Sekhsaria), Ambuja Cements (Suresh Neotia), Bata India (Thomas Bata), BP Ergo (Gita Piramal), and Zensar Technologies (Harsh Goenka). I sat on the ACC and Ambuja boards with my Holcim colleagues, Markus Akermann and Paul Hugentobler. Besides being one of the great entrepreneurial managers I have met, Paul has been a big supporter and provided me with many opportunities to observe Asian business at close quarters. I am most indebted to Holcim, and especially to Paul.

The Indian press is to be admired for its independence and energy. For some reason, they have also chosen to be very kind to me. Some of the journalists who have helped me keep in touch with India via e-mail are Indrajit Gupta (*Forbes India*), Gita Piramal (*Smart*

Manager), Neelima Mahajan (*Forbes India*), D. Murali (*Hindu Business Line*), Jagat Guru (*Hindu Business Line*), Sudipto Patra (*Business World*), Amit Sharma (*Times of India*), Inddrani (Rediff. com), Vivek Kaul (*DNA*), Irshad Daftari (*Economic Times*), Amit Bapna (*USP Age*), Vikas Kumar (*Economic Times*), and Alokananda Chakraborty (*Financial Express*). I am sorry if I have omitted anyone.

I was introduced to Suj Chandrasekhar by Philip Kotler. She and her team at Strategic Insights have played a valuable role in this book; they compiled briefing papers and much of the background research on the companies. They were also responsible for transcribing the audiotapes and drawing the salient lessons from each. Thank you, Suj.

Finally, I would like to thank three very special ladies for their incredible efforts on this book. Without any one of them, it would have been hard to complete this project. Donna Everett had the responsibility of taking the audiotapes of the interviews and my sloppy notes and turning them into first drafts. Without her efforts, it would have taken twice as long to complete this book. This was my fourth collaboration with Kirsten Sandberg, executive editor at Harvard Business Press, but I doubt she finds me any easier with time. We fight for our respective ideas, but hopefully our debates result in better books. Above all, thanks to Suseela Yesudian, the associate director of the Aditya Birla India Centre, who had the overall responsibility for managing the book project. She wrote several sections, rewrote many others, and helped conduct the interviews. With her charm, sensitivity, and intelligence, she is the only person who comes close to being able to manage me, and keep in the air all the balls that I keep throwing her way. Without her, it would be impossible for me to function effectively.

—Nirmalya Kumar,
London, November 2008

The Emergence of India's Global Powerhouses

IN MARCH 2007 I was checking into the Mena House Oberoi Hotel on the outskirts of Cairo, a palatial hotel that has enchanted guests since 1869 and played host to kings and emperors, heads of state and celebrities. In 1943, the Cairo Conference between President Franklin Roosevelt, General Chiang Kai-shek, and Winston Churchill was held here to bring the Second World War to a close with a plan to defeat the Axis forces. While I was settling comfortably into a room overlooking the Great Pyramids, hotel guests across the world were similarly checking into numerous prestigious properties like the Ritz-Carlton in Boston (renamed Taj Boston), Taj Crowne Plaza in London, and Oberoi Bali in Indonesia. All of these hotels are managed by India's two leading hotel groups, popularly known as Taj and Oberoi. In fact, four of the ten highest-ranked hotels in the world as voted by *Conde Nast* readers belong to the Oberoi Group, and it was also rated as the best hotel chain outside the United States. These two Indian hotel groups are evidence of the relatively new phenomenon of Indian companies spreading their wings across the world.

This book is focused on the emergence of India's global powerhouses. Like their German, Japanese, and Korean predecessors, Indian companies that go global will transform the world of business. Perhaps even more so, because Indian companies can leverage a domestic population ten to twenty times larger than in any of those countries for profits and revenues to support their globalization. Who are these Indian global powerhouses? How do they compete?

What should companies outside India know about them? These are the questions this book addresses, and all of us should become more familiar with the answers. Corporations in the developed world will increasingly see India and its companies emerge as acquirers of their assets, as global competitors using India's scale and cost advantages, as partners for enhancing the competitiveness of their global value chain, as a high-growth market, and as a source of new energy and dreams for the world economy.

India Inc. on Global Acquisition Spree

As late as 2001, Indian outward investment was less than $1 billion. Instead, India, like all developing countries, was actively courting foreign investment into the country. By 2006, India had reached the tipping point. For the first time, Indian outward investment of $10 billion had outstripped foreign investment into India. The spending spree continued unabated in 2007. Indian companies arranged or concluded $21 billion in forty foreign investment deals in January and February of 2007 alone.[1] Moreover, Indian foreign investment in the financial year closing March 31, 2007, exceeded the cumulative total foreign investment by Indian companies in the fifty-eight years between its independence in 1947 and 2005! In 2007, the Indian corporate sector was involved in $60 billion of M&A, up 109 percent over 2006.[2] Only the liquidity crisis of 2008 slowed down the pace.

The quest by Indian companies to be globally competitive is the driving force behind this accelerating foreign outward investment. With the opening of the economy and the easy entry of foreign players into the Indian market, domestic Indian companies realize that they must scale up to remain competitive. This is especially true for those companies that operate in what are global industries, like aluminum, automobiles, and steel. These are some of the recent large deals:

- Tata Steel's $12 billion acquisition of Anglo-Dutch steelmaker Corus in October 2006 catapulted it to becoming the world's fifth-biggest steel producer.

- Hindalco's February 2007 all-cash $6 billion purchase of Canadian Novelis made it the world's largest aluminum rolling company.

- Tata Motors drove away with Jaguar and Land Rover after paying Ford Motor Company $2.3 billion in 2008.

As one can see, these large deals are relatively recent. It was unimaginable even a decade ago that any Indian company could pull off a multibillion-dollar acquisition of a company in the developed world or buy a prestigious luxury brand such as Jaguar. And some of these deals, like Tata's acquisition of Corus, are particularly audacious. At the time of the merger, Tata Steel was the fifty-sixth-largest steel manufacturer in the world, while Corus was the ninth! How have Indian companies suddenly been able to pull off such large global deals?

The acquisitions reflect the rapid growth of the Indian economy since 1991. When combined with the restructuring efficiencies wrought by Indian companies since that time, this growth has resulted in average profit margins of around 10 percent, more than twice the global average. Indian firms have been minting money. For example, Reliance Industries, then India's largest company, doubled its profits between 2004 and 2006.

Growth and profits have left the Indian corporate balance sheets in robust health, with the consequent high market capitalization. By one estimate, 60 percent of India's two hundred leading companies are looking to spend their newfound wealth on foreign acquisitions and investments.[3] As an example, consider Vedanta, one of India's biggest producers of zinc, copper, and aluminum. Vedanta is the lowest-cost zinc producer in the world. Besides India, it has operations in Zambia and Australia. In 2007, Vedanta had revenues of $6.5 billion, an increase of 76 percent over the previous year, and nearly half of it was profit.[4] In the biggest overseas sale of shares by an Indian company at that time, 20 percent of the group's flagship company, Sterlite Industries, was floated in 2007 on the New York Stock Exchange for over $2 billion.

Besides enabling the high-profile deals, the burgeoning profits are encouraging many smaller Indian firms to seek foreign acquisitions.

For example, Bennett Coleman bought Virgin Radio Holdings for $100 million in 2008. At a time when Western media companies are struggling with falling advertising revenues and readership, Indian media companies are flush with cash because of double-digit growth rates. The relatively unknown Rain Group sprang a surprise by buying U.S.-based CII Carbon for $595 million in 2007. The acquisition helped them become the world's leading maker of calcined petroleum coke (CPC). CPC is a critical raw material, used by every aluminum smelter and manufacturer of titanium dioxide in the world.

The result is that Indians have already emerged as second only to Americans as foreign employers of Britons![5] Tata alone employs nearly fifty thousand people in the United Kingdom. Some of these purchases may have looked too expensive to outside observers. A potential acquisition target firm in the developed market, burdened with high operating costs and focused on a declining domestic market, may not seem attractive to a Western or Japanese suitor. But to an Indian company, the target can appear very different as it may have brands, customers, or technology that an aspiring Indian multinational covets. The current high operating costs of the target company do not deter Indian firms, because their vision is different. For example, VIP Industries, the second-largest luggage manufacturer in the world, dismantled the entire production lines of Carlton in the United Kingdom and rebuilt them back home in India.

Suzlon, India's leading wind energy firm, waged a takeover battle for REpower that perhaps best illustrates the power of Indian entrepreneurial models. To acquire REpower, a leading wind turbine manufacturer, Suzlon's founder, Tulsi Tanti, battled Areva, a firm controlled by the French government with annual revenues in excess of $13 billion. Despite owning 30 percent of REpower, Areva conceded defeat, allowing Suzlon to lock up 86 percent of the firm for $1.7 billion. Because of its cost structure, Suzlon was confident that it could acquire a company with a 4 percent margin and turn it into a company with a 20 percent margin, while Areva was not. Consequently, Tanti, when reflecting on his success, observed: "So I knew from the beginning: Whatever they offered, I could pay much more."[6]

The Indian global powerhouses profiled in this book have been large domestic players in the Indian market for some time. However, until recently they never had the confidence or the ability to be on the world stage. Forged in India's harsh environment, these companies are now increasingly seeking to secure the best of both worlds— access to the lucrative high-margin markets of the developed world by owning companies in Europe and the United States, while maintaining their low-cost bases in India.[7] Today, the remarkable thing that strikes one about Indian companies is that they have massive aspirations to be global companies, and they are extraordinarily confident, perhaps even over confident, about acquiring foreign firms and integrating them with their companies in India.

Indian firms have brought three unique traits to succeed in their acquisition spree. First, many Indian companies are part of a group of companies like Aditya Birla or Tata groups. They can leverage group assets to complete deals that would be difficult for any individual company. One or more of the group companies can lend or take an equity position in the company that is attempting to make the acquisition, or the entire group's assets can be offered to raise debt funds.

Second, Indian companies have historically had very high debt-equity ratios. This means Indian entrepreneurs can live with debt levels that many Western companies would find uncomfortable. Whether this is wise under the new debt regime is open to debate. Previously, Indian firms borrowed from nationalized banks whose mandate was to support India's economic development. Thus they were unlikely to be aggressive with respect to interest rates, debt collection, or valuation and revaluation of collateral. Now Indian firms are tapping global financial markets to fund their deals, and these lenders are going to be more exacting. High leverage increases risk. Nevertheless, the historical easy attitude toward debt has facilitated these acquisitions.

Finally, Indian firms, despite being public, are often controlled by powerful families and individual promoters, who have considerable management leeway. Such a promoter can swiftly decide to make an acquisition, knowing that the stock price may dip in the short run. This would be impossible for more conservatively managed companies run by professionals, whose compensation is significantly tied to increases in stock price. Furthermore, Indian promoters have considerable flexibility in negotiating postmerger autonomy issues with the managers of the acquired firms. As a result, Steven Spielberg and Dreamworks inked a deal with the Reliance Anil Dhirubhai Ambani Group (Reliance ADA Group) instead of with Hollywood because Western corporate investors are demanding faster payback schedules, better guarantees, and even a say in how the movie is made.

While it is only to be expected that some of these Indian acquirers will stumble because they have either paid too much or taken on large amounts of debt, the overall trend remains unaffected. For the developed world and its companies, the era of India as a major overseas investor is here. The question is not how to stop this trend but how to deal with it. There was a time when Westerners assumed that an Indian in the head office of a multinational or Western company was either an accountant or a computer nerd. Nowadays that person is just as likely to be the boss.

India Inc.'s Scale and Cost Advantage

Operating out of India gives Indian companies some advantages. As the economy has grown and many more Indians have moved into the middle class, companies with leading positions in the Indian market have acquired global scale. When combined with their relatively low costs, it becomes natural for them to seek further growth in international markets. Several Indian firms have leveraged their leadership in the domestic market to build world-leading positions:

- Essel Propack, the world leader in laminated tubes with a 30 percent market share, includes Procter & Gamble, Unilever, and Colgate-Palmolive among its global customers.

- Tata Tea, the second-largest branded tea company in the world, owns brands like Tetley.

- Mahindra & Mahindra is among the top three tractor manufacturers in the world with plants in Australia, China, and the United States.

- Reliance Industries Limited (RIL), a dominant Indian company, is the world's largest producer of polyester fiber and yarn; the fourth-largest producer of paraxylene (PX) and purified terepthalic acid (PTA); the sixth-largest producer of monoethylene glycol (MEG); and the seventh-largest producer of polypropylene (PP).

- Moser Baer is the world's second-largest producer of DVDs, after CMC of Taiwan, and exports 85 percent of its output.

Several other leading Indian companies are knocking at the door of globalization. Larsen & Toubro, India's leading heavy engineering firm, is building ten coal gasification plants in China. Bajaj Auto and TVS, two of India's leading manufacturers of two-wheelers (scooters and motorcycles), are exporters and aggressively seeking international growth. TVS has invested $50 million in setting up manufacturing plants in Indonesia, while Bajaj Auto, squeezed by Japanese competition in the domestic Indian market, is now taking on Japanese and Chinese rivals in markets like Indonesia, Egypt, and Brazil.

By operating in a demanding price environment, Indian companies are forced to innovate and build low-cost business models if they are going to reach the country's masses and still be profitable. Carlos Ghosn, CEO of Renault, has talked admiringly of India's frugal engineering, where costs are controlled more instinctively than in Europe.[8] The Indian mobile phone industry is a classic example of this. Arun Sarin, CEO of Vodafone worldwide, observed that in Europe, wireless operators average monthly revenues of €40 and make a 40 percent margin. In contrast, in India, mobile operators average revenues of only €8, yet manage to generate a 50 percent margin. That is why Sarin ordered his top global executives to fly to India and learn the secrets of the low-cost business model prevailing there.

The largest of India's mobile operators is Bharti Airtel, with 64 million-plus customers, which puts it among the top ten leading wireless companies in the world. The Reliance ADA Group, with telecom, financial services, and energy interests, reaches over 100 million customers in India. There is little doubt that companies like Bajaj, Bharti Airtel, Larsen & Toubro, Reliance, and TVS will be different—they

China and India

As expected, the competition between China and India has received considerable recent press attention. The objective data clearly demonstrates that China is ahead of India on most indicators. China leads India on share of world exports of goods (8% versus 3%) and services (3.1% versus 2.7%), current account surplus ($380 versus –$23 billion), foreign exchange reserves ($1,455 versus $265 billion), foreign direct investment inflows ($96 versus $19 billion), foreign direct investment outflow ($26 versus $13 billion), gross domestic product in purchasing power parity ($7,642 versus $3,389 billion), and GDP per head ($1,470 versus $640).[a] Beyond the numbers, China clearly has a far superior infrastructure, more developed manufacturing capabilities (13% of the global manufacturing output versus 2%), and better execution capabilities. We can't deny this reality or the fact that Chinese companies are going to be very successful. However, India has four relative advantages that are often overlooked when it comes to building multinational firms.

1.   The linguistic and religious diversity in India forces Indian firms to adopt the global language of business, English, in their operations. In addition, Indian firms are relatively more prepared to meet the challenges of a diverse workforce that running a multinational company entails.

2.   Despite China's dominance in manufacturing, India can compete in specific areas. As James McGill, head of Asia-Pacific for Eaton, a U.S. maker of automotive parts, remarked, there is "a lot of potential" in India for "low-volume" manufacturing, where design, engineering, and the ability to react quickly to specification

will be more global in five years. As a result, the list of companies that have leveraged India's scale and cost advantage to build leading global positions will only grow.

There is no reason why leading multinationals should emanate only from Europe, the United States, and Japan. As recently as 1996, none of the firms on the list of the five hundred largest global companies by market capitalization were from India or China. On the 2008 changes are critical.[b] Some global customers also like to have India as a second supplier in case there are political or economic problems in China. It reduces risk for global firms to locate some part of the supply chain in India, rather than have all manufacturing assets in China.

3. It is often remarked that "demographics is destiny" and, arguably, India has more favorable future demographics. In 2050, India will have 1.6 billion people, compared to 1.4 billion in China.[c] But because of China's one-child policy, China will have a much older population, and its workforce will look more like those in developed nations today, where fewer and fewer workers are supporting a relatively large retired population. China's overall working population will shrink after 2015.

4. India's greater democratic traditions, religious freedom, facility with the English language, privately owned firms, and more Western outlook mean that a majority of people in the European Union and the United States view India primarily as an "opportunity," whereas China is seen mostly as a "threat."[d] This makes it easier for Indian companies to both acquire firms and set up operations in Western developed nations.

a. From *Economist, Pocket World in Figures 2007: A Concise Edition* (London: Profile Books, 2006); and Martin Wolf, "A Waking Giant Tugging Hard at Its Chains," *Financial Times,* January 25, 2008, India and Globalisation special insert, 3.

b. Peter Marsh, "The Next Workshop of the World," *Financial Times,* July 3, 2007, 13.

c. *Economist, Pocket World in Figures 2007*.

d. Andrew Bounds, "Free Trade in Free Fall in Sceptical US," *Financial Times,* December 5, 2007, 7.

list, however, there were thirteen Indian and twenty-five Chinese companies.[9] In the emerging new global business order, companies from the old world of India and China will increasingly take center stage. While, relative to China, India may have some advantages when it comes to multinational firms (see "China and India"), there is little doubt that the old world is now the new world.

Partnering with India to Enhance Competitiveness

Much of recent world attention on India has focused on the *lower cost, high quality*, and *large quantity* of the skilled Indian workforce. Through the outsourcing lens, India is seen as the world's back office. The debate has unfortunately been about outsourcing jobs from the developed world to India, and has ignored how the Indian workforce is enhancing the competitiveness of global multinational companies.[10] As birth rates decline and population ages in the developed world, India's workforce becomes the world's workforce. No wonder that multinational companies are embracing India as integral to their global value chain.

The Indian outsourcing firms, especially the top three, Infosys, Tata Consultancy Services (TCS), and Wipro Technologies, have been responsible for unleashing the ambition of Indian companies to become both world class and global. Together, their annual revenues exceed $12 billion, and their average operating margins are 20 percent. Compare that to operating margins at IBM, which are half that figure. And IBM's margins are a bit higher than the average for the six largest U.S. technology companies, which include EDS and Accenture. No wonder that the market capitalization for Infosys, TCS, and Wipro at $50 billion is higher than Accenture, Cognizant, and EDS combined.[11]

Observing the success of Indian outsourcing firms in exploiting the skilled worker advantage, foreign companies have rushed to make India a critical part of their own value chain. The technology companies have been rather aggressive on this front in the hope of matching the operating margins and cost structures that Indian outsourcing firms enjoy. Consequently, Accenture India's facility, with fifty thousand employees, is now bigger than Accenture USA. In 2008, Accenture brought its entire board of directors to India to showcase the country's strengths.

IBM has more than fifty thousand employees in India, up from three thousand employees in 2002. In 2006, IBM held its first analyst meeting outside the United States in Bangalore. Sam Palmisano, then the CEO, showcased IBM's long-term commitment to India with plans to invest $6 billion over the next three years and have a hundred thousand Indian employees. When Hurricane Katrina ravaged the U.S. Gulf Coast in 2005, among the first outsiders to have an inkling of the extent of the disaster were a group of computer engineers in IBM, Bangalore. While managing computer networks for clients in the United States from the Indian city, they were assailed by thousands of alerts on the giant screens in their "command center" as the storm wiped out systems half a world away.[12]

It is important to see India's evolving competitive advantage as more than simply low costs and a steady supply of call center employees. As costs in India are going up, both Indian companies and Western multinationals are increasingly using India as a destination for high value and technologically sophisticated projects. HCL Technologies, the Indian outsourcing company specializing in research and development, is signing up big aerospace customers such as Boeing and EADS.[13] The company was heavily involved in the development of Boeing's 787 Dreamliner by designing two mission-critical systems—one to avert airborne collisions, the other to land in zero visibility. Ian Q. R. Thomas, president of Boeing India, was quoted as saying, "In theory, we could place the work anywhere. We're here because we found a level of sophistication."[14]

Nicholas Piramal India Limited (NPIL) in 2007 entered into a drug development deal with U.S. pharmaceutical major Eli Lilly, whereby NPIL would conduct clinical trials globally and also, in certain regions, market a select group of Lilly's preclinical drugs. Eli Lilly was impressed by the speed, quality, and costs at which clinical trials could be conducted in India.

Almost every *Fortune* 500 company is setting up or considering setting up operations in India that will be integral to its global value chain. Google, in 2004, chose Bangalore as the site of its first R&D center outside the United States. Google Finance is the first project born at that location. It started as a "20 percent project," a corporate attempt to tap employees' innovation potential by asking them to devote a portion of their time to a personal project. Google joins many other companies—including Flextronics, General Electric, General Motors, Hewlett-Packard, Sun Microsystems, Texas Instruments, and Yahoo!—that have engineers based in India working on important projects. Offshoring to India by multinational companies now rivals outsourcing to Indian companies.

The rush by multinationals to set up Indian operations and the rapid growth of Indian outsourcing companies has resulted in a war for talent. Only in India would T. V. Mohandas Pai, Infosys Technologies' chief financial officer for twelve years and member of the Infosys board of directors, make a career change to take over as head of human resources at Infosys! But the company hires twenty-five thousand people a year, and its growth is dependent on attracting and retaining the best talent.

Such competition requires a fundamental shift in the mind-set of multinational companies about the role of Indian talent.[15] They need to confront the question, Why should an Indian join a multinational instead of an Indian firm? In many multinationals, the local Indian operations are viewed as peripheral rather than central to the parent company's global agenda. As a result, knowledge, capabilities, and people flow from the headquarters in the United States, Europe, or Japan to India, but rarely vice versa. There is no career track for the Indian employee in the company's global operations. In contrast, at Infosys, TCS, and Wipro, the potential recruit can become the CEO of the firm and lead global operations. Unfortunately, only a handful of multinationals—Citibank, McKinsey, and Unilever being notable exceptions—have really grappled with the dilemma of remaking the talent management processes in face of the changing global workforce realities.[16]

The other war is for customers and business models. Indian outsourcing companies started from a low-cost basis, but are slowly moving up the food chain to more sophisticated projects. Companies like Infosys, TCS, and Wipro are starting to challenge the Western multinationals, such as Accenture, EDS, and IBM, head-on for the high-value global consulting deals. These Western IT consultancies are starting from a high-cost structure and are using their Indian back-office operations to move to lower-cost structures, while Indian outsourcing companies are making small acquisitions in the West to add to their front-end consulting capabilities.

Indian companies are also investing heavily in upgrading the capabilities of their people. Infosys spends $65 of every $1,000 in revenue on training, while IBM, in contrast, spends only $6.56.[17] Currently, the Western competitors are much larger, with stronger brands, and more upmarket than their Indian counterparts. But Nandan Nilekani, executive chairman of Infosys, says: "It's not about size, it's about the future, it's about who's got momentum, it's about new business models replacing old business models. Between 2000 and 2007, we grew at a compounded rate of almost 40 percent while the legacy players were growing in single digits."

The most frequently heard analogy in India is that of the Japanese automakers. These Japanese upstarts began in the United States by supplying lower-cost models, but retained a continuing cost and quality advantage as they moved into the luxury car segment. This is the aspiration of India's global powerhouses. They are not content to play in the low-cost segment forever. It is not where they see their future. It would be foolhardy to repeat the mistake that U.S. automakers made with respect to underestimating their Japanese competitors. Companies from the developed world would be wise to heed *Business Week*'s observation in its story on global giants from emerging markets: "They're hungry—and want your customers. They're changing the global game. Be afraid, be very afraid."[18]

India's Growth Drives Global Corporations

The *Economist* in 2008 argued that "India counts as one of liberalization's greatest success stories . . . without India's strength, the world economy would have had far less to boast about."[19] India as one of the fastest-growing economies seems like a paradox in a country where everything, especially the traffic, courts, and bureaucratic machinery, seems to move at a snail's pace. Regardless, with its neighbor China, India is where future growth and profits for multinational companies lie. Yet many global companies have been slow to respond to this shift in the locus of world opportunity to Asia. An analysis of several large Western firms found that, although an estimated 34 percent of the potential market for their goods is in Asia, the region accounted for only 14 percent of sales, 7 percent of employees, 5 percent of assets, 3 percent of research and development, and 2 percent of their top two hundred people.[20] Moreover, it found that these disparities were growing larger.

Numerous press stories document the importance of India to the success and growth of multinational companies:

- India has overtaken Japan as the largest Asia-Pacific market by sales for Turner Broadcasting, part of the Time Warner group, as television industry sales in India grew by 18 percent and movies 14 percent.[21] Given that the growth of the U.S. television industry is 2 percent, it is no wonder that companies like Walt Disney, NBC Universal, Viacom, and Sony are investing $1.5 billion in India.

- Walter Doran, president of Raytheon Asia and a former navy commander of the U.S. Pacific Fleet, predicts that India may be "one of our largest—if not our largest—growth partner over the next decade or so."[22] The Indian government is investing heavily in upgrading its armed forces to reflect India's emerging power.

- The M&A activity of Indian companies and private wealth creation make India an attractive market for financial services. India has become the biggest revenue contributor in Asia for Merrill Lynch and the second most important market in the world for Standard Chartered Bank. The Indian head of Citi is probably thanking his stars that he transferred from the U.S. operations to India five years ago. While the head office faces large losses, Citi's Indian operations were up 28 percent in 2007, with profits up 39 percent.[23] No wonder the 2007 joke on Wall Street was "Shanghai, Dubai, Mumbai, or goodbye!"

- As part of its $1 billion investment in India, Cisco in 2007 mandated that 20 percent of its top global talent must be located in India over the next few years. About twenty executives had already been relocated to Bangalore from the United States, Europe, and Singapore, including Wim Elfrink, Cisco's chief globalization officer, formerly based at Cisco's headquarters in San Jose, California.[24]

Luxury goods companies are acutely aware how rapidly relative wealth has migrated from the developed world to China, India, the Middle East, and Russia. Their change in focus has left U.S. luxury goods retailers frustrated. At a 2008 conference of luxury goods in Milan, Burt Tansky, chairman and CEO of Neiman Marcus, warned luxury goods manufacturers not to neglect U.S. consumer trends as they focus on emerging markets.[25]

A dramatic turnaround is taking place in multinational companies. I attend more than a few of the annual top management meetings of multinational companies, where typically all the country heads are present. Until a few years ago, the results from U.S. and European markets took center stage, with emerging markets barely mentioned. Today these meetings seem to be dominated by the potential growth from Asia, especially China and India. It is amazing for one who has been watching these meetings for more than a decade to see the executives running operations in North America, Europe, and Japan for European multinationals sitting silently and taking a back seat during these proceedings.

Consider the realities of the mobile phone business. With 260 million mobile phone subscribers in March 2008, India is second only to China, and ahead of the United States. In addition, 10 million new subscribers are being added each month in India. Arun Sarin, CEO of Vodafone, observed: "Just keep remembering that 75 percent of all incremental customers, revenues, and profits are coming from emerging markets—everybody is racing and rushing toward that."[26] He supervised Vodafone's exit from Japan in 2006. In 2007, he entered India by paying $11 billion for a controlling stake in Hutchinson Essar, India's fourth-largest mobile operator. Reflecting in 2008 on his tenure at Vodafone after announcing plans to step down, Arun Sarin remarked: "Being short Japan, and long India, was probably the best thing we did."[27]

New Dreams and Energy from Corporate India

Coming off a flight from London to India, one is struck by the obvious enormous infrastructure challenges. Yet one feels invigorated by the country's uplifting burst of energy and new dreams. India is of course not alone in this enthusiasm; it can also be observed in China, Dubai, Moscow, and Vietnam. We are at a historical inflection point. We cannot visualize the specific changes, but these places will be unrecognizable in a decade, and they will help remake the global political and economic landscape.

It is sometimes frustrating to explain these changes to many Americans and Europeans, who are usually unable to see them through their now obsolete lens on the world. Imagine in 1900 having to stand in front of a British audience and predict that the world was entering the American century. The audience would have considered such a prognosis mad, and probably countered with comments such as, "Do you know the vastness of the British Empire?" and "Have you ever been to America and seen the problems they have?"[28] In the seventeenth century, China and India accounted for more than half the world's economic output. After a pause, the pendulum is swinging back to them at a speed the West has not yet grasped.[29] Despite the countries' many challenges, this is going to be the China and India century.

How do you explain the gloomy feeling at the board meeting of an Indian company where annual revenues had grown by only 35 percent! Or, that Naresh Goyal, founder and chairman of Jet Airways, India's largest private airline, is sincere when he declares: "I want to produce a global Indian brand. That's the passion for me, that's what drives me. The people of this country, we have the capability to produce a global brand."[30] Jet Airways does not wish to compete on price, but on service against its more established competitors. A recent search on Expedia for business-class direct-return flights from London to Toronto served up British Airways at £2,357 and Jet Airways at £4,471![31]

The concepts, the constructs, and the mind-set that have prevailed over the past century in companies and countries need to transform as a new future with India and China as dominant powers comes into play. It is why Jeff Immelt, CEO of General Electric, sent the list of the hundred largest emerging-market companies to his underlings, ordering them to identify the companies it could sell to and buy from, as well as those GE would have to compete with.

Japan's geographical location has given the country a front seat to the developments of the last decade. Traditionally, it looked down on the rest of Asia after it became the first Asian country to achieve Western levels of economic development.[32] Recently, overshadowed by India and China, it has become more insecure. Today, Japanese bookstores are filled with titles such as *Extreme Indian Arithmetic Drills* and *The Unknown Secrets of the Indians*. Indian education is in fashion as Japanese parents in Tokyo rush to enroll their children in English-language schools taught by Indians and other Asians. The thought of viewing another Asian country as a model in education would have been unheard of a few years ago. In contrast, riot police had to quell protests by Dutch school students in 2007, when the government decided to increase their annual classroom hours by twenty-six to 1,040 hours.[33]

Support for free trade is falling as people in the developed world feel more alarmed than charmed by globalization. In a 2007 Pew Global Attitudes poll, the United States placed dead last out of forty-seven countries in the percentage of the population supporting free trade.[34] These ambivalent feelings toward globalization are also seeping into popular Western culture. The 2008 French movie *Summer Hours*, directed by Olivier Assayas, is about a successful French couple working abroad. Assayas in an interview was nostalgic but realistic when he observed: "It is not their own logic that takes them away from home, it is the logic of the world today. If you are young and successful, you look towards India or China . . . The world is changing in Russia, China, India, the Middle East . . . it's like an earthquake. They are absorbing all the energy. You don't feel that sense of change in Europe."[35]

During the Beijing Olympics, the *New York Times* carried a story about the changing architecture of the city: "If Westerners feel dazed and confused upon exiting the plane at the new international airport terminal here, it's understandable. It's not just the grandeur of the space. It's the inescapable feeling that you're passing through a portal to another world, one whose fierce embrace of change has left Western nations in the dust."[36] The article went on to compare the sensation to the epiphany that Adolf Loos, the Austrian architect, experienced more than a century ago. On stepping off the boat in New York harbor, Loos realized that he had seen the future, and Europe was now culturally obsolete.

The 2008 financial crisis only reinforces that growth is in the East and debts are in the West. According to 2008 surveys, in developed countries the outlook for future living standards is at historic lows. The fears expressed in the West for its economic future are diametrically opposite of the confidence and desire to succeed one observes in India. The *New York Times* columnist Roger Cohen provocatively wrote: "It's the end of the era of the white man. By 2030, India will probably overtake Japan as the world's third-largest economy behind the United States and China. But in the end, transformation is not about numbers. It's about the mind. Come to Asia and fear drains away."[37]

Research Process and Outline of the Book

To write this book on India's emerging global powerhouses, Pradipta Mohapatra, Suj Chandrasekhar, and I made several trips to India and conducted face-to-face interviews with the executives and owners who are leading corporate India's globalization.[38] As the list of the interviews conducted in table I-1 demonstrates, we were able to get access to the who's who of global Indian corporations.[39]

These interviews left little doubt that the emerging Indian multinationals and their leaders have the drive, passion, vision, charisma, and

TABLE I-1

Research interviews conducted

Company	Interviewees	Date
ArcelorMittal	**Aditya Mittal**, CFO	April 16, 2008
Bharat Forge	**Baba N. Kalyani**, Chairman and Managing Director	February 5, 2007
Dr. Reddy's	**Satish Reddy**, Managing Director and COO	July 19, 2008
Essel Propack	**Ashok Goel**, Vice Chairman and Managing Director	December 19, 2006
	R. Chandrasekhar, President, Medical Devices and Specialty Packaging	December 19, 2006
Godrej Group	**Adi Godrej**, Chairman and Managing Director	December 20, 2006

TABLE I-1   (CONTINUED)

Research interviews conducted

Company	Interviewees	Date
Hindalco Industries	**Kumar Mangalam Birla**, Chairman **Debu Bhattacharya**, Managing Director **Santrupt Misra**, Director, Human Resources	January 31, 2008 April 23, 2008 April 23, 2008
Hidesign	**Dilip Kapur**, President	April 19, 2007
i-flex solutions	**Rajesh Hukku**, Chairman	October 31, 2007
Infosys Technologies	**Nandan Nilekani**, CEO, President, and Managing Director	December 21, 2006
Mahindra & Mahindra	**Anand Mahindra**, Vice Chairman and Managing Director	February 7, 2007
Marico	**Harsh Mariwala**, Chairman and Managing Director	July 23, 2008
NASSCOM	**Ganesh Natarajan**, Chairman	June 23, 2008
Piramal Enterprises	**Ajay Piramal**, Chairman **Somesh Sharma**, CEO, Piramal Life Sciences	April 22, 2008 April 22, 2008
RPG Group	**Harsh Goenka**, Chairman	December 20, 2006
Suzlon	**Tulsi Tanti**, Chairman and Managing Director	April 23, 2008
Tata Group	**S. Ramadorai**, CEO and Managing Director, TCS **S. Mahalingam**, CFO and Executive Director, TCS **N. Chandrasekaran**, COO and Executive Director, TCS **S. Padmanabhan**, Executive VP Global Human Resources, TCS **Ravi Kant**, Managing Director, Tata Motors **R. Gopalakrishnan**, Executive Director, Tata Sons **J. J. Irani**, Director, Tata Sons **Alan Rosling**, Executive Director, Tata Sons **R. K. Krishna Kumar**, Director, Tata Sons	December 18, 2006 December 18, 2006 December 18, 2006 February 7, 2007 February 6, 2007 February 6, 2007 February 7, 2007 February 7, 2007 April 18, 2007
VIP Industries	**Dilip G. Piramal**, Chairman **Sudhir Jatia**, Managing Director **Suresh Menon**, CEO, Carlton International	December 18, 2006 December 18, 2006 December 18, 2006
Wipro	**Azim Premji**, Chairman and CEO **Sundip Nandy**, Chief Strategy Officer	November 03, 2006 December 21, 2006
24/7	**P. V. Kannan**, CEO	May 10, 2007

aptitude to emerge as global leaders. This new breed of Indian multi-national is eager to make its mark in the world of international business, just like its German, Japanese, and Korean predecessors. These firms are convinced of their global strengths of world-class quality, cutting-edge technology, cost competitiveness, and human capital. It would therefore not be a surprise if one day many of the companies featured in this book become as familiar as Allianz, Samsung, and Toyota.

Research Process

We developed a clear process for identifying the firms to include in the sample. First, we examined the Indian business press, various lists of emerging multinationals from developing countries, and global companies from India. Second, we discussed this list with a number of top Indian executives and academics to ensure we had not omitted any Indian company with significant global operations. Third, from this relatively long list, we excluded pure exporters. Instead, our focus was on companies with existing global operations and the desire to build multinational companies. Fourth, given our interest in the private sector, we excluded public sector firms such as Bank of Baroda, State Bank of India, and ONGC, despite their multinational presence.

Finally, we debated the presence of ArcelorMittal in our sample because of differences in opinion as to whether it could be considered an Indian firm. Given its incorporation overseas, Mittal Steel, the predecessor to ArcelorMittal, is technically not an Indian company. Yet it was the first "Indian" firm to acquire a world standing.[40] Observing Lakshmi Mittal become one of the richest people in the world by consolidating the steel industry had an enormous inspirational effect on Indians and Indian business. Watching Mittal Steel go from strength to strength, acquiring companies in various parts of the world and then operating these plants successfully, demonstrated to Indian businessmen that there was no reason why they could not aspire to do the same. It also led Indian businesses to question the diversified domestic model in the face of this successful focused global model. As the case study will demonstrate, the practice of poaching employees from the Indian steel industry contributed heavily to Mittal Steel's early success in difficult markets. As a result, the business philosophy behind Mittal Steel, regardless of its official domicile, is rooted in Indian business. There is little doubt that Mittal Steel was a great pioneer for Indian businesses going global. Therefore, consistent with Ramamurti and Singh's research on India's emerging multinationals, we decided to retain it.[41]

We investigated all the Indian companies that remained and refer to them in our general discussion of Indian global companies. Given the book's space limitations, we focused on nine in-depth case studies. For the purposes of individual case studies, we excluded the pharmaceutical sector (e.g., Cipla, Dr. Reddy's, Nicholas Piramal, Ranbaxy) because those companies were in the process of evolving their existing generic strategies to adapt to India's signing of the World Trade Organization (WTO) intellectual property protection laws. Furthermore, some cases, like Vedanta, Videocon, TVS, and the numerous outsourcing companies, were not chosen because more significant players like Hindalco, Mahindra & Mahindra, and Infosys were available. The two Reliance companies were seen as having a more domestic rather than international focus. Finally, we felt it was important that each of the nine case studies offered a relatively unique approach to globalizing Indian firms.

Outline of the Book

Chapter 1 provides a brief historical context on three phases that Indian firms had to go through to transform from local into global players. It describes the uniquely Indian, domestically focused business model that existed from India's independence in 1947 until the economic liberalization program of 1991. The reforms in 1991 necessitated a decade-long restructuring of Indian companies to make them globally competitive. The Indian companies that went global had to overcome the mind-set barrier and use a dominant lever to approach international markets.

Chapter 2 kicks off the case studies with ArcelorMittal. Its owner, Lakshmi Mittal, was the first Indian to build a global company. His globalization strategy was to consolidate a globally fragmented industry of national champions.

Chapter 3 features what India has become famous for in the globalization debate—outsourcing. The lead example here is Infosys, the poster child for the new India, being both global and technologically savvy. Infosys inspired many Indian companies that were created to serve a global opportunity using India's large pool of relatively cheap skilled talent. Some of these global companies mushrooming in the pharmaceutical, medical, legal, animation, and diamond industries are discussed briefly.

Chapter 4 introduces Bharat Forge, the world's second-largest forging company. It demonstrates how an old-economy manufacturing firm can obtain speed and flexibility advantages in the global market by exploiting India's technology talent.

Chapter 5 stars Essel Propack, the world's largest laminated-tube producer. How this small company achieved global leadership by following its largest customer, Procter & Gamble, all the way back to the United States makes for a unique story.

Chapter 6 demonstrates how Hindalco leapt into the world's top five aluminum players and became a global *Fortune* 500 company in one fell swoop through its transformational acquisition of Novelis.

Chapter 7 showcases Mahindra & Mahindra, one of the top three tractor manufacturers in the world. The case suggests that it is only natural for dominant Indian companies to go international because domestic leadership in a large market like India gives them global scale.

Chapter 8 searches for a global consumer brand from India. Although no such brand exists yet, some firms are slowly building up to it. Five companies with different approaches are profiled. Godrej and Marico have the leading world position in the two specialist categories of powder hair dye and coconut oil, respectively. VIP is the world's second-largest luggage manufacturer, while United Breweries Group, with 140 brands, is the world's third-largest spirits marketer. Finally, in the luxury business, where size is not the most important criterion, Hidesign has adopted a niche strategy for building a global brand without large advertising expenditures.

Chapter 9 has the exciting story of a relatively new company called Suzlon. By adopting a distinctive concept-to-commissioning strategy in the industry, Suzlon has come from nowhere to become the world's fifth-largest player in the wind energy sector. Perhaps new industries will offer greater opportunities to build multinationals from emerging markets, as there are relatively fewer first-mover advantages for the developed world.

Chapter 10 presents the last of our cases, the Tata Group. It highlights how a century-old, highly decentralized and diversified group, one that was relatively sluggish and domestically focused, could suddenly be prodded into becoming a global player. Ratan Tata's mandate to go global has already seen several group companies, such as Tata Tea, Tata Steel, Taj Hotels, and Tata Motors, transform into major international players within this decade.

Chapter 11 argues that as more Indian companies go global, India and the world will need to grow closer together in the years ahead. As such, it behooves us all to have a deeper understanding of how Indian companies behave as customers, competitors, and collaborators.

Finally, the conclusion reflects on the future of Indian multinationals. In their quest to become more global, Indian firms will have to overcome some significant challenges along the way.

Welcome to India's global powerhouses.

Transforming Indian Business from Local to Global

THE TRANSFORMATION of Indian companies from domestic to global players went through three phases. In the prereform phase, prior to 1991, Indian business was under shackles, first from British colonialism and later, postindependence, from socialist policies. In the second phase, post-1991 economic reforms necessitated a decade-long corporate restructuring to make companies globally competitive. Now in the third phase, Indian companies are increasingly going global. Of course, these time periods do not describe any particular company but rather the general thrust of Indian business.

Indian Business 1947–1991: Rich Owners, Poor Companies

Indian business from the country's independence in 1947 until the economic liberalization program of 1991 was uniquely shaped by the constraints imposed by three factors—Indian culture, British rule, and postindependence socialist policies. It resulted in a domestically focused, unique, and somewhat perverse Indian business model that left companies in poor shape, but their owners relatively wealthy.

Influence of Indian Culture

Indian business has been highly dynamic, thriving under different, and often difficult, circumstances. But change is slow in ancient cultures like India's, and key aspects of India's cultural and social history, especially Hinduism, practiced by 85 percent of Indians, played an influential role in shaping the traditional Indian business model. In articulating the effects of Hinduism on business, it is important to note a caveat. As Fareed Zakaria observed in his excellent book *The Post-American World*, Hinduism is not a religion in the Abrahamic sense since it does not believe in universal commandments.[1] The only clear guiding principle appears to be "ambiguity," and over centuries, Hinduism's remarkable absorptive capacity has allowed it to evolve continually. We cannot do justice to Indian culture and religion in a couple of pages. Therefore, the treatment here covers only what is relevant to our thesis and is open to other interpretations.

A crucial element of Hinduism, the system of castes and sub-castes, functioned like medieval European guilds. It ensured division of labor and provided for training of apprentices. Over time, the caste system became a source of hierarchical differentiation in Indian society, where traders (Vysyas) and those engaged in business were placed above only the lowest Sudra caste, but below the priests (Brahmins) and warriors (Kshatriyas). Furthermore, as the four-caste system fragmented into hundreds of subcastes, it restricted people from changing their occupation or aspiring to a higher caste.

Scholars believe that the caste system throttled initiative, instilled ritual, and restricted the market.[2] It also played two vital roles in shaping the Indian business model. First, respect for higher caste members was unquestioned. This laid the foundation for deference to one's superiors in the workplace. Typically, Indian organizations were, and many still are, hierarchical and feudalistic. Second, entrepreneurial aspirations were not encouraged. In fact, an acceptance of the natural order of one's position in society meant that except for those belonging to the trader class, historically, Indians did not aspire to be entrepreneurs.

Another significant aspect of Indian culture is the traditional joint family system, which infused the Indian business model. The joint family is a unit consisting of the patriarch, his younger brothers, and their children and grandchildren, all living together under a single roof. The family pooled their resources and invested in business ventures with the goal of allowing each member to earn a respectable livelihood.

In the Western world, nepotism holds unflattering connotations because competing on merit is a strongly held virtue. In contrast, Indian family businesses held responsibility for and respect of family members as superior norms. The entire family participated in the business. When a son grew up, his elders would either assign him a role in existing businesses or launch him in a new venture, not only financed by existing businesses but often engaged in significant commercial transactions (e.g., supplying, buying, or distributing) with those businesses. Consequently, family business houses, especially from the two trader communities, Gujarati and Marwari, disproportionately dominated Indian business.

Impact of British Rule

For centuries, Indians had traded with Europe, the Middle East, and Southeast Asia for manufactured products such as silk, textiles, and handicrafts as well as agricultural products like pepper, cinnamon, and indigo. British rule unfortunately stifled and distorted India's trade with the rest of the world, barring Indian industry from competing with the British, especially in global markets, and thus forcing Indians to focus either on developing cheap raw material for British factories or on distributing British products in India. Although the British developed the railway, postal, and modern legal systems in India, this infrastructure supported the management of Indian resources for British gain.

For example, by 1830, India's thriving textile industry had been all but destroyed. By the mid-1800s, India was importing one-quarter of all British cotton textile exports. In the decades that followed, the British compelled Indian farmers to grow indigo, cotton, and wheat for export to Britain. During British rule, imported products received tariff and tax benefits while Indian industry was suppressed. The British focus on its interests hindered the development of a free trade environment in which Indian multinational companies, similar to those sprouting elsewhere in the world in the late 1800s and early 1900s, could be born.

Yet, beyond the obvious benefit of imposing English as the national corporate language, British rule conferred another unintended benefit for Indian companies when they finally decided to enter global markets. Early in their rule, the British realized that it was impossible to transplant enough of their own citizens to India. Instead, Thomas Macaulay, who was advising the then governor general of India, argued in 1834 that the British must "train a class of people Indian in blood and color but English in taste, in opinions, in morals, and in intellect."[3] Even today, "Macaulay's children" refers to Indians who adopt Western culture as a lifestyle. Though usually used with a negative connotation, this process meant that when the British did leave, a significant segment of Indians in the corporate sector had superficially adopted British habits (e.g., dressing in well-tailored suits, using a knife and fork) that allowed them to interact with Westerners with relative ease. This was especially true for the Indian elites at the time of the country's independence, most of whom had been educated in England. At times, these Indians even tried to outdo the British at their own game, and it is still jokingly said that the last Englishman on earth will be an Indian.

Postindependence, large Indian firms that could have adopted an Indian language or the Indian national dress as organization-wide practices chose not to do so. Instead, most Indian firms with national presence adopted the English language and British Indian work practices that were considered more neutral. This allowed them to avoid having to negotiate the conflict between the large regional and language differences that existed within the workforce. Because of British rule, Indians learned to manage the duality of their work and home lives. At work, the managers were all similarly "British"; at home, they reverted to the language, dress, and food of the region from which they originated.

Perhaps this duality explains why Indian managers have been more successful, compared to their Chinese or Japanese counterparts, in reaching the higher echelons of Western companies. Indian expatriate communities have maintained their racial and social identities regardless of whether they have been settled for more than a century and a half, as in Mauritius, Southeast Asia, and the West Indies, or whether they have emigrated in the past fifty years, as in Canada, the United Kingdom, and the United States.

Postindependence Socialist Model

At the end of colonial rule, India inherited an economy that was one of the poorest in the world. India suffered from one of the world's lowest life expectancies and a largely illiterate population. By 1950, Britain's legacy of profound structural economic issues—a stagnant economy, stalled industrial development, and an agricultural base that could not feed the rapidly accelerating population—proved a significant challenge for India's first prime minister, Jawaharlal Nehru.

Influenced by the British socialist Fabian Society, Nehru adopted the socialist economic model, hoping for strong growth through a centralized economy to increase the standard of living among India's poorest and to encourage the growth of critical manufacturing and heavy industries. Tragically, the earnest romantic vision of the socialist ideal proved wholly inadequate in dealing with the real challenges in the Indian economy.

In India's centrally planned economy, government planners determined the output allowed in each industry because they did not want to see "overinvestment" and "waste" in a country with limited resources. Therefore, companies needed licenses for everything—from setting up a business and expanding capacity to laying off workers and closing down a factory. As a result, the central bureaucrats in Delhi became enormously powerful and were popularly known as "License Raj," translated as "license rule." Favored entrepreneurs formed large groups during the License Raj though some, like the Tata and Birla groups, date from the early twentieth century.[4] Yet even the Tata Group received several projects as rewards for the group's consistent support of Nehru's freedom movement.[5]

Indian Business Under License Raj

Licenses were so precious that to obtain one you needed either a "connection" to a major politician (e.g., the only new automobile manufacturing license granted between 1950 and 1980 was to Sanjay Gandhi's Maruti Udyog) or the ability to pay a large bribe, or both.

Exploitation of licenses by established business houses. The large family business houses learned how to game the system by using their "connections" to get follow-up on their files, organize bribes, and win licenses.[6] They used the licensing process to foreclose competition, often by applying for a competitor's license; the competitor's application would then be rejected because industry capacity had already been licensed. Then the company with the license would simply sit on the license without using it to build any capacity.

A license for a new business gave the owner the right to establish an operation capable of producing a predetermined level of output specified on the license. Because banks and financial institutions were nationalized by the 1970s, the license owner then approached these public sector lenders for financing. A substantial part of the public sector financial institutions' mandate was to aid the economic development of the country. Therefore, they frequently loaned as much as 90 percent of the total investment required. This meant that the promoter or owner of the license needed to invest only 10 percent of the project costs to control the company. Usually this 10 percent was funneled through cross-holdings from the promoter's existing companies, supplemented by money raised in the domestic capital market from individual investors. This was necessary because with individual income tax rates of 90 percent-plus and a punitive wealth tax, few promoters could openly demonstrate the ability to fund large projects with their personal wealth.

Most of the licenses granted were for major industrial and infrastructure projects.[7] Setting up these operations required having a foreign multinational company build a large plant since these capabilities typically did not exist within India. International vendors would be invited to compete for these capital projects. One of the conditions for being awarded the order, which of course would not appear in the contract, was that the foreign supplier would fully or at least substantially reimburse the promoter's initial equity investment by placing funds directly into the promoter's offshore and undeclared bank account. As a result, the entire project would be completed without requiring the promoter to have any of his own real money in play, but allowing complete management control despite shareholdings of less than 10 percent.

For example, if the project was budgeted at $100 million, the promoter would be obliged to invest $10 million, with the remaining $90 million obtained as loans from public sector financial institutions and banks. A $100 million contract would then be awarded to the winning international vendor for building the factory or power plant. The understanding was that the vendor would have hidden into its winning bid a $10 million transfer to a foreign bank account of the promoter. After the plant was operational, if it made a profit, then the promoter owned a profitable company. On the other hand, if the company became unprofitable, the promoter would hand over the "sick" firm to the public sector institutions who had loaned the $90 million and walk away with no real losses out of pocket. The government would then continue to operate the company to avoid dismissing the existing workers and adding to the large pool of unemployed people. No wonder licenses were so coveted that the bureaucrats sanctioning them as well as the bank managers approving the loans required a "facilitating" payment.

A second bonanza to the established Indian business houses accrued in 1973, when the Foreign Exchange Regulation Act (FERA) was passed. The government restricted foreign companies from holding more than a 40 percent share. This required foreign multinationals to rapidly dilute their holdings in their Indian subsidiaries. Since most foreign companies were uninterested in minority shares, they began looking for the exits. Not surprisingly, established Indian business houses were able to acquire these Indian assets of foreign companies, especially British companies, at throwaway prices. Often these transfers were done at ten to twenty cents on a dollar.

Impact on corporate sector and consumers. The prevailing policies led to concentrated family ownership of Indian business assets, exercised through pyramids, with significant divergence between the promoter family's almost complete "control rights" and typically much smaller "cash flow rights."[8] Institutional gaps meant that new ventures by established business groups could not only rely on capital infusion from the group, but also benefit from the group brand name, internal talent transfers, and reduced contractual costs.

To grow, Indian business groups had little choice but to pursue unrelated diversification.[9] For example, the Aditya Birla Group operated in diverse industries such as automobiles, cement, dairy, electricity, jute, newspapers, plastics, sanitary ware, shipping, steel, sugar, tea, and textiles. Meanwhile, RPG Group had interests in agribusiness, cable, carbon black, electricity, engineering, fiberglass, financial services, music, radio, tea, tires, and typewriters.

A focus on core competencies leads to "product relatedness" within a group to exploit linkages between the different lines of businesses. In contrast, diversified Indian groups relied on "institutional relatedness," a dense network of ties with dominant institutions, which allowed them to exploit nonmarket forms of capital such as social, political, and reputational.[10] Unlike the results for American companies, where diversification resulted in lower returns, there was a "diversification premium" for Indian companies during this postindependence era.[11]

Research demonstrates that during this era, because of policy distortions, informational imperfections, and entrepreneurial scarcity, groups with high institutional relatedness and low product relatedness, such as Tata, performed best. In contrast, groups with high product relatedness and low institutional relatedness, like TVS, suffered from the worst relative performance. In other words, groups pursuing unrelated diversification strategies were more successful than groups that were focused on related products or industries.

Despite the domination of Indian business by established business groups controlled by powerful families, there was some room for entrepreneurial ingenuity. Existing business heads and new entrepreneurs differed in their ability to cultivate close relationships with politicians and in their business acumen. As a result, there was turnover in the relative rankings of the Indian business groups. Only three of the top ten groups in 1964 also featured in the top ten in 1990.[12] Furthermore, new groups did form, the most famous of which was Reliance. Unknown in 1964, Dhirubhai Ambani, in a classic rags-to-riches story, built Reliance into the third-largest Indian group by 1990, behind only Tata and Birla.

Unfortunately, because of the omnipresence of state planning, controls, and regulations, Indian business focused on dealing with the state planners. Indian companies were characterized by poor quality and productivity, neglect of customer needs, and short-sighted attitudes toward product development.[13] The widely quoted observation of Indian business at the end of this era was "Indian businesses may be poor, but their owners are rich."

The production controls imposed in the face of India's burgeoning population led to chronic shortages. To obtain a scooter one had to wait two years, for a car one year; a telephone line could easily take four years in the late 1980s. Even an everyday product like butter, where two companies controlled most of the production, was in very short supply during the summer, when consumption rose. Black market prices for these items could be 50 percent higher, and the government response was to institute a policy where every company had to state the maximum retail price at which an item could be sold. Of course, consumers immediately circumvented this by paying bribes to the middlemen.

The highly favorable climate for large Indian business houses and the resulting strong monopolistic positions made them more prone to stay at home in the sheltered domestic market. The institutional environment of licensing and limited competition led to domestic success without developing the unique competencies, the resources, or the viable scale necessary for competitive advantage in international markets.[14]

The severe shortage of foreign exchange meant that companies had to apply to the country's central bank, the Reserve Bank of India, for any expenditure denominated in foreign currency. If an Indian businessperson wished to travel overseas in the 1970s, the government limited the purchase of foreign exchange currency to $8 a day! Foreign capital was in such short supply that the question of overseas acquisitions by Indian firms never even arose.

There was, however, a small silver lining. Although the greater technological self-reliance and import substitution forced on Indian companies by regulation led to inefficiencies, it did help create some unique assets. Indian companies had to learn how to run imported capital equipment in the absence of ready availability of spare parts and service networks. And, frequently, import substitution meant having to reverse-engineer foreign products. Thus, Indian companies were forced to develop a very broad base of technological competence.[15] They were quite innovative in adapting and improving existing technologies for the local Indian context. Even after technologies were abandoned in developed markets, Indian companies were still improving them for their resource-constrained market. As a result, a few business houses found opportunities to expand operations on the back of such technological competence into other emerging markets in Africa and Southeast Asia.

The total equity overseas investment by Indian companies rose from $2 million in 1970 to around $100 million in 1980.[16] Not a large amount and highly concentrated—the top seven Indian investors accounted for at least three-quarters of the total foreign equity. The Birla Group alone accounted for 40 percent and Tata, another 9 percent.

In this postindependence era, until 1991, everything was loaded against Indian firms with global aspirations. Indian companies were not in great shape to compete in global markets or even at home against global competitors.

Corporate Restructuring 1991–2001: Becoming Globally Competitive

In 1991, India suffered a major economic crisis from the combined effects of oil price shocks (resulting from the 1990 Gulf War), the collapse of the Soviet Union (a major trading partner and source of foreign aid), and a sharp depletion of its foreign exchange reserves (caused mainly by large and continuing government budget deficits). Also in 1991, India had to service the country's $70 billion external debt, which had trebled over the previous decade, as well as pay for the burgeoning costs of imports, especially oil. The country's foreign exchange reserves dipped below $1 billion, barely enough to pay for two to three weeks of imports. In addition, with the collapse of the Berlin Wall in November 1989, the viability of socialism as an alternative model to capitalism had crumbled before the world's eyes.

Economic Liberalization

The government was forced to accept that the socialist model that had prevailed since independence had to be abandoned. Fortunately, the Indian government had in place what is now considered an economic dream team of Manmohan Singh (finance minister), P. Chidambaram (commerce minister), and Montek Singh Ahluwalia (commerce secretary). To reform the economy, the government adopted several new policies:[17]

- Industrial licensing was drastically reduced, leaving only eighteen industries subject to licensing.

- Import tariffs were reduced from an average of 85 percent to 25 percent, combined with a rollback of quantitative controls on imports.

- The rupee was devalued, and made convertible on the trade account.

- The Controller of Capital Issues, which decided the prices and number of shares firms could issue, was abolished.

- Indian firms were permitted to raise capital on international markets by issuing global depository receipts (GDRs).

- India's equity markets were opened to investment by foreign institutional investors.

- Procedures for foreign direct investment approvals were streamlined, and in at least thirty-five industries, allowed for automatical approval of projects within the limits for foreign participation.

- Foreign direct investment was encouraged by increasing the maximum limit on the share of foreign capital in joint ventures from 40 to 51 percent, with 100 percent foreign equity permitted in priority sectors.

The effects of the reforms were immediate and dramatic. The GDP growth rate between 1950 and 1991 had averaged between 2 and 3 percent per year; since 1991 it has averaged about 6 percent per year. More recently, since 2004, growth has exceeded 8 percent. The foreign exchange reserves that had dipped to a low of $1 billion are now approaching $300 billion.

More importantly, the economic growth has had a significant impact on the reduction of poverty levels. Within two decades, between 1985 and 2005, the percentage of the population living on a dollar a day was reduced by almost half, from 93 to 54 percent.[18] Based on that reduction, it is estimated that 431 million fewer Indians live in extreme poverty today. McKinsey expects Indian incomes to triple over the next two decades, lifting another 290 million people out of poverty and boosting India's middle class to 580 million. More optimistic surveys show even greater progress on poverty reduction, with estimates as low as 319 million Indians currently living at under a dollar a day.[19]

In the 1990s, India was one of the fastest-growing economies in the world in terms of productivity, with average productivity levels doubling every sixteen years.[20] It was estimated in 2001 that if that pace of growth were maintained, in sixty-six years (2066) India would reach the real GDP per capita level of the United States prevailing in 2001. The contrast with the pace of growth before 1980 was remarkable, when average Indian productivity levels were doubling only every fifty years. At the 1980s rate, India would have expected to approach America's 2001 GDP per capita level not in 2066, but in 2250![21]

Corporate Restructuring

The post-1991 reforms changed the environment for Indian business. Indian companies realized that the traditional Indian business model appropriate for "sheltered firms" had to be abandoned. First, the liberalization of industrial licensing meant that new domestic players could easily emerge in what were previously tightly controlled industrial sectors. As a result, companies went through a tough corporate restructuring program to enhance *domestic competitiveness* in the face of a more aggressive marketplace. Second, as import tariffs were cut and entry barriers for foreign companies were reduced, international players began to view India as a potential market. Subsequently, they brought to India their world-class products and services.

This forced even Indian firms with no global ambitions to become *globally competitive* to survive this foreign competition.

The transformation of Indian companies and business houses post-1991 was a crucial step in preparing Indian companies for the global marketplace. And, not surprisingly, some of them have become global players. The decade-long Indian corporate restructuring program had four essential elements: cleaning the balance sheet, improving competitiveness, focusing on core businesses, and strengthening management.

Cleaning the balance sheet. The balance sheets of most Indian companies in 1991 were poor. Established companies had the ability to raise money from banks, and many had done so at relatively favorable rates. These borrowed funds exceeded what the business itself could utilize. Instead the money was placed in an investment portfolio and invested in other group companies. As mentioned earlier, these cross-holdings allowed the ultimate promoters of these companies to control a vast network of group companies with very little of their own funds. The other shareholders in these companies disliked this arrangement, but could do almost nothing about it as the regulatory regime did not empower them or protect their interests.

As the Securities and Exchange Board of India (SEBI) began adopting reforms in corporate governance and empowering small shareholders along the lines of the American stock markets, companies were forced to shed these investments and cross-holdings. Given the complexity and ubiquity of corporate cross-holdings, their disentanglement was a time-consuming process. But every major Indian business group had to address it.

The balance sheets also suffered from substantial distortions in the valuation of assets. Many firms had assets with inflated values on their books. These needed to be recorded at their real market value. On the other hand, certain other assets on the books—usually property, cars, and art—were valued much below their market price. The logic here was that these undervalued assets would at some stage be sold to the promoters at book value. It was essentially a mechanism for transferring funds from the firm to the owners with the controlling interest, at the cost of the minority shareholders. Large Indian companies had to go through a painful process of cleaning up their balance sheets to bring the assets in line with market values. The boom in property and the resulting revaluation to reflect the rising prices helped companies write down the overvalued assets.

Strong balance sheets were essential for companies to attract new share capital from domestic and foreign sources. The infusion of capital helped reduce the historically high debt-to-equity ratios in Indian firms. More critically, it was needed to make the necessary capital investments to become competitive in the new deregulated marketplace. Finally, funds were also required to ramp up capacity to keep pace with the rapid domestic growth that followed the liberalization program.

Improving competitiveness. Under the protection of the benign environment pre-1991 and without the discipline of a tough competitive marketplace, Indian companies had become bloated. Costs, productivity, and quality had all become victims as companies could simply pass on inefficiencies to the consumer. Companies had little choice but to seek dramatic improvements on these fronts if they were to survive in the new marketplace.

To reduce costs and improve productivity, companies became more demanding of their suppliers and employees. Traditionally, Indian firms, because of the high import duties, had relied exclusively on Indian suppliers, and frequently substituted the available cheap labor for sophisticated capital equipment. Baba Kalyani, who led the transformation of Bharat Forge from a labor-intensive to a technology-intensive manufacturing firm, observed the conditions that forced firms to make inappropriate choices: "You waited a year for an equipment-import license, got less than you wanted, then paid an 80 percent import duty."[22] Even computing the import duties was a nightmare. For example, a new Burroughs computer imported by TCS in 1974 attracted a tariff of 101 percent, including import duty, auxiliary duty, countervailing duty, and a levy to help pay for the war in Bangladesh![23]

In the 1980s, Maruti, through its partnership with Suzuki of Japan, brought to India the concepts of tight cost control and process engineering. At that time, there were no auto component manufacturers in India capable of producing to Japanese standards. Yet the Indian government required Indian-made parts in Maruti cars. Suzuki was responsible for the first wave of modern component technology in India with its concept of Indian entrepreneurs and Japanese companies together supplying Maruti plants. It launched a Japanese-backed supplier development program, where Japanese component manufacturers often took small stakes in the Indian auto component manufacturers, helping them achieve world-class quality and cost standards.

In family-controlled firms, suppliers were frequently relatives of the promoter. The promoter had set them up in business to allow them to make a decent living. The procurement managers were keenly aware of these relationships, and therefore did not lean too hard on the suppliers with respect to prices, quality standards, or delivery reliability. The new competitive environment forced, and liberalization allowed, firms to access the global supply chain and obtain inputs on a par with global standards at competitive prices.

Most Indian firms were overstaffed with strong, militant unions that protected the employees. In the new environment, companies began downsizing the workforce by providing incentives for workers to retire early. In addition, even unions began to be more flexible in the private negotiating rooms. Union bosses initially realized that layoffs were inevitable, and later that jobs were available elsewhere as the economy was rapidly expanding. For example, at Mahindra & Mahindra, in 1991 it took 1,230 workers to manufacture seventy engines a day; in 1994 productivity had improved to the point where 760 workers could produce 125 engines a day.[24]

Finally, India always had a very poor reputation for quality and customer focus. Pre-1991, the problem was for consumers to find products rather than for companies to find customers. Reflecting on this era, Baba Kalyani, chairman of Bharat Forge, remarked: "The concept of quality used to be that if it works somehow, it's okay, but it doesn't need to work all the time."[25] Clearly this had to change if Indian brands were going to compete not just with each other, but also against the multinational companies entering the country.

The IT sector in India was a beacon in demonstrating that India could achieve world-class standards. The Capability Maturity Model

(CMM) from the Software Engineering Institute at Carnegie Mellon University assesses software companies for quality. Level 5 is the highest level on the maturity scale; in 1994 Motorola's software center at Bangalore became the world's second CMM Level 5 unit (the first was at NASA). By 2003, there were eighty software centers in the world assessed at CMM Level 5, and of those, sixty were in India.

Focusing on core businesses. The highly diversified Indian business groups quickly realized that they needed to focus on a few industries where they could obtain leading domestic positions. Building these positions would require significant investments. Focusing the portfolio would not only free up resources from noncore companies but through their divestment would also generate additional capital for the core business. In the early 1990s, many large business groups in India went through an exercise of identifying their core businesses. For example, the RPG Group went from twenty to six areas. In 1998 even Tata reduced the number of group-affiliated companies from eighty to thirty by trimming its lines of business from twenty-five to a dozen.[26]

The focus on a few core areas allowed companies to consolidate their domestic positions and had a subtle impact on their aspirations. Firms were no longer satisfied by claiming that they were number one or two in India; instead they began touting their world ranking. For example, MRF started asserting it was among the top fifteen tire manufacturers in the world, while Ranbaxy emphasized its position among the top ten generic pharmaceutical producers in the world. Slowly but surely, Indian companies began benchmarking themselves against world competitors. It was a first step toward global ambitions for Indian firms.

Strengthening management.   In a populous country with relatively few opportunities in the corporate world, Indian companies never saw managerial talent as an important source of competitive advantage. Compensation levels were extremely low. In the 1980s, it was not surprising for top executives to earn as little as $5,000 per year! Relationships, loyalty, and trust were valued in professional managers more than talent and competence. This was especially true in family-owned firms where many critical positions were occupied by family members. This explains the common usage of the term *professional manager* in India to distinguish such a leader from the "owner manager" and family members.

Often these family firms were run on feudalistic norms whereby all important decisions had to flow through a powerful promoter. This frustrated competent professional managers, and their only options were the few Indian subsidiaries of multinational companies. Some of these multinational companies, like Unilever and Imperial Tobacco, recognized that managerial talent was available in India at a relatively low cost and raided their Indian subsidiaries for overseas operations.

Post-1991, Indian firms, especially the family business houses, realized that professional managers had value as they could take responsibility and deliver results. Not surprisingly, they began to scour the Indian subsidiaries of multinational companies for management talent and move away from "one-person" rule. In the ensuing war for talent, professional manager salaries shot up dramatically. In addition, variable pay and stock options were introduced. In addition to competing for the best talent, managers were empowered and firms began investing in their training. Today, Indian managers, relative to their peers in other countries, probably have the highest standard of living in the world. These managers brought the world-class practices and processes they had learned at multinational companies to Indian firms, thereby preparing Indian business to be globally competitive.

The role of owners. As would be expected, the general corporate restructuring program described here varied considerably in how business groups and companies implemented the corporate restructuring program. Some firms started the restructuring process even prior to 1991, while others are still struggling with it. There were substantial differences among the owners, and to a large extent, the owner's philosophy determined the degree to which the painful restructuring medicine was adopted by the group. Some of the heads of family business groups and companies were rather aggressive in changing the old ways. Other business groups suffered from poor leadership and family splits of assets. As a result, some renowned family business houses witnessed an unprecedented decline in the 1990s. The important point here is that owner-promoters in Indian companies, rather than the corporate resources available, played the major role in distinguishing between subsequent winners and losers.

The new regulations made it impossible to exercise control of companies with small equity stakes and helped spur consolidation within industries. Furthermore, the liberalization allowed new companies to emerge in sectors such as IT, media, pharmaceuticals, and property. Several of these relatively new companies and groups, like Dr. Reddy's, Subhas Chandra, and Wipro, had by 1999 entered the list of the top twenty Indian business groups. This was possible because with liberalization, unlike in the prereform era, groups with high product relatedness and low institutional relatedness were the relative top performers in the 1990s.[27] The ability to exploit institutional gaps became less critical than the ability to effectively manage a business. Instead, more traditional, textbook business success factors of articulating a clear vision and strategy, understanding customer needs, whilst focusing on core competencies, innovation, and implementation became most important.

Unleashed—How Indian Companies Are Taking On the World

The corporate restructuring brought confidence to Indian business. Indian companies transformed themselves from domestic players, scared of global competitors and constantly seeking government protection in domestic markets, into confident players capable of building Indian multinationals. As they have gone from being passive resisters to active promoters of globalization, Indian firms are continuing to force a change in government policies toward a more open Indian market and business environment.

As stated in the introduction, we conducted interviews with the leaders of global Indian companies in our sample. We supplemented these interviews with secondary research and follow-up telephone interviews to ascertain how Indian companies went global, what challenges they faced in doing so, and how these challenges were overcome. Two factors clearly emerged as drivers of globalization: overcoming the mind-set barrier and having a dominant lever.

Overcoming the Mind-set Barrier

"We asked ourselves: Why don't we become one of India's MNCs in manufacturing? By doing so we will have better access to the market, better access to knowledge, better access to new developments," explained Baba Kalyani of Bharat Forge, elaborating on the firm's incentive to go global.[28] Nevertheless, he added, it took Bharat Forge seven years to find its first customer because, coming from a so-called underdeveloped, low-cost country, the company had to battle all kinds of doubts regarding its capability and technology. The Bharat Forge experience raised three issues about overcoming the mind-set barrier that came up repeatedly in our interviews: making a leap of faith, persistence in the face of initial setbacks on the path to globalization, and overcoming the liabilities of "Made in India" origin.

Making a leap of faith. For an Indian company to go global requires, at some level, a leap of faith into the unknown. In the face of skepticism, the entrepreneur or owner made the decision to go for it despite what to unbiased observers may have seemed like long odds. Anand Mahindra, in his interview, mentioned that, while pursuing his MBA at Harvard Business School, he was disappointed that there were no case studies or examples of Indian global brands. It fired his ambition and led him to decide that when he took over the family business, Mahindra would be a global brand. Much later he did just that: "We decided that we weren't going to be in any business that wasn't global . . . You're not safe if you're only at home. You can't compete in a small pool anymore."[29]

Similarly, Ranbaxy, a generic drug maker in India, had been exporting its products since 1975, but had never really made any money on these international sales.[30] In 1993, the then CEO, Parvinder Singh, challenged his organization to become an international research-based pharmaceutical firm. When his managers questioned whether it was possible to build such a firm in a country like India, he responded that Ranbaxy cannot change India but what it can be is a pocket of excellence. Ranbaxy, he argued, must be an island in India. Today it is one the world's top ten generic producers with presence in twenty-three of the twenty-five largest markets and manufacturing facilities in eleven countries.[31]

Persistence in the face of initial setbacks. Becoming a global corporation is a learning game. In most of the companies that we researched, it was not a straight-line process. There were initial setbacks. For example, in Essel Propack's first attempt to acquire a piece of land for its operations in China, the vendor absconded with the money. Anand Mahindra described his firm's first international incursion into Greece as a chapter on "how not to do it!"[32] Staring at these initial setbacks, in light of a growing and profitable domestic business, it would have been easy for all of these companies to retreat from global markets. Yet they persevered, and learned from their mistakes.

The initial hotel properties acquired in the 1980s by the Taj Group in cities such as Chicago, New York, and London were "B" level properties. But they were what the Taj Group could afford given the foreign exchange limitations the government placed on Indian companies. These subpar properties were not consistent with the upscale Taj image. Taj executives were not motivated by these international properties, and as a consequence, these hotels soon deteriorated in terms of customer experience and became largely unprofitable. Taj realized that its competence was in running five-star hotels. Later, when Taj became serious about its international operations in the developed markets, it had to shed all of these initial acquisitions.

Learning from this experience, in the Taj Group's next sortie into developed markets, it acquired prestigious hotels—including the Ritz-Carlton in Boston, Campton Place in San Francisco, and Blue Sydney in Australia—at top dollar. What made Taj persevere was the realization that going global was an imperative. R. K. Krishna Kumar, vice chairman of Taj Hotels, said: "The Tata Group has always recognized that the world marketplace is not divisible . . . There's a strategic compulsion to go outside India for many of our businesses because we believe the global market is one marketplace."[33]

Overcoming the liabilities of Indian origin. Until the late 1990s, before the IT outsourcing boom, the image of India was detrimental to Indian business. At its worst, India was identified with abject poverty. Most images and stories of India in the international press reflected this with pictures of starving masses, natural disasters, and famines. At its best, India was seen as an old and mystical culture. The images most frequently associated with this view featured snake charmers, historical palaces, temples, and holy men. While both of these were, and still are, reflective of India's reality, they missed another India—an India populated by pockets of technological sophistication, an entrepreneurial private sector, and a well-educated workforce.

Given India's image, it was extremely difficult to convince global customers that an Indian supplier could be a reliable source of good-quality products made by a technologically sophisticated company. When Indian companies began knocking on the doors of large multinational firms, which had many choices within their global supply chains, it was difficult to close the sale. Imagine an Indian executive a decade ago, trying to convince the big three U.S. automakers to buy from Bharat Forge, or persuade Procter & Gamble that Essel Propack should be its supplier in the United States.

Indian entrepreneurs learned that, in competitive global markets, there was always another supplier willing to match the Indian firm's low prices. Therefore, Indian companies had to recognize that price as a weapon could take you only so far. To obtain the order required more than that: Indian firms had to demonstrate they had the world-class capabilities (assets, processes, and knowledge) to compete in international markets. Only then would global customers be reassured.

Dominant Lever

After conducting their research, the hope of academics is to discover some common patterns so as to group firms according to a few generic global strategies. For example, Ramamurti and Singh propose four generic international strategies that characterize India's emerging multinationals, with an illustrative example for each: local optimizer (Mahindra & Mahindra), low-cost partner (Infosys), global consolidator (ArcelorMittal), and global first mover (Suzlon).[34] We were unable to fit all our cases neatly into this typology, and in some categories, such as global first mover, were unable to identify any Indian company beyond Suzlon. Instead, we discovered that the companies in our sample chose very different strategies in their paths to having an international footprint. Moreover, they could not be faithfully arrayed in any simple typology. Each company in our sample had a dominant lever that they exploited to access international markets.

We were interested to see how these companies used their dominant lever to launch their globalization once they overcame the country-of-origin liability. While no company used a single dominant lever exclusively, our nine case studies demonstrate nine different dominant levers.

ArcelorMittal saw an opportunity in the fragmented steel industry, recognizing that national champions would lose to a global champion. Consolidating the fragmented steel industry created a truly global company with the ability to reduce risk and leverage capabilities across markets. Mittal's unique vision changed the industry.

Companies like Infosys and i-flex solutions were *born* global, because they understood that while there was a huge human capital advantage in India, the fulfillment had to be global. "Infosys started with no brand, no technology, no faith in marketing capability, and no access to foreign exchange," recalled Nandan Nilekani.[35] Infosys and, more generally, the IT sector (TCS, and Wipro in particular) were instrumental in sparking the imagination of Indian entrepreneurs to seek "born global" business models that exploit India's large pools of reasonably priced skilled workers. From Hollywood studios outsourcing animation to lawyers outsourcing preparation of briefs, the potential for India's skilled workers to be the world's workforce are substantial.

Bharat Forge employed reasonably priced engineering talent to transform itself from an 85 percent blue-collar workforce to an 85 percent professional workforce. Replacing unskilled workers with engineers on the plant floor led to a significant advantage in design capabilities. The product development time of two to three weeks (versus industry standards of six to twelve months) delivered the "wow" factor to prospective clients.

Essel Propack's induction into the global circle began once it convinced Procter & Gamble that it could be P&G's best supplier—a quality supplier and a process-oriented supplier. The company went out of its way to build a relationship with P&G, which subsequently allowed Essel Propack to enter Egypt, China, and finally the United States as a supplier.

A transformational merger is a frequently employed strategy to become a global firm. Hindalco did exactly that with its 2007 acquisition of Novelis, a world leader in aluminum rolling and can recycling. By combining its previous upstream focus with Novelis's dominance of downstream operations, Hindalco became an integrated global major in the industry. Several other Indian firms, such as Tata Tea and United Breweries, have also used acquisitions as a path to globalization.

Other companies, like Tata Motors, Godrej, and Marico, have utilized the specific product competencies developed for India to enter other emerging markets. Given India's size, domestic leadership often confers global scale, as seen at both Mahindra & Mahindra and VIP. As Anand Mahindra observed, "India is the largest tractor market in the world, and if you are the largest tractor maker in India, it is a disservice to India if you are not a global force."[36]

Ratan Tata, the group chairman, has been a transformational leader in making this relatively sleepy giant dance in the global markets, making bold acquisitions for individual group companies that leverage the combined financial muscle of the entire group. As in Suzlon and the other companies we examined, the role of the leader has been an important catalyst for those Indian firms that have made the transition to global.

Conclusion

The first seminal study of India's multinationals was done twenty-five years ago by Sanjaya Lall, who discussed the patterns of foreign direct investment by Indian companies in the 1970s.[37] We can contrast the global strategies of Indian companies today with those Lall identified. Four dramatic changes are evident in how Indian companies are pursuing global strategies in this decade vis-à-vis the 1970s.

First, in the 1970s the pattern of foreign direct investment was highly concentrated, with seven family business groups accounting for at least three-quarters of it. In contrast, the companies featured as case studies, except for Hindalco (Aditya Birla Group), Tata Group, and Mahindra & Mahindra, either did not exist or, if they did, were not included on the list of the largest twenty Indian business houses of 1980. What has really inspired Indian companies to go overseas, including the more aggressive internationalization of the Birla and Tata groups, is the success of the "born global" IT sector and Lakshmi Mittal. It is these latter two, rather than any of the old family business groups, that are responsible for waking up Indian business to seriously examine global opportunities. Today, the overseas footprint of corporate India is drawn from a much broader set of Indian firms.

Second, prior to 1980, 80 percent of Indian overseas activity was manufacturing based. The success of Indian outsourcing has instead tilted the nature of Indian global operations toward the service sector. It reflects the change in India's economy over the past three decades. Services now account for 50 percent of India's gross domestic product; industry and agriculture account for 25 percent each.[38] This is a very unusual profile for a developing country, where the economies, and especially exports, tend to be dominated by manufacturing (e.g., China), natural resources (e.g., Middle East), or agriculture (Latin America).

Third, observing the success of the IT sector in the United States, Indian companies are now focused on expansion opportunities in the developed markets of North America and Europe. This is in contrast to the 1970s, when most of the foreign investment of Indian firms flowed to other developing markets like Africa and Southeast Asia. Indian firms today have the confidence that they can succeed in the most demanding markets of the world.

Fourth, as they focus on the developed world, Indian companies recognize that they do not have the appropriate brands, product lines, or distribution networks. As many of them are impatient to go global, they have chosen to acquire these resources. Almost every

Indian firm in our study has made some acquisition in the developed markets. And instead of taking minority positions in foreign joint ventures, as was the practice in the 1970s, Indian companies are now either setting up wholly owned subsidiaries or buying majority interests. They seem to have no interest in being a minority partner. Thus, the *relative* focus of Indian companies' globalization has shifted from favoring greenfield operations and minority stakes in developing countries to taking controlling positions through acquisitions in developed countries.

Indian companies are no longer the traditional low-price bidders for foreign assets and companies, slow to appoint international advisors. Instead, they have become self-assured and savvy investors, financing large deals and paying global prices. World-class management and improved earnings have given them the ability to access global liquidity and financial markets. Despite the global financial crisis of 2008 and the meltdown of markets worldwide, the future will no doubt bring financing of foreign acquisitions with their own stock. And, who knows, future rupee convertibility may lead to rupee acquisitions! All of this was unimaginable in 1991, even by the biggest of India bulls.

ArcelorMittal

Consolidating the Globally
Fragmented Steel Industry

Today every Indian businessman has the same opportunities
as me. India is open. Indian businessmen can go global, whether
they live in India or not. It's a small world now.

Lakshmi Niwas Mittal, Chairman and CEO, ArcelorMittal

ARCELORMITTAL IS A *Fortune* 500 company with corporate
headquarters in Luxembourg. It is listed on the New York
Stock Exchange (NYSE) as well as several European exchanges—but
not on the Mumbai stock exchange.[1] Its chairman and CEO,
Lakshmi Mittal, holds an Indian passport, but resides in the United
Kingdom. The company established its position as the largest steel
company in the world by leveraging low-cost production operations
in emerging markets throughout the globe, and thrived for decades
without establishing operations of any kind in India. The absence of
operations in India was largely due to an earlier family split, but now
Mittal plans significant investments in India.

Company History

ArcelorMittal is a global company in the truest sense; it employs
310,000 people in sixty countries. Producing over 116 million metric
tons of output and generating revenues of over $105 billion in 2007,

ARCELORMITTAL SNAPSHOT

- With revenues of over $105 billion in 2007, ArcelorMittal is the largest steel producer in the world by far (about three times the size of its nearest rival).

- It is the only truly global steel company, employing 310,000 people in sixty countries.

- ArcelorMittal owns steel-making facilities in sixteen countries, spanning four continents. It produces 116 million metric tons of steel, 10 percent of the world's steel output.

- In 2006, ArcelorMittal announced a $9 billion investment in India, the country's second-largest greenfield production and mining operation.

ArcelorMittal is the largest steel company in the world, by a wide margin. The company is the leading supplier for several major industries, including automotive, construction, consumer goods, and packaging, among others.

The company achieved global domination not only through production scale, but also by making significant R&D investments to ensure cutting-edge technology applications and production efficiencies. Suceess is also due to controlling sizable amounts of captive supplies of raw materials and an extensive international distribution network. Further, an expansive industrial presence—in Europe, Asia, Africa, and America—gave the group exposure to all key steel markets, from emerging to mature.

The outcome of building the steel company is that Mittal was ranked in 2008 as the richest Indian and the fourth wealthiest person in the world.[2] As the founder and CEO—not to mention a 44 percent shareholder—of what at its high was a $100 billion company, one might reasonably ask . . . where next? But in 2008 Mittal seems well poised for an encore surpassing even his previous achievements. Further industry consolidation is likely to be a strong strategic thrust, as is heavy investment in fast-growth markets of Asia. In the world of steel nothing happens on a small scale—production is measured in millions of tons, and investment in billions of dollars. In the larger-than-life world of steel, Mittal is the one to watch.

For a company with an Indian CEO, the most interesting aspect of Mittal's next big move was only that it hadn't occurred earlier; in 2006, Mittal announced a $9 billion investment in India. Mittal's journey back to his homeland was a circuitous one, two decades in the making.

The Birth of a Global Giant

Mittal began his career in the family's steelmaking business in India. In 1976, Mittal was sent to manage a recently acquired run-down plant in Indonesia, leading to the establishment of Ispat Indo and, concurrently, the LNM Group.[3] The country was chosen for its growth potential and the fact that there were fewer governmental and economic restrictions than in India. However, the plant was inefficient and faced significant production issues, such as reliable access to electricity. Using his instincts from working in a similarly challenging environment in India, Mittal secured a reliable source of energy to operate the plant. With the plant up and running, Mittal stayed on in Indonesia instead of divesting the operation and returning to India as originally planned. With the support of his father, Mittal ran a profitable operation for the next fourteen years.

The formative struggles in Indonesia would provide Mittal with important lessons in his plans for global expansion. He identified the vulnerability of the industry as its dependence on an uncertain supply and was anxious to rectify this weakness. Along with the rest of the industry, Mittal knew that good-quality scrap, the raw material for making steel, could be both difficult to source and costly. By supplementing his supplies with a substitute, direct-reduced iron (DRI), he found a solution to his raw-material problem that was both financially and technologically viable. His search for a supplier of DRI led him to the Caribbean, and his first of many big breaks came in 1989 with the acquisition of the Iron & Steel Company of Trinidad and Tobago.

The next phase of Mittal's international growth followed quickly in 1992, with the privatization of the steel industry in Mexico. Mexican government officials courted interest throughout the world and were impressed by Mittal's record in Indonesia and his pioneering use of DRI technology. A deal was struck and Mittal acquired Sibalsa, renaming it Ispat Mexicana. This was a key turning point for Mittal, not only in terms of international exposure but also in terms of production volume.

Although Mittal himself had a vision beyond his family's operations in India, Mittal's father and two younger brothers back in India were interested in concentrating solely on the domestic market. In 1985, Ispat Industries was established, becoming the flagship of the Mittal family's Ispat Group, which M. L. Mittal had set up in 1952. A few years later, in 1989, Lakshmi Mittal established Ispat International, and by 1994 he had formally split from the family steel business. With a distinct parting of ways from his family business back in India, nothing held Mittal back from executing his vision—global domination.

The dramatic turnaround and generation of high-profit margins by Ispat Mexicana would fund a series of acquisitions in the 1990s. Mittal Steel had begun to change the way the steel industry conducted its business. Until then, the industry had been largely fragmented and inward-looking; national steel companies catered mostly to their domestic market. This resulted in a volatile marketplace such that even when steel prices dipped, excess national production continued, which only compounded the problem and drove global steel prices down further. Mittal understood early on that companies needed to operate on a worldwide basis, and he therefore pursued a strategy of globalization. In doing so, he went against the prevailing industry belief that steel was regional and could not be global.

The Mittal Turnaround Competence

Mittal showed that the strategy of operating globally, which meant having proximity to raw materials and growing markets, was highly lucrative. Shipping raw materials vast distances was financially crippling and inefficient. Mittal recognized that a change in operations was critical and that proximity to raw-material suppliers or, better still, acquiring nearby coal and iron ore mines was the way forward. This strategy led him to serial acquisitions of underperforming companies, often government owned, that no one wanted to touch and in locations where few wanted to venture.

The acquisition of Karmet in Kazakhstan in 1995 was clear evidence that Mittal was prepared to take risks that no one else in the industry was willing to take. Along with the steelworks, Ispat International had *de facto* acquired the bleak company town of Temirtau and its numerous problems, including an inefficient power plant, hotel, and television station.[4] The spectacular turnaround of Ispat Karmet provides an excellent model of how Mittal is able to make otherwise doomed, money-losing companies hugely successful.

A number of elements make up the winning formula, including targeted investment, cost cutting, import of modern management practice, and the sharing of best practice among all plants. In the case of Ispat Karmet, though Mittal retained the local workforce, he also brought in skilled managers and executives from India. The huge resource of highly skilled managers and engineers working in the Indian public sector at the state-owned Steel Authority of India Limited (SAIL) for a meager wage had not gone unnoticed by Mittal. He poached some of their best managers, offering them very attractive salaries in return for outstanding performance and for having to work in some very unpleasant and at times dangerous environments.

One high-profile example is Malay Mukherjee, who joined the LNM Group in 1993 after a long career with SAIL. He was executive director of the largest integrated steel plant in India, Bhilai Steel Plant, when he left to run Mittal's operations in Mexico.[5] Another former SAIL employee, Narendra Chaudhary, was part of the top management team sent in to Kazakhstan when the Karmet plant was acquired, and he was later instrumental in the Ispat Sidex start-up in Romania. The SAIL managers proved to be highly skilled and prepared to work extremely long hours in remote and difficult locations.

Apart from demonstrating an eye for a bargain, Mittal has shown his skill at managing problem assets rejected by other steel producers. When considering an acquisition, Mittal looked not only at low-cost inputs and an expanding market but also whether the company to be acquired would fit with his growth strategy. This strategy required the company under consideration to have production, marketing, or cost synergies and the potential to become a low-cost producer. Further, as the industry changed, Aditya Mittal, son of Lakshmi Mittal and CFO, noted that "employee commitment, capital-expenditure commitment and media perception" were even more important than financial measures.[6]

Key to reducing costs and improving performance was the Knowledge Management Programme. By benchmarking against the best in the Mittal Group, valuable knowledge transfer with respect to cost reduction occurred daily between plant managers.[7] By pooling global expertise on a regular basis, the Mittal Group was able to share and implement best practice, technical knowledge, and target setting more quickly and efficiently than its competitors. The process of knowledge sharing occured on various levels in the company and was coordinated at the corporate level.

At the shop floor level, "twinning" has proved highly effective in the exchange and implementation of best practices between plants. Once plants are twinned, the interaction between them is continuous and systematic. Operational and technical managers visit both plants regularly to benchmark key performance indicators, review technological needs, and compare operating and maintenance practices.[8] The consistency and regularity of this interactive process allows twinned plants to implement and benefit from each other's best practices. Consequently, improvement at the plants continues in a structured manner.

So why has Mittal been so successful in bidding for and acquiring plants where other steel producers have failed? In the case of the state-owned plant in Trinidad, where there were few serious rival bidders, Aditya Mittal believes that what fundamentally differentiated them was their "ability to present a revival plan." The management team believed that by drawing from their previous experiences they could turn around what was a failing operation. As a result, he said, they could "revive the facilities, invest in the facilities, and provide stability not only to the community but also the company and the country." In addition to offering a credible revival plan, they also paid the best price. According to Aditya Mittal, these two components go hand in hand: "If you believe that you can turn around a facility, you can include some of that value in the bidding."

Paying the best price clearly paid off in the landmark acquisition in Mexico. The Mexican government had originally invested $2.2 billion in the start-up of the plant in 1972.[9] When Mittal acquired the plant in 1992 for $220 million, paying twice as much as the next highest bidder, it was making an annual loss of $20–$30 million.[10] The turn-around was dramatic. The plant's annual shipments exceed 3.7 million metric tons and it is now one of the world's largest DRI producers. What under state ownership had been a loss-making plant operating at only 25 percent of capacity became, under Mittal, a hugely successful operation that would help fund the plans for global expansion.

Another important factor in Mittal's successful bidding history has been its strategic alignment with national and local governments in the bidding process. This approach proved essential for Mittal's first major opportunity in the former Soviet Union, its ambitious acquisition of the Karmet plant in Kazakhstan. Mittal was faced with an entrenched state-owned cultural legacy and a crumbling plant. What was once the third-largest steel plant in the Soviet Union was now run down, making huge losses, and the employees had not been paid for six months.[11] Mittal's revival plan was not only to turn around the plant but also the nearby town of Temirtau. The success-ful bid in 1995 would reap rich rewards. Within a year the plant became profitable, and within eight years annual steel shipments rose from 2.5 to 4.1 million metric tons.[12] Moreover, with the Karmet plant as the main provider of heat and electricity, many other services were restored as well, and the once crumbling town of Temirtau was brought back to life.

So what is the key to such dramatic turnarounds of these previ-ously failing state-owned assets, and what made Mittal Steel so con-fident of its turnaround strategy? According to Aditya Mittal, there is no magic to a successful turnaround.

It is simple and strong management. First you have to diagnose what is the real issue, and then you have to make sure that the manage-ment team and the company is completely focused on resolving the critical issue. Often when you do a turnaround, you think that everything is wrong with the company and try to change everything, and then you are in a quagmire. The focus has to be on understand-ing the number one critical issue and resolving it first with all focus, dedication, and time. As each turnaround situation has a different focus issue, identification of that focus issue and resolving it is the most important aspect.

Many of these acquired plants were located in challenging environments, a fact that put off many rival bidders, but not Lakshmi Mittal. He looked beyond the widely held perceptions of the location as trouble spots to the reality of each situation. In the case of Kazakhstan, Mittal met with political leaders and understood that the steel industry was not at odds with the government. Kazakh president Nursultan Nazarbayev was from the area and a former employee. Nearly 90 percent of the steel being produced in the country was being exported, so Mittal did not have to rely on the domestic economy for success but rather on the global steel industry. What the domestic economy did ensure was that Mittal would have a good cost base. Understanding, respecting, and working with the local culture were crucial, first, to not being put off by these challenging environments, and second, to the subsequent implementation of the revival plan. Sensitivity to the local working environment and turning it to an advantage, whether in emerging or developed markets, has been an important competence in the turnaround strategy.

Though a number of key elements contribute to turnarounds, Mittal's knack for dramatic transformations is based largely on the company's tremendous wealth of knowledge and experience. The Mittal competence, as explained by Aditya Mittal, is the knowledge they have gained over many years of experience, a resource that would be difficult for another steel company to replicate.

As you gain experience, you have fine-tuned your methods. Often we have made mistakes; now we have learned from those mistakes. It is the knowledge that we have. For example, when we did the acquisition in Romania, the turnaround plan was not a three-year plan but a twelve-month plan. So, clearly we can do something that is much faster because we knew what the issue was, we were able to take the actions, and not repeat the mistakes.

The art of turning around a steel plant is clearly a skill that Mittal has used to great effect. Being prepared and willing to take calculated

FIGURE 2-1

Mittal Steel international growth milestones

1989	Acquisition of Iron & Steel Company of Trinidad and Tobago.
1992	Acquisition of Sibalsa, Mexico.
1994	Acquisition of Sidbec-Dosco, Canada.
1995	Acquisition of Karmet, Kazakhstan, and Hamburger Stahlwerke, Germany. Formation of Ispat Shipping.
1997	Ispat International NV goes public.
1998	Acquisition of Inland Steel Company, United States.
1999	Acquisition of Unimétal, France.
2001	Acquisition of Sidex, Romania, and ALFASID, Algeria.
2002	Business assistance agreement signed with South African Iscor.
2003	Acquisition of Nova Hut, Czech Republic.
2004	Acquisition of Polski Huty Stali, Poland, and BH Steel, Bosnia. Acquisition of rolling mills from Balkan Steel, Macedonia. Merger of LNM Holdings and Ispat International to form Mittal Steel and proposed takeover of International Steel Group, United States.
2005	Buys 36.67% stake in Hunan Valin Steel Tube & Wire, China. International Steel Group, United States, acquisition completed. Mittal Steel Europe created. Mittal Steel makes *Fortune* 500. Mining development agreement with Liberian government. Acquisition of Kryvorizhstal, Ukraine. Memorandum of understanding signed with state of Jharkhand, India, for $9 billion investment. Purchase of Stelco subsidiaries, Canada. Stake lifted in Mittal Steel Zenica, Bosnia.
2006	Acquisition of Sicartsa, Mexico.

Source: Adapted from company Web site, www.arcelormittal.com.

risks that others in the industry are reluctant to consider along with the ability to make these acquisitions perform have set Mittal apart from the rest. Figure 2-1 shows the steady pace of Mittal's acquisitions since 1989.

Nevertheless, 2001 was a critical period for the steel industry as it experienced a dramatic downturn, leaving it close to bankruptcy. The fragmented industry, global overcapacity, and nationalized industry mentality of the early 1990s saw the average growth of global steel demand down to a derisory 2 percent by the close of the decade.[13] In 2001 Mittal's share price was only $1; the company was experiencing a cash crunch and producing 12 million metric tons. Mittal turned the global slowdown into an opportunity to acquire assets cheaply with sellers' credit. By the time the recession ended, Mittal's production had risen to 29 million metric tons per year and the company had momentum coming out of the recession. It was a big bet that paid off.

Arcelor Merger

By the end of 2005, Mittal was forced to change strategic direction, as there were few remaining privatizations of the large state-owned steel companies on which Lakshmi Mittal had built his burgeoning empire. At the same time, the prices of acquisition targets were being bid up to high levels, as the steel industry experienced a boom from 2001 onward. The fiercest competition often came from Mittal's most hard-hitting rival, Arcelor, a steel giant based in Luxembourg.

The path was paved for a bold strategic move. In early 2006, Mittal Steel launched an unexpected $22.7 billion hostile bid for Arcelor, the second-largest steel company in the world. The bitter battle between the two companies would go down as one of the most acrimonious takeover bids in European history. Allegations of racism and vocal hostility on the part of Arcelor as it fought against the takeover featured heavily in the five months prior to the creation of ArcelorMittal. Cultural differences were highlighted and Guy Dollé, Arcelor's CEO, went so far as to claim that "Arcelor was producing aristocratic perfume while Mittal was making plebian eau de cologne."[14] The personal attack went further and Dollé added that he did not "want his shareholders to be paid with the Indian-born Mr. Mittal's 'monkey money.'"[15] Politicians from France and Luxembourg also stepped into the fray in a bid to protect European interests, ignoring the fact that Mittal Steel was a European company. Despite reassurances from Lakshmi Mittal that there would be no redundancies or cost cutting, resistance continued, and the negative effects of any possible merger were emphasized by both governments. Though legally a European company, clearly the perception was that Mittal Steel was an Indian company.

After a much-publicized and dramatic five-month battle, the Arcelor board unanimously accepted Mittal's offer of €27 billion ($33.6 billion), creating the world's largest steel company. Lakshmi Mittal was made CEO of the merger of the world's largest and second-largest steel producers. The "merger of equals" automatically created a company three times the size of its nearest rivals—Nippon and JFE Holdings of Japan and Posco of South Korea—and more than four times the size of the leaders in the developed markets, including United States Steel and British/Dutch Corus.[16] (See figure 2-2.)

FIGURE 2-2

Market share of top ten steel producers

1995 = 752 million metric tons

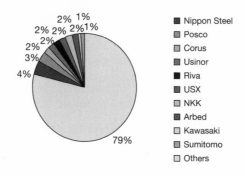

- ■ Nippon Steel
- □ Posco
- □ Corus
- ■ Usinor
- ■ Riva
- ■ USX
- □ NKK
- ■ Arbed
- □ Kawasaki
- ■ Sumitomo
- □ Others

2007 = 1,344 million metric tons

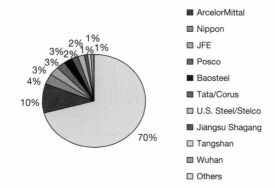

- ■ ArcelorMittal
- ■ Nippon
- □ JFE
- ■ Posco
- ■ Baosteel
- ■ Tata/Corus
- □ U.S. Steel/Stelco
- ■ Jiangsu Shagang
- □ Tangshan
- ■ Wuhan
- □ Others

Source: Adapted from Metal Bulletin/IISI (International Iron and Steel Institute) and IISI, Laplace Conseil Analysis.

Nearly two years since the creation of ArcelorMittal, how has the merger and integration of the two companies developed? Aditya Mittal described the process so far: "It has been better than what we dreamed. We always knew it was a fantastic combination and that on all parameters would alter not only our company but the steel industry. And the way it has played out, it has surpassed all our expectations. The strength that the new company has, building on the advantages of both, is tremendous. The weaknesses that each of these companies had on their own have been eliminated. On a combined basis we are much stronger."

Aditya Mittal explained that the merger altered the steel industry by making people understand the importance of consolidation and globalization, which fundamentally upgrades stability in the steel industry. The merger "demonstrated that through consolidation you can reduce the cyclicality," a problem that historically had beset the steel industry. The reduction in cyclicality allows more investment in people and technology, attracting better talent and so changing the image of the steel industry. This view complements the message from Lakshmi Mittal in the ArcelorMittal company brochure:

A new era has dawned for the world steel industry. The consolidation process of recent years, which was led in large part by ArcelorMittal and its predecessor companies, has transformed the steelmaking landscape—creating a more stable and sustainable market environment. We are proud to have played our role in this process.

We have long believed that size and scale are vital, both to compete in a global marketplace and to manage supply and demand through the economic cycle. A strong, sustainable industry benefits all its stakeholders—employees, customers and investors alike.

Back to India

The United States, Britain, and Germany made the bulk of the world's steel until the 1970s, when competition from Japan and South Korea, coupled with lowered demand and oil price shocks that adversely affected automobile production, sent Western steelmakers into a downward spiral. The late 1990s brought closures of many plants in western Europe and North America.

Thus the scene was set at the turn of the century for a series of mergers and acquisitions, fueled by steadily rising demand for steel in rapidly industrializing nations, including China and India, which resulted in a trebling of steel prices.[17] Both countries were also becoming major sources of steel production. Thanks to explosive growth in Asia, global steel consumption increased by an average of nearly 6 percent a year between 2000 and 2005, compared with an anemic 1.9 percent annual average growth between 1970 and 2000.[18]

In 2005, ArcelorMittal, despite its global dominance, had no operations in India and China. The next step was clear: new strategies were needed to tap the growth areas in these markets. Production facilities in Asia would allow steel companies to be close not only to massive natural resource supplies but also to key markets. According to Aditya Mittal, "the developing markets of Asia are those of great significance as we look to take advantage of the forecast per capita steel consumption increase in these countries."

In 2006, Mittal announced a memorandum of understanding for an investment of 300–400 billion rupees ($6.7–$9 billion) for a 12-million-ton greenfield steelmaking and mining facility. The operation would be one of India's largest. Though it had been a while coming, the investment made strategic sense. Orissa, the mineral-rich northeastern state, was the proposed site. National demand for steel was widely forecast to rise as the country's economy boomed, with strong growth in the automobile and construction sectors in particular.

The Indian investment signaled a new strategic thrust for Mittal as well as for the industry as a whole. Since its inception, industry attention had been focused on developed nations, but the future belonged to the rapidly expanding economies in Asia.

Is there still room for further consolidation? The steel industry remains fragmented but that is largely limited to China, where 40 percent of the steel industry is located. If China is taken out of the equation, ArcelorMittal's global market share is 20 percent.

What does the future hold for ArcelorMittal? Today the company is producing roughly 110 million metric tons and the goal is to grow shipments to 150 million metric tons in five years. According to

Aditya Mittal, this target will be achieved: "Twenty million tons through organic growth, i.e., brownfield expansions at our existing facilities, such as in Ukraine, Brazil . . . then another 24 million tons from the India project where we want to set up two greenfield facilities—12 million tons each." Excluding any acquisitions, this growth in production exceeds the size of the second-largest steel company in the world.

How does ArcelorMittal view itself? Lakshmi Mittal states:

We are the only truly global steel producer, with a leadership position on four continents. A quarter of our production comes from plants that figure among the lowest-cost producers in the world. High-end and specialty products account for more than 60 percent of shipments. We are not just a steel producer. At one end of the value chain, we are an integrated metals and mining business. At the other, we operate a significant service and distribution business that transforms finished products and delivers a bespoke service to customers.

THREE

Infosys

Born Global to Exploit the Skilled Workforce Advantage

Our industry has been global from day one because when we
all began in the IT industry, there was no Indian IT industry
and thus there was no competition. But we knew we had a great
human capital advantage and that the fulfillment of that
advantage had to be global.

For people like us, going global was not a choice.

Nandan Nilekani, Cochairman and cofounder, Infosys Technologies Limited

THE INDIAN OUTSOURCING industry has helped put India on
the global corporate map. It is populated by many famous Indian
IT companies, the three most famous of which are Infosys, TCS, and
Wipro. Of them, Infosys was born global, and therefore this chapter
starts with its story. Then the rest of the Indian IT industry and its evolution are examined. Finally the copycat outsourcing strategies that the
IT industry has sparked in a variety of sectors are briefly discussed.

Infosys: The Poster Child for Indian Outsourcing

Infosys Technologies was created in 1981 by seven software engineers
with start-up capital of $250, borrowed from the savings the wife of
one of the founders had put aside.[1] Each had walked away from a safe
corporate career to pursue an entrepreneurial dream. It was a bold step

INDIA'S IT OUTSOURCING SNAPSHOT

- Overall sector revenues are projected to grow 33 percent, to $64 billion in 2008.

- As a proportion of GDP, the Indian technology sector revenues have grown from 1.2 percent in 1998 to 5.5 percent in 2008.

- Direct employment in the sector has grown at 26 percent annually between 1998 and 2007, and in 2008 almost 2 million skilled workers were employed in the sector.[2]

in an environment where Indian businesses were shackled by a controlled economy with underdeveloped capital markets, foreign exchange controls, and a poor technological infrastructure.

But audacity makes for a compelling story, and Infosys is no exception. By the financial year-end of March 31, 2008, Infosys was a $4 billion company, with more than ninety-one thousand employees and over 98 percent of its revenue from international clients. Several of those founders—N. R. Narayana Murthy, Nandan Nilekani, and Senapathy Gopalakrishnan—are all now billionaires.

Infosys is truly a company that was born global. According to Nilekani, "We were the only guys from day one that felt the real opportunity was outside India." Infosys's business model—now the gold standard for an entire industry—was an innovation in the delivery of IT services. According to Murthy: "When we founded the company, we knew that India, with its vast pool of English-speaking, analytically strong technical talent and the excellent work ethic among its professionals, had the essential ingredients for global success in customized software development. Thus, our idea was to produce software in India for clients in the G7 countries."

Specifically, the company's initial strategy was to transfer some of that Indian talent abroad to the client site to do basic (and time-consuming) software coding and development work. This became known as "bodyshopping," where Indian companies like Infosys exploited the wage differentials between Indian IT workers and their counterparts in the United States. Infosys hired skilled IT workers in India and then sent them to the U.S. client site for particular projects.

Infosys focused on creating relationships with a few large customers, the first of which was Data Basics Corporation in New York in 1983. Eventually, in 1987, the company opened an office in Boston through a joint venture with an American firm to build the U.S. client base. By this time, Infosys's head office had moved from the front room of Murthy's home to a corporate headquarters in Bangalore. Yet, with 1989 sales at less than half a million dollars, the founders had faced a grueling struggle to build a company. Gopalakrishnan recalled those challenging early years: "We had nothing after eight years of trying to bring up a company. Those who studied with us had cars and houses."[3] With the company on the verge of collapse, one of the founders left, but the other six were unwavering in their ambition.

Being a first mover meant significant challenges in overcoming the deep-rooted skepticism among multinational corporations (MNCs) regarding an Indian company's ability to manage projects eleven time zones and tens of thousands of miles away from the client site. But from the start, Infosys was always focused on world-class quality, helping to set the company apart from India's image. Slowly but surely, major companies like Digital Equipment Corporation and Reebok became Infosys clients.

Sharpening their teeth on client-site projects, Infosys by 1994 had convinced MNCs to move low-end basic maintenance and system migration projects to India, enabled by the emergence of faster Internet connections and improved telecommunications infrastructures. Over the next couple of years, Infosys's offshoring (work done in India for clients abroad) revenue grew, but at a modified pace. That is, until a once-in-a-lifetime opportunity came along, one that could not have boosted Infosys's fortunes more if it had been designed explicitly to do so: "Y2K" mania. By the late 1990s, with the Internet and e-commerce booming and Y2K threat looming, Infosys was on its way. Nilekani described Infosys's growth:

The combination of the environment changing, the technology enabling, and the global clients understanding made everything come together. Global clients began to see the value in India, so selling became easier, and that is how we were able to grow.

The nineties made us sufficiently competitive to make the leap into the global market. As late as 1992 we were only a $3 million company, but by 1999, after taking advantage of liberalization, we were at $121 million. Since then growth has been phenomenal, but the nineties allowed us to move up.

Infosys ended the millennium in style. Besides surpassing $100 million in revenues, it had also become the first Indian company to be listed on an international exchange—the Nasdaq. Nilekani explained the reasoning behind this: "Ultimately, the conclusion for us was to list in the U.S. in 1999. We said that if we're going to be a global company and our clients are going to be global, then being listed in their market is going to give our customers confidence that this is a company that can be trusted. Plus it gave us the ability to raise capital abroad." Born global, Infosys had become a source of national pride while becoming a superstar on the international stage—all before its twentieth birthday. (See the growth summary in table 3-1.)

Y2K turned out to be an imaginary threat, but one thing was real: business-critical projects of a huge scale were well managed by Infosys's cost-effective engineering talent. Further, with the attainment of the highest possible quality ranking—a Capability Maturity Model (CMM) Level 5 certification in 1999—Infosys's high standards of service quality, intellectual property protection, and data security were widely acknowledged. Only twenty-one IT services companies had achieved such recognition at that time.

As Infosys gained scale and experience, it built increasing competence and scope, offering more complex solutions in shorter turnaround times, at a significant cost savings and often a quality advantage to a *Fortune* 2000 company's internal IT departments. Infosys had long ago abandoned bodyshopping and a fee-for-service business model. Instead, it was moving up the value chain, positioning itself as a strategic partner, sharing risk, and codeveloping innovative products and services with its key clients.

The latest maturation of services involves outsourcing noncore business processes, which often have a large IT component, including human resource, supply chain management, and finance and accounting

TABLE 3-1

Infosys ten-year employee and revenue summary

Fiscal year	Employees	Revenues ($ million)
1996	1,172	27
1997	1,705	40
1998	2,605	68
1999	3,766	121
2000	5,389	203
2001	9,831	414
2002	10,738	545
2003	23,377	754
2004	32,178	1,063
2005	44,658	1,592
2006	59,831	2,152
2007	73,490	3,090
2008	91,000	4,176

Source: Adapted from company information.

functions, as well as marketing and research services. For example, Infosys believes that 35 percent of consulting projects (elements such as proposal preparation, presentation preparation, research, and analysis) can be done in India. Clients of engineering services include Airbus and Boeing, both of whom outsource design work to Infosys. Infosys's integrated performance management and compensation solution for a top independent software vendor will enable that company to streamline employee rewards, ratings, and assessment while helping its employees and managers to enjoy a better user experience. In 2007, Infosys signed its biggest deal to date—a $250 million contract from Philips Electronics of the Netherlands. Contracts such as these heightened the pace of Infosys's growth: revenue doubled in 2004 (to $1 billion), 2006 ($2 billion), and again in 2008, reaching over $4 billion.

Infosys faces challenges too, of course. A rise in the rupee adversely impacted exporters. And a slowdown in Infosys's key markets is expected to curtail IT expenditures among *Fortune* 2000 firms in the near term. In the domestic market, a profound talent shortage, due to explosive growth rates and an insatiable appetite for Indian talent, means that Infosys faces annual wage increases of 15 percent and attrition rates of 13 percent.

Infosys has refined human resource management strategies to improve retention rates, not the least of which is a significant investment in training and development. Infosys Center is one of the largest training facilities in the world, capable of training 13,500 candidates every quarter, with accommodation for ten thousand candidates and teaching staff. The $120 million facility has been referred to as a combination of Disney World, Club Med, and a modern American university. Its amenities include movie theaters, hair salons, a huge gym and pool, and a high-tech bowling alley, situated among well-manicured, landscaped vistas. Infosys's reputation and best-in-industry training make it easier for the firm to attract high-caliber candidates, despite lower salaries. According to the company, Infosys received over 1.3 million applications in 2007, but hired less than 3 percent of those applicants.

In 2008, Infosys's client base included over five hundred *Forbes* Global 2000 companies. North America generated over 60 percent of overall revenue, whereas Europe contributed 26 percent; the rest of the world, 9 percent; and India, just 2 percent. It was on the strength of its international client base that Infosys pioneered the Global Delivery Model (GDM). Indeed, it was an interview with Nilekani that sparked Thomas Friedman's now ubiquitous description of the forces of globalization as a "flat world."

Infosys's Global Delivery Model

Infosys's GDM concept is based on the principles of "sourcing capital from where it is cheapest, producing where it is most cost-effective, and selling where it is most profitable, all without being constrained by national boundaries."[4] Nilekani explained: "Our GDM allows us various locations to leverage global capacity, resources, and strengths to desegregate sophisticated software work and get parts of it done in Bangalore, Beijing, and Boston in a seamless manner."

Fifty-two global development centers support Infosys's GDM, the majority of which are located in India. Development centers in Australia, Canada, China, Japan, Mauritius, Mexico, and Poland and at multiple locations in the United States and Europe simultaneously work with Indian centers to collaborate on client projects, allowing work to be done 24/7. Effectively, individual projects are carved up, apportioned to suitable global development centers, and reassembled for client delivery. It attempts to do for services what Henry Ford's assembly line process did for manufacturing.

Infosys's global development centers are often used as "nearshoring" locations. As the name implies, nearshoring involves offshoring to a location that is nearer in distance to a client company. Benefits of proximity include possible temporal, cultural, linguistic, economic, political, or historical alignment. According to Nilekani:

> *To improve our ability to connect with Infosys customers, we have to get geographically closer to them. This will require a much more local presence and much more diversity than we currently have. As we develop multiple locations outside India we want to be multicultural and to be seen as a good local company in the markets where we operate. When we do acquisitions or buy out the employees of a client, we de facto diversify. As we require more creative business solutions, we need diversity beyond left-brain Indian engineers.*

Infosys: Inspiring Corporate India

Without doubt, no company has had as big an impact in inspiring corporate India as Infosys. It has raised the bar for ethical Indian business practices. The company's founders inculcated frameworks for corporate governance, education, social responsibility, and inclusive growth into the spirit of the company from inception. They believed that a corporation's success must be shared by its employees and society alike. This has led to many firsts among Indian corporations. For instance, Infosys was the first company in India to adopt a code of corporate transparency and offer stock options to employees, in 1993.

Legend has it that the founders were intent on creating "a thousand millionaires," epitomizing an organizational culture that was a complete departure from the top-down organizational structure that most of corporate India seemed quite content with. A culture infused with entrepreneurial spirit could be supported only by leading the way in creating a culture of meritocracy. In its 2007 article "Meritocracy Is the Model," *Time* magazine commented, "So many big Indian companies remain family-run that their board meetings might as well be held at the dinner table."[5] Infosys, by contrast, has always had a strict ban on nepotism and a compulsory retirement age of sixty. Leading by example, when Murthy turned sixty, after serving as the CEO for twenty-one years, he handed over the reins to cofounder Nandan M. Nilekani in March 2002, and moved back to his first, more modest office. Murthy's oft-uttered statement "the softest pillow is a clear conscience" is a summary of Infosys's corporate reputation.[6]

Infosys has committed to the highest standards of disclosure and voluntarily provides financial statements in compliance with the GAAP requirements of Australia, Canada, France, Germany, Japan, and the United Kingdom (in addition to those of India and the United States). During 2008, Infosys continued to voluntarily fully comply with the U.S. Sarbanes-Oxley Act (2002). As a result, Infosys placed in the top ten among *Fortune*'s Top Companies for Leaders. Such high-profile recognition, combined with a sustained brand management campaign, has created a valuable global brand.

Infosys has demonstrated that it is possible to be from India and be world-class. Accordingly, as Murthy stated: "Today, no matter where you go in India, if you talk to entrepreneurs in the country, they would say, 'We want to be like Infosys.'"[7] And why not? Infosys has sparked the entrepreneurial dreams and confidence of an entire nation, while creating a whole new generation of middle-class Indians. In creating a highly respected, world-class company that provides excellence in customer service, adopts best management practices from around the world, has a strong corporate brand, voluntarily adopts transparency and wealth sharing, and invests significantly in human resources development and training, Infosys has offered a model for entrepreneurial success in the new Indian economy. But as impressive as it is, Infosys is just one of the Indian IT outsourcing success stories.

The Indian IT Outsourcing Industry

India is the primary recipient of global IT outsourcing; over two-thirds of *Fortune* 500 firms engaged in offshore activities in India in 2008.[8] (See the ten-year growth summary in figure 3-1.) The IT services industry in India can be divided into "captives" because the companies are subsidiaries of non-Indian MNCs, such as IBM, or Indian home-grown third-party suppliers, like Infosys. The latter category—Indian IT services providers—is further segmented into the six major billion-dollar-plus firms and the remaining sub-billion-dollar firms.

The Six Major Players

The top three IT vendors—Tata Consultancy Services (TCS), Wipro, and Infosys—account for nearly half (46 percent) of Indian IT services exports, almost doubling from just a few years ago (26 percent in 2004).[9] These three firms differ from the next twenty-five top IT services exporters not only in revenue and scale, but also in strategy. Their success has established the rules of the game; the end game is becoming a top global outsourcing player, rivaling the likes of Accenture and IBM Global Services. Key success factors of these three firms include profitability, revenue per employee, and growth through service proliferation as well as the ability to scale up operations, especially in terms of talent as employee bases expand both in India and abroad.

The largest Indian IT services exporter is TCS. With over 111,000 employees in fifty countries, TCS created revenues of $5.7 billion in 2008.[10] In rounded numbers, about half of TCS's overall revenue was generated from the United States, $1 billion from the United Kingdom, and $500 million from Europe. New growth markets—Asia-Pacific, India, Latin America, the Middle East, and Africa—grew by over 40 percent in 2008, crossing $1 billion in revenues.

FIGURE 3-1

Indian IT services industry: Ten-year revenue and employee growth

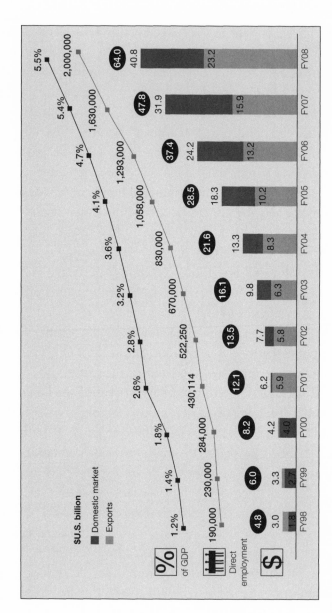

Note: Growth data based on annual revenue aggregate estimates of the IT services sector, comprising IT services, software, engineering services, hardware, and business process outsourcing.

Source: National Association of Software and Services Companies (NASSCOM), 2008. Reprinted with permission.

The third-largest IT services exporter is Wipro Technologies, with over eighty thousand employees. It posted revenues of almost $5 billion in 2008.[11] Wipro has over three hundred customers across the United States, Europe, and Japan, including fifty of the *Fortune* 500 companies, served by operations based in China, Portugal, Romania, Saudi Arabia, and other locations. Its founder, Azim Premji, is one of the richest men in the world, with a personal fortune once estimated at $12.7 billion.[12]

Cognizant, Satyam Computer Services Ltd., and HCL Technologies Ltd. round out the top six Indian IT players. These three firms offer a similar array of services to the top three, each with revenues exceeding $1 billion, about fifty thousand employees operating from diverse geographies, and a client list of *Fortune* 1000 companies. Having established an impressive scale and scope, the strategic choices of these firms are less clear—should they try to compete with the top three on a global level, or establish themselves with more specialized services? They are at a crossroads.

The Specialized Players

The top six Indian IT services firms have, through economies of scale and market share, effectively created high barriers to entry. Other new and existing incumbents have therefore had to specialize by developing software and IT services for a niche market. Thus, the second main category of Indian IT firms comprises the many sub-billion-dollar companies, such as i-flex solutions, 24/7, Minacs, Genpact, and Zensar (see table 3-2). To survive, these firms have had to pursue a strategy of product, process, or business model innovation (or sometimes, a combination thereof).

I-flex, with its focus on financial services, is an example of a specialized firm that has succeeded through product innovation. Founded in the mid-1980s as a division of Citicorp, i-flex was acquired by Oracle in 2005.[13] I-flex now operates in over 130 countries and had revenues in 2008 of over half a billion dollars.[14] The 1997 launch of FLEXCUBE, an end-to-end complete banking product suite, put the company on the global map and brought it industrywide recognition. Since its launch, FLEXCUBE has become the product of choice of 340 financial institutions in over 115 countries.[15]

TABLE 3-2

Top twenty IT software and service exporters from India (2006–2007) (excludes Information Technology Enabled Service-Business Process Outsourcing)

Rank	Company
1	Tata Consultancy Services Ltd.
2	Infosys Technologies Ltd.
3	Wipro Technologies Ltd.
4	Satyam Computer Services Ltd.
5	HCL Technologies Ltd.
6	Tech Mahindra Ltd.
7	Patni Computer Systems Ltd.
8	i-flex solutions Ltd.
9	L&T InfoTech Ltd.
10	Polaris Software Lab Ltd.
11	Hexaware Technologies Ltd.
12	Flextronics Software Systems Ltd. (Aricent)
13	Mphasis BFL Ltd.
14	Mastek Ltd.
15	Siemens Information Systems Ltd.
16	NIIT Technologies Ltd.
17	Prithvi Information Solutions Ltd.
18	Genpact
19	iGate Global Solutions Ltd.
20	Birlasoft

Source: National Association of Software and Services Companies (NASSCOM), 2007.

Rajesh Hukku, the chairman and managing director of i-flex, explained: "I was fed up with Indian brains being labeled as cheap, English-speaking labor when I knew we were capable of innovating."[16] He further described how i-flex sets itself apart from its competitors: "With our product strategy, we generate the added value ourselves and don't just earn the money by helping companies run other people's software."[17]

Hukku was often met with resistance when trying to market his two award-winning products, FLEXCUBE and Reveleus, to Western banks. One European executive quipped that only God could figure out the complexity of the banking systems. To which Hukku responded: "Sir, we are Indians. We are very religious, and very close to God."[18] He closed the deal!

Process innovation is developing specific domain expertise on a process level to improve the customer's operational efficiency. A case in point is the development of Zensar's "solution blueprinting framework" (SBP), which automates the software development life cycle and accelerates software development. Zensar has also increased the efficiency of software development by creating a common platform for experts to collaborate on individual projects. SBP is delivered through a global development platform that spans five centers in four countries, which facilitates real-time collaboration among global customers and partners.

In the business process outsourcing (BPO) sector, 24/7 has brought its own brand of process innovation to the call center industry since its launch in 2000, building a profitable, rapidly growing business. Starting with just one call center in Bangalore, the company now has eleven global delivery centers, including locations in the Philippines and Guatemala. The demand for greater customized outsourcing services was understood by P. V. Kannan, the CEO and cofounder of 24/7. It was the first BPO firm to offer a multishore global delivery model and an integrated customer life cycle management service. Similarly, Genpact, with over thirty centers in nine countries, is becoming a major player for outsourcing telephone debt collection. The company employs thousands of debt collectors not only in India, but also in Romania, Mexico, and the Philippines. The somewhat surprising result is that debt-stricken Americans find themselves receiving calls from Delhi asking very politely for money in an Indian accent.

An example of business model innovation is Minacs's broad geographic footprint. As with many Indian IT services firms, the company's success is based on an effective global services delivery model with nearshoring locations in Canada and Europe. One example is Minacs's dealer support programs for an automotive company, operating throughout forty-three countries in twenty-four languages from three main European locations in Germany, Hungary, and the United Kingdom. Technical assistance centers help with diagnostic calls from dealer technicians, marketing assistance centers help with outbound marketing, and dealer assistance centers support dealer parts and warranty departments. By centralizing such a range of multilingual services through Minacs, the auto company is able to service multiple markets with higher consistency and lower costs across European operations, while improving communication and knowledge sharing across the organization.

Leveraging Competence, Not Costs

One could say that India is offshoring its own offshoring. It is estimated that Indian IT services providers are expanding their U.S.-based operations at an annual rate of roughly 40 percent and their European operations by 60 percent.[19] According to Sundip Nandy, vice president of strategy at Wipro, for example, "If Shell wants us to follow them somewhere, we follow them there." Each remote Wipro site behaves as an independent organization with the primary purpose of understanding customers and/or mastering a domain integral to deepening the company's service offerings. "We have a whole bunch of talented people who can build businesses on their own," said Nandy.

But it is not only Europe and the United States that are growing as recipients of Indian IT outsourcing investment. Bangladesh, the Philippines, Eastern Europe, Vietnam, and Mexico are fast expanding as offshoring locations. Indeed, these regions are not only becoming valuable offshoring locations for Indian IT services firms, but are at the same time becoming increasingly viable competitors to India for offshore services investment. Indian companies have responded with a twofold strategy, expanding to these developing countries before their clients do while deepening the Indian advantage. According to Ganesh Natarajan, the chairman of the National Association of Software and Services Companies (NASSCOM), Indian IT services firms are moving "from labor arbitrage to value arbitrage by creating a hub of world-class processes." He explained: "Indian IT services firms are developing competencies to assemble new processes. We are not simply reengineering existing processes. Rather, we identify a desired outcome, design a new process to achieve it, then build the technology around it. Indian innovation is not a fluke. It's captured by a very deliberate process which supports a virtuous cycle fostering greater innovation."

Endless Possibilities for Indian Outsourcing

The incredible success of IT services firms has sparked the imagination of Indian entrepreneurs, who have applied the process, product, and business model innovation at the heart of this success to service-specific non-IT niches, including the medical, pharmaceutical, legal, and animation industries, to name just a few. All of them attempt to exploit the cost, quality, and scale of the skilled workforce available in India.

In medical services offshoring, highly skilled radiologists in Bangalore analyze not only X-rays but, increasingly, more sophisticated CT scans, ultrasounds, and MRI images. Teleradiology Solutions services dozens of hospitals and clinics in the United States, for example. Its clients save money and the patients receive accurate readings within a day or two—arguably a key benefit for patients used to waiting up to two weeks to hear perhaps one of the most important results of their lives.

Medical tourism has become big business as patients from the developed world go to India for complex operations, like heart surgery, at a fraction of what it would cost back home. It is estimated that 150,000 foreigners are treated annually in India, the majority from the United Kingdom and United States. The increasing popularity of health tourism is predicted to create revenues of $1 billion for the Indian economy by 2012.[20]

The pharmaceutical industry also is increasingly turning to India for offshoring. Indian companies specializing in research and development, clinical trials, medical data analysis, and lab services, for instance, are reducing drug development times and helping to contain escalating R&D expenditures for Western drug companies. With more than eighty manufacturing facilities approved by the U.S. Food and Drug Administration, India is a preferred location for outsourcing drug manufacturing as well.

The Indian pharmaceutical industry has become a global success story and is a market leader in producing low-cost, high-quality generic drugs. It is predicted that its current market share will rise from 14 to 50 percent by 2010, with revenues of $20 billion by 2015.[21] The leading players in the Indian pharma industry include Caraco, Ranbaxy, Dabur, Dr. Reddy's, Wockhardt, Cipla, Lupin, and Nicholas Piramal.

In the fast-expanding legal process outsourcing niche, legal firms around the world are reducing costs and increasing productivity by offshoring to India (where high-quality work is done around the clock). This leverages a large pool of law graduates in a country where the legal system is similar to those in the United States and United Kingdom. In addition to IT, human resources, document management, and litigation support, legal firms are increasingly outsourcing knowledge services such as case law research, precedent checking, drafting legal documents, reviewing contracts, and filing patent applications.

Demand for animation production services from India is growing with the emergence of an organized animation production sector, capable of the state-of-the-art work required for international TV and film production, at substantially lower costs. Overseas entertainment giants like Walt Disney, Warner Brothers, and Sony are leveraging Bollywood's infrastructure, second only to Hollywood's. Once a script and storyboard have been created by, say, Walt Disney in the United States, production (drawing cells, hand-coloring, inking, painting, and camera work) is done in India and sent back to Disney for postproduction (visual and audio editing). Companies such as Crest Animation, UTV Toons, Pentamedia Graphics, Padmalaya Telefilms, Moving Picture Company, Toonz Animation, and Jadoo Works offer such services. An Indian newspaper headline captured the boom in film production outsourcing to India: "A Hollywood movie set in Switzerland . . . made in India."[22]

IT was not the first industry to leverage India's pool of skilled workers. The rather low-tech diamond cutting and polishing industry is considered to be India's first "born global" industry. In fact, India is home to the world's largest cutting and polishing sector, employing 3 million people or 94 percent of the world's diamond workers. India's average $10-per-carat labor cost for cutting and polishing is much lower than the per-carat rate of $17 in China, $100 in Tel Aviv, and $150 in Belgium. Nine out of ten diamonds under one carat are cut and polished in India, with exports worth $17 billion in 2007.[23] India's share of global diamond polishing is 57 percent, and 40 percent of the trade in Antwerp, the diamond-trading capital of the world, is now controlled by expatriate Indians.[24]

Conclusion

Indian outsourcing touches the daily lives of consumers around the globe, whether they know it or not. Imagine a household in the United States. The stories in the newspaper that landed on the family's doorstep at dawn were researched overnight in India, as was the analysis of the family's equity portfolio that arrived in the morning mail. Patient notes from the daughter's visit to the family doctor in the early afternoon were typed up on the other side of the world and placed in her file before she'd finished watching her Walt Disney DVD (created with animation cells drawn in Bollywood) in bed that evening after taking a prescription for a medication that was manufactured in Ahmedabad. Meanwhile, Dad is downstairs on the phone with a polite, knowledgeable, and patient customer service agent with an ever-so-slight Indian accent and an American name of Polly who is helping him download a new online banking software application (developed in Bangalore, of course). In the living room, Mom is reviewing the income tax filing by the local branch of a national accounting firm and the details of the car insurance claim she submitted to her bank, both efficiently processed in just two days despite being ten time zones away.

But just when one might think "what else can be outsourced to India?" another innovative outsourcing services niche pops up where you might least expect it. Think of a service that doesn't need to be fulfilled physically in the same place as the consumer is located, and India probably can do it—at equal quality, often with improved processes, and almost always a lower cost. And yet just 4 percent of the world's outsourcing investment ended up in India in 2008. Astonishingly, we have seen only the tip of the iceberg.

FOUR

Bharat Forge

Bringing Technology and Speed to the World Forging Market

Confidence is essential to globalization . . .
and it grows with every success.

Baba N. Kalyani,
Chairman and Managing Director, Bharat Forge

DETROIT. STUTTGART. Tokyo. Shanghai. Pune.[1] These cities
have one thing in common: they're manufacturing hubs of key
players in the global automotive industry. But Pune? And high-tech
manufacturing in India? In the past decade, manufacturers in Eastern
Europe, China, and Southeast Asia have established reputations for
quality, reliability, and cost efficiency. But manufacturing-led, export-
driven growth bypassed India . . . until now.

Whereas Indian manufacturing has generally been associated
with belching machines, clanking equipment, flooded mud roads,
and dodgy power supplies, a few companies are emerging as contenders for domination of global markets after securing large chunks
of the domestic market. One such company—Bharat Forge—has
transformed itself from a basic manufacturer for domestic consumption into the second-largest forgings (bending metal into finished
shape) company in the world, with sales of more than $1 billion in
2007. Bharat Forge's goal is to surpass ThyssenKrupp of Germany
and become number one in the world.

BHARAT FORGE SNAPSHOT

- Second-largest forging company in the world behind ThyssenKrupp of Germany and ahead of Sumitomo Metal Industries of Japan.
- Supplier to thirty-five of the world's forty largest automotive original equipment manufacturers and Tier I suppliers.
- Listed on *Forbes* Asia's 200 Best Under a Billion from 2003 to 2006.
- Operates ten manufacturing plants in six countries.

A seminal advertising slogan of the 1970s was "This is not your father's Oldsmobile." Well, Bharat Forge is not your father's supplier to General Motors, the parent of Oldsmobile, either. Several elements have been instrumental in its quest to conquer world markets— a bold overseas acquisition strategy, a focus on human resource management, and a significant investment in developing superior technology. Technology services companies have proved that "Indian high-tech" is not the oxymoron it once was. And Kalyani has not only understood the imperative but has also successfully implemented the technology and quality controls necessary to compete in markets where precision is measured in .001 millimeter. It might not mean much to many of us, but if you're an engineering nerd, a technology geek, or especially if you're a Daimler or Chrysler purchasing manager placing a $15 million order, a fraction of a millimeter can make or break the deal.

So just how did a Nehru-era socialist company break from the shackles of the past to develop the capabilities to lead the hypercompetitive, highly cyclical, volatile, and demanding world of parts manufacturing for global automotive manufacturers?

One confident step at a time.

Thinking Global

Bharat Forge was established in 1961 with a government mandate to produce engine parts to meet India's domestic automotive production needs. The initial company strategy was born in a centrally planned socialist environment of production quotas, price controls, and strong employee rights—not customer service, quality, and innovation.

Change came in the 1970s, with a period of growth and consolidation within the Indian forgings industry. Bharat Forge emerged as the undisputed domestic leader throughout the 1980s. Thus, in 1991, when India began liberalizing, Bharat Forge found itself in a favorable position. The company was well poised to be the supplier to the many global auto giants rushing to establish manufacturing operations in India. The potential of the vast and expanding market of India's middle class, along with the promise of the country's low-cost manufacturing base, was highly compelling.

It was Bharat Forge's chairman and managing director, Baba Kalyani, an MIT-trained engineer with bold vision, who realized that his company's current capabilities would become obsolete in the new economic environment. Kalyani bet heavily that the future of Indian manufacturing would be driven by sophisticated production to meet the quality requirements of global original equipment manufacturers. Further, Kalyani knew that to leverage economies of scale and manage cyclical risk, Bharat Forge would have to be closer to the buzz of new scientific and technological development.

In response to Kalyani's prescience, an audacious global strategy was born. By successfully competing with multinationals in post-1991 India, Bharat Forge laid the foundation for overseas growth. First, Bharat Forge experienced dramatic success through export-driven domestic growth by changing the workforce of the firm from muscle power to brain power. Then the company adopted an aggressive international acquisition strategy, thereby gaining credibility, customers, and production capacity and, most important, achieving Kalyani's goal of acquiring technological expertise.

From Muscle Power to Brain Power

Well before the Infosys, Tata, and Wipro success stories, India's best bet for economic development was thought to be in leveraging its low-cost manufacturing base, employing legions of workers in low-skilled jobs on basic production lines. By contrast, Kalyani's vision, which began in the late 1980s, involved an aggressive international strategy that would develop technological advantage through sophisticated production lines employing highly skilled Indian engineers at relatively low cost. He hoped to realize his vision of technological superiority in a country with vast pools of manual laborers, an unreliable infrastructure, and a reputation for low quality. It's not a stretch to imagine that at the time, Kalyani's strategy would be considered daring and risky at best, foolhardy at least, and, at worst, a disaster in the making.

The availability of cheap manual labor in the country combined with high capital costs led Indian companies to make an archaic trade-off. Instead of investing in technologically sophisticated production equipment, they preferred to employ a large blue-collar workforce in a labor-intensive manual production process. Bharat Forge was no exception, and most of its hammer shop operations for making forgings were manual. But Kalyani realized that it was impossible to make world-class products on a consistent basis utilizing this manual process.

Kalyani correctly identified the core competencies in which Bharat Forge would need to invest to become a player on the world stage: speed to market, high quality, low cost, volume, production flexibility, and a distinctly customer-focused orientation. And these competencies would not be possible without a highly trained, motivated, and productive workforce. He needed to replace muscle power with brain power. To actualize his vision, Bharat Forge would have to make considerable investments in technology in the hope of gaining a future advantage.

In the late 1980s, Bharat Forge acquired a couple of new, state-of-the-art, fully automated press lines for manufacturing forgings.[2] But the existing manual workforce in the hammer shop did not know how to operate them. Bharat Forge decided to place these machines in a new workshop that would be run by freshly recruited young white-collar employees with science degrees. Unlike the old forging shop, where workers had narrow specializations like machinist, grinder, fitter, and so on, this new workforce was multiskilled, having the ability to do several jobs at very high levels of productivity. The older manual employees were given an option to retire early, and many chose to do so. The remaining employees received extensive training to upgrade their skills.

The impact of this transformation was dramatic. The company went from an 85 percent blue-collar workforce in 1989 to an 85 percent white-collar workforce in 2000, with more than seven hundred engineers. The modern facility also helped make global customers feel comfortable with the idea that Bharat Forge could potentially be their supplier. Automation lowered variable production costs considerably. In addition, the life of the dies used to make forgings increased. A die that previously would make a thousand forgings in the hammer shop could now make 2,500 forgings in the press line. Quality and speed increased, while simultaneously lowering costs. Figure 4-1 outlines the company's transformation.

FIGURE 4-1

Bharat Forge: Then and now

That was then . . .	This is now . . .	Key points
Indian socialist beginnings	Capitalist player in India—a fast-growing economic global powerhouse	Customer-centric strategy, profitable growth
Old economy	New economy	Driven by brain power versus muscle power; reliance on computing power as much as heavy-duty presses; Engineering and Design Centre as critical as the shop floor
Associated with Indian manufacturing (poor infrastructure, basic, unreliable, low quality)	Well-established reputation for quality, innovation, and speed to market redefining Indian manufacturing	High-tech, six sigma processes and ISO 9000 registered, high-speed machining and automated, computerized production lines
Narrow product range and capabilities	Enhanced product range—600–700 products	Sophisticated and flexible manufacturing processes producing everything from 350 kg crankshafts to tiny transmission parts
Product design, development, and production in 6–8 months	Product development in 2–3 weeks (the "wow" factor and speed to market) Key clients invited to witness the process	Successful client development strategy ensures flow of new clients and provides them with unexpected levels of presales service
First international customer took 7 years to secure	Confronting notions about India and Indian companies as a risky place to do business, with outdated manufacturing and poor infrastructure	Perceptions being replaced by spotlight on Indian technology enhancing Indian manufacturing

FIGURE 4-1   (CONTINUED)

Domestic market for 30 years, overreliance on single export customer (90% export revenues from a single customer in 2002)	Export revenue of $150 million in 2007 Exponential growth in export revenue, spread across three regions	Spreading of business risk geographically Roughly half of export revenue in 2007 from North America, a third from the United Kingdom and Europe, and 20% from the Asia-Pacific region
Blue-collar workforce (85%) in 1989—1,800 manual laborers	Professional workforce (85%) in 2000—over 700 engineers	Led by MIT-trained engineer turned entrepreneur—chairman and managing director Baba Kalyani
No contact with customers below senior management level	Integrated client servers for interactive real-time design and collaboration	A collaborative multilevel partnership with customers
Largely self-reliant	Strategic partnerships to ensure manufacturing excellence, be close to market, keep abreast of key industry trends and the latest in technological developments	European and U.S.-based manufacturing sites bringing technological expertise and building the client base, transferring knowledge to lost Indian and Chinese manufacturing bases
Diversity across Indian subcultures	45% non-Indian workforce	Dealing with diversity within India was valuable experience for managing highly diverse workforce throughout the world
Single manufacturing site for domestic market	"Dual-source" manufacturing capacity Manufacturing facilities in 11 locations and 6 countries—3 in India, 3 in Germany, 1 each in Sweden, Scotland, North America, and 2 in China	Goal of design and engineering and forging manufacturing capability for core products in at least two locations globally (and in most cases more than two)
De-risking strategy	17% of total revenue in 2007 from nonautomotive business	Goal of 40% revenue from nonautomotive sectors within five years

Source: Adapted from company information.

Realizing Global Strategy

Kalyani displayed almost unimaginable patience in executing the global strategy—it took a full seven years to sign his first international customer, Rockwell International (now known as ArvinMeritor) in the United States. Kalyani attributed this to two key factors. "First," he acknowledged, "India was perceived as a high-risk environment in manufacturing." There was tremendous negative publicity about the existing system in India. Indian manufacturing was often associated with low-quality, inefficient production processes and insufficient, unreliable infrastructure and distribution/logistics. "Second," he added, "nobody outside of India had heard of Bharat Forge." Kalyani explained how they overcame these barriers:

> *We brought in one simple strategy of speed to market to overcome challenges. We created a process to do things in a third of the time a European or American company took to do similar tasks, using technology. ArvinMeritor, a Tier 1 automotive supplier, visited our plant and found us producing a part for their automobiles in just three weeks from scratch. They were blown away. We used speed to market to develop the confidence. We did the same thing with Caterpillar. Low cost, high technologies, and speed of delivery have all helped us to be accepted in the Western markets.*

Bharat Forge also confronted the prospective customer's more legitimate fears with respect to supply. An Indian supplier would be far away in an industry that does not like to hold inventory and expects frequent delivery. To allay this problem, Bharat Forge deputed a resident engineer to the United States, where he was based in a warehouse that was located close to the customer and stocked thirty days of inventory.

Global Ramp Up Through Acquisitions

Bharat Forge was among the first Indian automotive component manufacturers to pursue a strategy of inorganic growth as a means to establish itself as a global winner. In this decade Bharat Forge had been on a spending spree, investing in six overseas companies.

Kalyani's global acquisition strategy was two-pronged. The first goal was to expand the company's product range and thus its customer base. Second, with facilities closer to its clients, Bharat Forge could develop closer client partnerships as well as ensure more efficient logistics.

The first big step in Bharat Forge's journey toward global leadership was the 2002 agreement with Dana Corporation's United Kingdom operation in Kirkstall, Leeds. Dana wanted to divest this business for £10 million, but was unable to find a buyer at anywhere close to that amount. Bharat Forge was not interested in the physical assets of the firm but in its order book. Creatively structuring a deal, Bharat Forge helped Dana find other buyers for the physical assets of land, buildings, and plant, while acquiring the order book as well as some tools and dies for £3 million. The tools and dies were moved to Pune, while the order book brought with it a dozen new customers with long-term contracts worth £10 million a year for the next seven years.

The next step, in 2004, was more a leap than a step: a bold investment of well over a billion dollars for a sophisticated engineering manufacturing facility—Carl Dan Peddinghaus GmbH (CDP) in Germany, the original home of the auto industry and the source of many technological developments. The successful integration of CDP with Bharat Forge's operations—an ROI within three years and growth over the same period from a €100 million to a €160 million company—was a real boost in confidence, fuelling further growth. Table 4-1 outlines the nature of the merger.

In 2005, a particularly big year for the company, Bharat Forge acquired a U.S. manufacturer to gain traction in one of its largest markets. That same year, Bharat Forge signed a joint venture agreement with the largest automotive group in China. China alone added one hundred thousand metric tons of capacity. By 2007, Bharat Forge's exports to the United States, United Kingdom, Europe, and Japan reached $150 million. By 2008, Bharat Forge's manufacturing facilities were spread over eleven locations and six countries, with the United States accounting for over 50 percent of the annual revenue.

According to Kalyani: "The ongoing process of Indian companies becoming global is driven largely by confidence. I'm beginning to see a picture develop where Indian companies are in a leadership position in their domestic markets, and want to expand. And the only way they can expand is by going global."

Kalyani's vision was becoming a reality and Bharat Forge was well on its way to becoming an Indian multinational corporation with a truly global customer base. As table 4-2 demonstrates, the

TABLE 4-1

Bharat Forge Limited and Carl Dan Peddinghaus merger

	CDP	BFL	Combined entity
Size	Germany's second-largest company	Third-largest forging company in the world, with largest single facility	World's second-largest forging company
Geographical spread	Europe-centric operations	Asia and U.S.-centric operations	Global footprint
Product breadth	Primarily focused on passenger car components (50%+) with limited commercial vehicle business (20%)	Primarily focused on commercial vehicles (60%+) and diesel engines (15%)	Broad coverage of product markets
Facilities	Capacity focused on small forgings	One of the world's only two companies in heavy forging	Complete range of forging facilities
Value proposition	Renowned for high-end technology operations with strong design and engineering capabilities; located close to the customer	Destination for low-cost operations, suitable for certain limited types of components	Ability to provide a complete solution to major customers

Source: Adapted from J. Ramachandran and Sourav Mukherji, Bharat Forge Limited, "Forging Leadership," case study (Bangalore: Indian Institute of Management, 2005).

ten-year transformation from an Indian firm with one international customer to a diversified customer base comprising almost all the blue-chip companies in the automotive sector has been remarkable. However, embracing the culture of a sophisticated technological global company has required massive organizational change.

"Very Basic Tools" to Win Over Employees

In contrast to sophisticated production and manufacturing processes, Kalyani's approach to human resource management (HRM) was decidedly low-tech. Kalyani referred to HRM as "people systems," thus highlighting his down-to-earth approach.

For systems integration of new companies, headquarters in India standardized operations, systems, and structures while leaving a wide margin for local adaptation. Bharat Forge placed a high degree of trust

TABLE 4-2

Bharat Forge global customers, 1994 and 2008

	Asia	Europe	North America
1994			ArvinMeritor
2008	Eicher	AkerKvaerner	ArvinMeritor
	First Auto Works China	Audi	Axle Alliance
	Honda	BMW	Cameron
	Toyota	Caterpillar Perkins	Caterpillar
	Yuchai China	Cummins	Dana Corporation
		Daimler	Detroit Diesel
		Dana Corporation	Ford
		DAF	GE
		Ford	GM
		IVECO	Halliburton
		MAN	Ingersoll-Rand
		New Holland	MWM International
		Renault	
		Rexroth Bosch	
		Saab	
		Scania	
		Wartsila	
		Vestas	
		Volvo	
		Volkswagen	

in local management teams, keeping them in place as part of its integration strategy. "We rely on local management entirely," said Kalyani.

To ensure integration of key processes and systems, Bharat Forge's operations team visited each acquisition site every six to eight weeks or so to ensure efficiency. Finance personnel from Pune reviewed the books in person on a monthly basis, and business development teams also visited monthly to ensure activities were proceeding according to agreed-upon plans. According to Kalyani: "We have developed a structured relationship process with management teams in our international operations that works by integrating our processes locally, while leaving the local managers to do what they do best."

With every international acquisition, Bharat Forge paid a great deal of attention to the people integration processes. According to Kalyani, "We did individual interventions to increase the trust and confidence of the people working there." In dealing with employees other than management, Bharat Forge used what Kalyani referred to as "very basic tools. We have a very simple employee integration process—we constantly communicate (sharing information, being very open), we involve employees actively in the company's activities and direction-setting, and ensure there's a strong community involvement on behalf of the company."

Kalyani recounted one story in particular that highlighted the success of a simple, commonsense approach to gaining buy-in from employees:

> *Recently, we bought a company in Lansing, Michigan, with a strong union presence: the United Auto Workers. They're powerful, and are a tough nut to crack. Lansing is an area where, in the last decade, plants have been shutting down in large numbers. And that's where this one was heading—we bought it out of a bankruptcy process, so it was really in terrible shape. I went there myself to visit the two hundred employees. I spoke with them—they were grumpy, nasty, unhappy, mistrustful . . . everything. I also walked around the plant—it was filthy. I couldn't believe it was a plant in the U.S. I have a habit of going into locker rooms in plants because I believe that the locker rooms really tell you the story of what is going on. I couldn't believe how people would use that place—stinking, smelly, in really bad shape. The first thing I did was to build a new locker room with very clean and modern facilities. It became a symbol of hope, new beginnings, and was a symbol of our commitment.*

In a single simple act, he won over the employees and had an organization that previously had often faced bankruptcy, but was now better motivated and suddenly able to believe there was a future.

The Future: Opportunities and Challenges

Global auto manufacturers are facing tough challenges associated with sluggish sales, poor financials, and fierce competition. Prices are forecast to remain flat at least until 2013. With the auto industry in crisis, how successful and profitable auto component suppliers can be is debatable. Thus, global OEM and component manufacturers will continue to expand their supplier base in low-cost countries in a never-ending search for effective cost-cutting strategies to resist profit erosion.

India is well-positioned for global sourcing, currently exporting just $2 billion in auto parts annually, less than 10 percent, on average, of the exports of Mexico, Canada, and Japan. Indian auto component manufacturers' relatively lower labor costs and overheads have resulted in a 20 to 30 percent cost advantage over their U.S. counterparts.[3] This is despite the fact that the Indian manufacturers average significantly higher margins of 36 percent, versus 13 percent for their global peers.[4]

Already dominating the domestic market, owning 45 percent of India's $615 million market for forgings, Bharat Forge by 2008 was particularly well positioned to capitalize on the projected 25 percent annualized growth in the auto parts exports sector. According to Kalyani: "We have a de-risked business model. We operate in both the commercial vehicle and passenger car segments; increasingly, we will operate in nonautomotive sides of the business, and we now have operations spread throughout three continents—North America, Europe, and Asia."

All too often, manufacturing stories are cautionary tales. Systemic issues remain in the Indian manufacturing sector—poor infrastructure development in a highly sensitive JIT (just-in-time) manufacturing environment, traditionally low levels of productivity, a countrywide reputation for low quality, heavy reliance on foreign sources of technology, and a need for stronger investments in home-grown R&D. However, Bharat Forge through a modular approach—confident and shrewd strategies that leveraged past victories—has succeeded where others haven't even dared. With a strong focus on innovation, a customer service orientation based on client collaboration, cost-effective yet people-sensitive systems, and the successful implementation of a bold international acquisition strategy, Bharat Forge is well on its way to becoming number one in the world.

Not bad at all for a once modest Indian manufacturer from a city not many outside India had heard of before.

FIVE

Essel Propack

Following a Global Customer Across the World

If you have a product you truly believe in that is global in terms of competitiveness, then just do it. Find a way to play on the global stage.

Ashok Goel, Managing Director and Vice Chairman, Essel Propack

"HELP THY BROTHER'S *boat across and, Lo! Thine own has reached the shore.*" This Hindu proverb sums up Essel Propack's route to global success—hitch a ride with a sterling customer, in Essel's case most notably Procter & Gamble, and reap reciprocal benefits.[1] The story of Essel's evolution from a one-unit company in Vasind, India, to global leader in laminated tubes is the story of the power of a fortuitous partnership that evolved as most relationships do—through a series of accidents, opportunities, and mutual gain.

The Beginning

Essel's origins were as an agricultural trading group. In the 1970s, the Indian government needed to store food after several bumper crops and so, with government support, the Essel Group began making giant envelopes out of polymers that could store up to a hundred tons of grain. Dovetailing this experience, Subhash Chandra, great-grandson of the company's founder (now chairman of Essel Group)

ESSEL PROPACK SNAPSHOT

- A manufacturer of laminated and plastic tubes, medical devices, and specialty packaging, Essel Propack is number one in the world in laminated tubes with a 32 percent global share.

- Global operations achieved a turnover in excess of $300 million for the year 2007 with a five-year target of $500 million.

- Twenty-five plants located in India, Egypt, China, United States, United Kingdom, Russia, Germany, Mexico, Colombia, Venezuela, Philippines, Indonesia, Nepal, and Singapore.

- The company's 2,700 employees represent more than twenty nationalities.

- Customers include Colgate-Palmolive, L'Oreal, Procter & Gamble, and Unilever.

explored alternative business opportunities in packaging and in 1984 settled on laminated tubes.

Essel Propack began as Essel, a single-unit company in Vasind, India, that combined both lamination and tube manufacturing. Significantly, in the late 1980s, its capacity for laminating tubes far exceeded that of manufacturing them—lamination capacity equivalent to 1.4 billion tubes versus production capacity of 53 million tubes—so Essel's first opportunity was matching tube production to lamination capacity. In 1990 Essel added two manufacturing units close to Bombay, and in 1994 opened a third in Wada, all dedicated solely to tube production.

Essel's key client in India was Procter & Gamble (P&G). Paradoxically, P&G did not sell toothpaste in India at all due to the foreign exchange balancing system that existed at the time. As part of their ongoing relationship, P&G proposed a potentially mutually beneficial arrangement with Essel that would mark the company's first foray out of India. In the words of R. Chandrasekhar, chief global operating officer: "P&G suggested we join hands with one of their existing suppliers and set up a packaging facility to make tubes in Egypt. It was to be a very small facility—only 20 million tubes—of which P&G said they would underwrite 9 to 12 million. The balance we could sell."

The deal seemed to be an excellent opportunity for Essel to explore international manufacturing, mitigating some of the financial

A Primer on Laminated Tubes

Most tubes were fashioned out of flexible aluminum sheets. However, when aluminum mixed with fluoride, the reaction formed a toxic chemical, and therefore, nontoxic laminated tubes were more appropriate for oral care products. Laminated tubes also could be decorated more easily than metal tubes. Thus, aluminum tubes were manufactured for pharmaceutical and industrial uses, whereas laminated tubes were used in oral care products (and plastic tubes for cosmetics).

Manufacturing of laminated tubes was not technologically challenging. However, making money in it was. A tube sold for roughly one rupee (three cents), with a net margin of 14 percent. In a mostly automated operation, a low-cost Indian workforce was not much of an advantage.

Today, Essel Propack has 32 percent of the global market for laminated tubes. Its key global competitors included manufacturers in France and Britain, which control about 25 percent of the market. The remaining market need was met by consumer packaged goods firms as part of their vertical integration process.

Rising per capita GDP in developing countries, especially Southeast Asia, is expected to accelerate to dental hygiene products. The entire consumer goods market in India is experiencing double-digit growth due to rising disposable incomes. As demand for consumer products escalates, increased competition among consumer products companies is expected to result in the use of packaging as a marketing tool—a trend that favors the industry and Essel Propack.

---

risk while deepening the relationship with a key client. It would be a learning experience.

Passage from India

In Egypt, Essel entered into a joint venture (JV) with a local partner—P&G's existing supplier in Egypt. In exchange for a minority (35 percent) share, Essel provided know-how and raw material to Osama Mashoor, the local partner who ran the business.

The first year Essel made a profit. Then for the following seven years, expenditures seemed to eat up profit, and the JV was in the red each year. With just two months' notice, P&G pulled out entirely, leaving Essel with several million laminated tubes in search of a customer. As the local partner had no other supplier relationships, Essel was forced to recapitalize operations and spent the next five years in survival mode.

Despite the challenges in the relationship, Mashoor remained Essel's local partner in Egypt, though Essel subsequently took control of the JV with a 75 percent share. In Chandrasekhar's words, Mashoor was "a good partner." Acting as a silent partner, Mashoor developed into a valuable human resource consultant. Specifically, he identified qualified technical people, avoiding a shortage of skilled labor. Thus, in the final analysis, rather than fruitlessly pointing fingers, Essel's leadership saw the value in an ongoing relationship (which was solidified with Essel's majority ownership of the JV).

According to Chandrasekhar, mistakes were made in Egypt, but the experience was not in vain. He explained:

> Unless you have a relationship with the customer and understand how the customer's organization works, you cannot succeed. Our partner in Egypt knew only the buyer of P&G who buys the tube . . . nobody knew the matrix they reported to or whose door we were supposed to knock on.
>
> We also learned we should no longer be a minority partner in a JV. But most of all, it fired our imagination to become a global company. We were on top of the world. We had made a success in a tough place like Egypt and now we should be thinking bigger. Hence, in a way, the loss of the P&G order helped us to look at other opportunities.

Interesting Times in China

Essel recognized the tremendous market potential in China and began scouting the Chinese market from early 1995. "Interesting times" is how Goel characterized the mid-1990s, as China was opening up for business and multinationals such as Essel were trying to figure out how best to take advantage of the opportunity.

With no exposure to the local market or knowledge of the Chinese regulatory labyrinth, Essel initially sought a (majority) JV with a local Chinese company. This strategy was soon abandoned, however, as Chandrasekhar felt that potential local partners were predominantly driven by a short-term "hit and run" money-making mentality rather than the desire for an investment for the long haul.

Essel leadership opted for 100 percent ownership. This was a weighty decision, carrying substantial risk. Essel was familiar with developing market dynamics, but China was entirely alien. Chandrasekhar outlined some of the challenges: "None of us spoke the language, which was a big issue. The regulatory environment was very different—different courts. We had a couple of bad experiences . . . somebody sold us a piece of land which was owned by the state and walked away with the money. We quickly learned that China had a very unique corporate environment."

But Essel's leadership did not give up and grew more steadfast in their determination for 100 percent ownership, particularly when it seemed to them that in practice, minority shareholders enjoyed the same rights as the majority.

Essel faced challenges not only in China, but back home in India as well. As one of the first Indian companies to invest in Chinese manufacturing facilities, Essel faced foreign exchange hurdles and had to convince a bureaucratic government committee to allow them to take money out of the country for investment in China. In exchange for a release of $2.5 million, the committee wanted Essel to return dividends to India. Essel knew it could not make such assurances and replied that it could export raw material to China and return the money as export income. The words *export opportunity* immediately appeased the committee, and the project was cleared.

In China, Essel faced yet another challenge: in the province of Guangdong, a foreign company had never been given 100 percent ownership. Essel convinced the Chinese that the technology transfer to China was unique. Further, Essel would help them solve the problem of excess capacity (150 million tubes) in a plant that was lying idle because too few workers knew how to use the machinery.

Initially the Chinese stipulated that Essel should export 10 percent of production, but Essel managed to convince them that exporting empty tubes was not feasible, and permission to manufacture in China was granted. In Chandrasekhar's words: "The local authorities were very supportive. It was a bit of luck. We had not a single consultant to set up our business. We did it on our own. We went straight to local authorities and told them what we needed. We didn't know the ABCs of how to get it. But we asked them to help us . . . I think they appreciated the clarity and transparency of our approach."

Within months of receiving an operating license, Essel was in commercial production. The Chinese said they couldn't believe it because most American companies took one to two years to become operational. Essel's efforts were rewarded with profit the first year of operation, 1997–1998.

However, Essel's story in China was far from over. Almost immediately after Essel was up and running, the Chinese toothpaste market became "very interesting." (See figure 5-1 for a snapshot of the market.) The customer base of international JVs was growing at the expense of the Chinese toothpaste manufacturers with which Essel had initially aligned.

It soon became clear that by aligning with domestic manufacturers, Essel had, despite its success in securing a wholly owned Chinese

FIGURE 5-1

The Chinese toothpaste market circa 1995

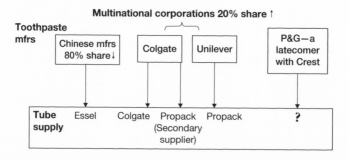

Essel's initial strategy was to sell to Chinese toothpaste manufacturers (more specifically, a company called Measles) and hope for a bandwagon effect with the other Chinese manufacturers. However, multinationals were making significant inroads and Propack had just locked Essel out of the growing MNC segment . . . or had it?

operation, hitched its wagon to the wrong horse. In a characteristically bold move, Essel acquired Propack, the competitor that had recently outbid it on a Unilever contract. Essel bought out Propack on a global level, but China was a key piece of the puzzle. Interestingly, Unilever production dropped by 50 percent. In the midst of this nose-dive, P&G entered China. Domestic tube manufacturers were emerging and presented a significant threat. Essel knew that to avert the disaster of declining volumes it had to do everything in its power to align itself with P&G and hope for growth. According to Chandrasekhar: "The second phase of our success in China is related to P&G. They had one of the most fantastic entry strategies in China. From virtually a small start-up, they grew their volume by ten times in five years—a most fantastic growth story . . . and we rode on that success. On one hand we lost Europe. On the other hand, the entire Chinese toothpaste market was getting churned, and our major customer was consolidating its position in the changing market."

In hindsight, targeting P&G was a brilliant strategy because P&G took off with Crest—reformulated, repriced, and repositioned for the Chinese market from a female brand to a common man's toothpaste. Consumers saw this as a good value proposition. Essel, now Essel Propack, had bet on the right horse and was well positioned for the future.

Essel Propack Enters Acquisition Mode

Chinese success was the launching pad for Essel's global ambitions. A number of strategic acquisitions around the globe followed in rapid succession.

Essel entered Nepal as a preemptive move against the looming free trade between Nepal and India that would put its North India market at risk. Essel was under pressure from Colgate as well, which also decided to invest in Nepal.

Colgate was also instrumental in a South African acquisition and subsequent relocation of four lines of capacity. Colgate had recently abandoned MCG, and the company went bust. Essel picked up the assets and part of this capacity was relocated to Nepal as a gesture of support for Colgate, with the remaining assets augmenting India. The South African plant was subsequently closed down.

Then, Neopack in Switzerland invented a new technology, the polyfoil tube, that Essel felt would revolutionize tubes. Again, lines were shifted to Nepal. In Romania Essel picked up a high-speed tube line and printer. These machines and the person who ran them were relocated to China.

Essel got a foothold in Europe based on a joint venture with Dental Cosmetics of Germany. Dental Cosmetics had its own brand and also made tubes. Chandrasekhar tells the story as follows:

> We approached them with the idea that making tubes is about plastic processing. So we agreed to a JV and invested in the tube line in Germany. And from there we serviced the entire European market. The sweetener in the deal was the German government, which gave us a 40 percent capital grant. So in Europe, where in our business capital cost is one of the significantly important things, when you get a significant grant you become viable straight away. So that's how we started in Germany.

From a global perspective, most of these acquisitions were not very large, but to Essel each deal was big in its own right. (See figure 5-2 for a summary of Essel's growth.)

Subhash Chandra's appetite for risk is considered legendary within Essel and was translated organizationally into an entrepreneurial mentality. According to Goel: "Most of the managers, the senior team, used to believe they were truly entrepreneurs. Once you are able to inculcate that feeling, then people get charged to do things." This type of "just do it" entrepreneurial drive was demonstrated by Essel's leadership in its move to its next big market—North America.

Let Us Show You Who We Are: Essel Propack in America

In 2002 Essel's leadership heard that P&G was floating a request for quotation for the majority of its tubes business in North America.

FIGURE 5-2

Essel Propack international growth milestones

1984	Essel started the first company producing laminated tubes in India.
1993	Initiated first overseas venture in Egypt.
1997	Established a wholly owned subsidiary in Guangzhou, China.
1999	Entered joint venture with Dr. Rose Linger in Dresden, Germany.
2000	Set up a wholly owned subsidiary in Nepal.
	Acquired the tubing operations of Swiss company Propack (the fourth-largest manufacturer of laminated tubes in the world), expanding Essel's reach in China, Philippines, Columbia, Venezuela, Indonesia, and Mexico.
2003	Established operations in Danville, Virginia.
2004	Acquired plastic tubes manufacturer Arista Tubes, United Kingdom.
2005	Established facility near Moscow.
2006	Entered medical devices business by acquiring Tacpro Inc., United States, and Avalon Medical Services, Singapore.
2006	Announced manufacturing of plastic tubes at plants in Danville, Virginia, and in Poland under the brand name Arista Tubes.
2007+	High-end specialty packaging opens doors to pharmaceutical and food industry clients as Essel moves up the value chain.

Source: Adapted from company records.

Essel's senior managers realized the acquisition was a bit of a long shot, but they chose to go for it, recognizing that strategic opportunities like this—to enter the U.S. market by piggybacking on an elite customer such as P&G—presented themselves only rarely. Further, landing the P&G contract was a strategic imperative for Essel's U.S. success, and thus its global aspirations. The other two key clients— Colgate and Unilever—were not viable options; Colgate had its own expertise and Goel believed (correctly, as it turned out) that Unilever would soon abandon the U.S. market. P&G, meanwhile, was already an excellent client, and would likely continue to be in the United States as it had used the same U.S. supplier for over twenty years. Would Essel have to wait another twenty if it let this opportunity slide?

The challenge was that Essel had no particular price advantage, did not know the North American market, and had only regional relationships with P&G, in China and Egypt. To throw another curve ball, P&G had expressly stated that the company to be awarded the five-year contract was to be up and running within months in a location relatively close to North Carolina. It seemed to Essel's leaders a bit like the China experience all over again, with one key exception—this time, language was not a barrier.

Ultimately, for Essel leadership, the question was: Are P&G managers mentally prepared to accept an Indian firm supplying their home market? Essel was confident it could meet price and quality expectations. It also believed it had an advantage over U.S. companies: Essel's operations were not constrained by a five-day workweek when a job had to be done, making capacity a flexible concept. "If we had to," Chandrasekhar said, "we would work seven days for twenty-four straight weeks."

All Essel had to do was convince P&G that it was a quality- and process-oriented supplier—there were processes in place for almost all aspects of the business, from procurement to manufacturing. Essel leadership invited a multifunctional team from P&G to visit plants in Germany, India, and China, and what they saw amazed them. Clearly, the "let us show you who we are" strategy won valuable allies, and Essel won the contract.

From P&G's perspective, why did Essel win the contract? In the end, it was not so much a question of pricing, but rather of meeting manufacturing specifications since not meeting specifications is far more costly than the price of the tubes. P&G meticulously assessed Essel's plants to ensure they could produce the same tubes everywhere. Essel passed the test.

Essel also found a city government in Danville, Virginia, willing to move quickly to meet P&G's deadline. Within five months ninety employees were hired and trained in India, and the first tubes were rolling off the Danville line.

Interestingly, sixteen Danville machinists—some of whom had never been on a plane, much less a plane to India—were trained in Wada, India. Essel's senior managers took great care in ensuring the culture shock was not too much for the trainees, to the point of booking an entire hotel, hiring security to give a sense of comfort, and ensuring food was not too oily or spicy. Essel even spoke to the phone exchange to ensure the hotel phone never went down so that employees could call home every few days to talk to their families. Chandrasekhar sums up the visit as follows: "I still remember that on the last day, when the first group left, we had a dinner party. The flight was in the middle of the night. Every senior guy from our team was there to send them off. It took us two hours to reach there. We sat at the same table with them and had a drink—experience sharing. We saw them board the bus, said bye to them, and then came back. It helps."

Call it Indian hospitality as a means to globalization. It was a model of outsourcing in reverse and a model for Indian companies going global.

Go and Grow with the Customer

Essel's route to global success is embodied in its "go and grow with the customer" philosophy. It was a strategy founded in economic reality. It simply did not make economic sense to transport "air" (the content of laminated tubes before they are filled) over large distances; therefore Essel had to be physically close to the customer. Being tied to the customer in a more profound, strategic sense evolved out of physical closeness and the need to preserve the relationship. Losing a customer could have devastating financial consequences, as Essel had learned in Egypt.

Chandrasekhar cites the "3Rs" as integral to maintaining a close relationship with the customer—reception (listening to customers' opinions), reaction (reflecting on customers' opinions), and response (analysis and action relative to customers' opinions). To this end, Essel has two R&D teams—one focused on new products, working closely with customers to develop products in line with specifications, and another focused on improvements to existing products made within existing factories. And what of P&G? According to Goel: "P&G is now an ongoing relationship, no big or small issues. The challenge is that customers like P&G have continuous expectations on how competitive you can be. That really keeps us on our toes. They have pressure from their customers. They openly say that in internal meetings."

Not content to rest on its laurels, Essel plans to become even more involved with the customer and the entire process of putting product into tubes, insinuating itself deeper into the value chain and leaving the client to focus on product development, brand building, and distribution. Future success will be predicated on goals such as fully exploiting opportunities with existing customers and geographies as well as aggressively taking on the plastic tube segment.

Goel and his team have a global vision: through acquisition and strategic client relationships, to establish Essel Propack as a leading player in plastic tubes across all geographies by 2010 with a 20 percent market share (in 2006 they had a 3 percent share). Expansion into medical devices is anticipated to further spread the considerable risk of Essel's business model, as is expansion into new customer segments such as pharmaceuticals, cosmetics, and food.

In a logical extrapolation of the "go and grow with the customer" philosophy, Chandrasekhar states, "Our approach is that of a service enterprise, one that brings value to our customers through creative applications of knowledge of science, technology, design, and marketing."

Essel Propack is a manufacturer with a service provider mentality. Indian hospitality has been taken to a whole new global level.

SIX

Hindalco

Globalizing Through
a Transformational Merger

*The acquisition of Novelis is a landmark deal for Hindalco and
our Group. It is in line with our long-term vision of taking India
to the world. With Novelis, we gain immediate scale and a global
footprint. We were attracted to Novelis by its sheer size, scale, and
cutting-edge technology, which would have taken us over a decade
to build. In aluminum, one needs to invest downstream to go up
the value chain. India does not at this time offer suitable downstream investment opportunities of a global scale.*

Kumar Mangalam Birla, Chairman, Hindalco Industries Limited

THE STORY BEHIND Hindalco's $6 billion acquisition of Novelis
is of particular interest because of its boldness.[1] When Hindalco
made the bid in 2007, Novelis represented the largest Indian investment in North America and the second-largest overseas investment
by an Indian company, behind Tata's purchase of Corus just two
weeks earlier. So, why was Hindalco's bid for Novelis so bold?

First, the valuation was controversial: Hindalco's bid valued
the shares at almost $45, though the stock had never passed the $30
mark, even in 2005 when the company posted positive earnings.
Second, the structure of the deal put Hindalco in a potentially difficult position; Hindalco would have to borrow $2.85 billion, with
debt repayments that were forecast to amount to a third of its profits
in 2007.[2]

HINDALCO SNAPSHOT

- Total turnover of Hindalco was around $16 billion in 2007, putting the company among the world's five largest aluminum players.

- Hindalco owns forty-six manufacturing facilities, spanning thirteen countries and employing thirty-three thousand workers of more than fifteen nationalities.

- Its subsidiary, Novelis, is a world leader in:

  - Aluminum rolling, producing 19 percent of the world's flat-rolled aluminum products

  - Rolled products, operating plants in Europe, South America, and Asia as well as being the number two producer in North America

  - Recycling of used aluminum beverage cans, recycling more than 38 billion used cans, enough to circle the earth more than one hundred times

But was the rationale behind the deal solid? "Absolutely," Kumar Mangalam Birla, chairman of Hindalco, said at the time: "This deal secures Hindalco's position as the leading aluminum company in the world. Novelis adds global reach and scale. Importantly, Novelis brings critical technological expertise. And by moving downstream, we are hedging the volatility of aluminum prices."

Specifically, via its flat-rolled aluminum manufacturing plants in different locations throughout the world, Novelis's operations would build a strong platform for Hindalco to sell value-added products to many more global customers. The acquisition of Novelis would give Hindalco a more diverse portfolio of premium products, positioning Hindalco's operations further downstream and into more finished, higher-value-added rolled aluminum products.

It was a very big bet—would it prove an effective way to go global and ensure long-term profitability by merging downstream and upstream operations? Birla remained adamantly confident in the role the acquisition would play in realizing his strategic global vision for Hindalco.

The Aditya Birla Group and Hindalco Industries Limited

Created in 1958, Hindalco Industries Limited is the flagship company of the Aditya Birla Group. Established in 1857 as a cotton trading company in Rajasthan, by 2008 the group was a $28 billion conglomerate operating in diverse industries, from clothing to mining to financial services (see figure 6-1). The group employed one hundred thousand employees throughout twenty countries: India, Thailand, Laos, Indonesia, Philippines, Egypt, China, Canada, Australia, United States, United Kingdom, Germany, Hungary, Brazil, Italy, France, Luxembourg, Switzerland, Malaysia, and Korea. Over half of its 2008 revenues flowed from overseas operations.

Group operations included the Hindustan Aluminum Corporation Limited (HACL), which was established in 1958. In 1989, the company was restructured and renamed Hindalco. Through brownfield expansions and modernization, Hindalco established itself as the largest domestic integrated aluminum company. In 2000, it acquired a majority stake in Indal, a subsidiary of global major Alcan, to consolidate its position as a leading player of aluminum in India. This acquisition also led to Hindalco's dominance in the downstream aluminum market in India.

Indeed, since 2000, Hindalco has undertaken seven acquisitions, with each one working its way up to the complexities and scale of the Novelis deal. Debu Bhattacharya, the managing director of Hindalco, explained:

> *In 2000, we acquired a 74 percent stake in Indal. At the time, it was the biggest cash deal concluded to date within India. Indal became a subsidiary of Hindalco, providing expertise in downstream products, complementing Hindalco's upstream operations. It was a big deal for us. There was a lot of apprehension, but since then, we've turned a "comfortable" blue-chip into a growth machine, showing top and bottom line growth of 25 percent year on year. This was followed by a small acquisition, that of a foil business in India, Annapurna Foils.*

FIGURE 6-1

Aditya Birla Group operations

Company	Products/services
Grasim	Viscose staple fiber, rayon-grade pulp, cement, chemicals, sponge iron, textiles
UltraTech Cement Ltd.*	Cement
Hindalco	Aluminum, copper
Bihar Caustic and Chemicals Ltd.*	Caustic soda
Aditya Birla Nuvo	Garments, viscose filament yarn, carbon black, textiles, insulators
Idea Cellular Ltd.**	Cellular telecommunications
Birla Sun Life Insurance Co. Ltd.**	Life insurance
Birla Sun Life Asset Management Company Ltd.**	Mutual funds
Birla Sun Life Distribution Company Ltd.**	Mutual fund distribution
PSI Data Systems*	Application development, IT/systems maintenance, and data enhancement solutions
Aditya Birla Minacs Worldwide Ltd.*	Customer relations management (CRM), integrated marketing services, knowledge process outsourcing
Birla Global Finance Ltd.*	Asset-based finance, corporate finance and investment banking, capital market and treasury
Birla Insurance Advisory & Broking Services Ltd.	Non–life insurance advisory and brokering services
Madura Garments Life Style Retail Co. Ltd.*	Apparel, retail
Peter England Fashions and Retail Ltd.*	Apparel, retail
Madura Garments Exports Ltd.*	Apparel, exports
Aditya Birla Retail Limited	Multiformat stores
Tanfac Industries Ltd.**	Chemicals
Essel Mining & Industries Ltd.	Iron and ore mining, ferro alloys

*Subsidiaries
**Joint ventures
Source: Adapted from company records.

Our next complexity in terms of acquisition was to acquire a new business in an alien country—a copper mining company in Australia. We didn't know anything about copper mining, and were familiar only with open-cast bauxite ore mining (for aluminum). But it has been a great success. The opportunity came along at the right time, at the right cost. Now, it is a debt-free company, and we have since opened one of the largest underground mines developed in a decade.

Then came the Novelis acquisition, which represents the latest step and a very systematic way of Hindalco advancing through the acquisition learning curve.

In addition to the many acquisitions (see the summary in figure 6-2), the past few years (notably, 2005) have brought significant investments in brownfield projects, substantially increasing Hindalco's low-cost production capacity. In 2007, Hindalco was a leading domestic player in both aluminum and copper, with a 28 percent and 43 percent domestic share, respectively. Exports accounted for 20 percent of total aluminum production and 58 percent of copper production. Birla Copper, Hindalco's copper division, exported to the Middle East, Southeast Asia, China, Korea, and Taiwan. Yet, a review of the global aluminum industry left the leadership of Hindalco and the Aditya Birla Group relatively unsatisfied with their position in the industry.

FIGURE 6-2

Hindalco international growth milestones

2007	Novelis becomes a Hindalco subsidiary. Takes/acquires Alcan's 45 percent equity stake in the Utkal Alumina project.
2006	Hindalco enters joint venture with Almex. Copper mining subsidiary Aditya Birla Minerals Limited listed on the Australian Stock Exchange.
2004	Announcement of merger with Indal.
2003	Hindalco acquires Nifty Copper Mine. Hindalco acquires the Mount Gordon copper mines. Hindalco becomes the majority stakeholder in Utkal Alumina (a joint venture with Alcan).
2002	The amalgamation of Indo-Gulf Corporation's copper business, Birla Copper, with Hindalco.
2001	Hindalco appears on the Asia Top 25 list of the *CFO Asia* Annual Report Survey, the only Indian company listed in 2001.
1995	Kumar Mangalam Birla takes over as chairman of the Indal board.
1962	Production commences at Renukoot (Uttar Pradesh) with an initial capacity of 20,000 million metric tons/year of aluminum metal and 40,000 million metric tons/year of alumina.

Source: Adapted from company records.

The Global Aluminum Industry

Aluminum has been produced in commercial quantities for just over a hundred years. During that time, aluminum—a multipurpose metal with several key benefits over steel, including its light weight and corrosion resistance—has become essential in various industries, including infrastructure building, heavy industry, and a wide variety of consumer goods industries, from kitchenware to automobiles.

Countries all over the world are exploiting aluminum deposits to infuse growth in the industrial segment. Electric power represents 20 to 40 percent of the cost of producing aluminum (depending on the location of the smelter). Thus, smelters tend to be situated either close to a bauxite mine/alumina refinery to reduce transportation costs or in regions where electric power is both plentiful and relatively inexpensive. Though global aluminum consumption grew by over 7 percent in 2006, it was powered mainly by growth in Asia (specifically in China), estimated at 20 percent.

For any global aluminum player, key success factors have included low-cost production (there was significant price competition amongst strong global players), access to bauxite deposits (which often meant owning mines), successfully leveraging efficiencies of scale in production capacity, and capturing new markets.

In 2003, when Debu Bhattacharya became managing director of Hindalco, he inherited a relatively small company that was profitable, but had a primarily Indian focus. Hindalco executives conducted a strategic review of the world aluminum industry. They observed that at a general level, the value chain of the industry consisted of three main steps: bauxite mining, aluminum production, and manufacture of value-added products. This value chain led companies within the industry to adopt four different types of business models:

- Upstream companies like Rio Tinto, which concentrate primarily on bauxite mining and conversion to aluminum

- Production companies like Dubal, which make aluminum products leveraging cost-effective power advantage

- Value-added downstream producers like Novelis and SAPA, which buy aluminum and then covert it into recognizable customer products

- Integrated giants like Alcoa and Alcan, which combine the benefit from scale and integrated operations, with dominant presence across the value chain

This strategic review raised some interesting insights for Hindalco. First, it noted that world-class companies existed in each type of business model, and thus, no one business model was inherently preferable from a strategic standpoint. Second, though Hindalco, with its more recent domestic acquisitions, had some downstream exposure, it was still primarily an upstream player. Third, the profitability analysis of upstream and downstream companies revealed an interesting conclusion, as Bhattacharya explained:

Profitability in the upstream business is generally higher, but selling a commodity is subject to high volatility as the prices are set on the London Metals Exchange [LME]. On the other hand, the profitability of the downstream business is lower than upstream but it is also less volatile. So our objective became to "optimally balance" the portfolio with downstream operations to increase profits consistently, rather than relying on the volatility that accompanies the higher profitability of upstream operations.

However, upstream and downstream required different competencies, as Bhattacharya realized:

The key success factors for upstream operations are very, very different than those for downstream manufacturing. For instance, with downstream operations, size is not everything; the name of the game is differentiation. Quality and delivery are important, and you have to be close to the market and key clients to foster strong client relationships. But with upstream manufacturing . . . aluminum is aluminum; it's a commodity and hence low cost of production is the key. And the price is set on the LME.

For sustained long-term profitability, Hindalco required competencies in process development for upstream operations and in product development for downstream operations. The Novelis acquisition was a one-time opportunity to immediately gain what Bhattacharya referred to as "optimal balance" (between upstream and downstream operations) as a natural hedge against volatility in the commodity pricing of aluminum on the LME. It was the key to developing Hindalco's sustainable competitive advantage in order to achieve Birla's strategic vision of being a major global aluminum player.

The Novelis Acquisition

Novelis was headquartered in Atlanta, Georgia (United States), but registered as a Canadian company, with shares listed in both Toronto and New York. In 2007 the company was the world's largest producer of rolled aluminum and a significant recycler of aluminum cans, with 12,500 employees in eleven countries. Though Novelis had recorded a profit of $90 million in 2005, its latest financial statements prior to its acquisition showed a loss of $170 million (for the nine months prior to September 2006). At that time, Novelis management was projecting a loss of $240 to $285 million for fiscal year 2006. Indeed, Novelis had faced profound financial troubles from the time it was created, in 2005.

Novelis was born when its parent, $23 billion Canadian-based aluminum giant Alcan, launched a hostile takeover of the French aluminum company Pechiney. Specifically, antitrust proceedings dictated that Alcan's rolled aluminum business must be spun off from its parent. In the forced spin-off, Novelis inherited a mountain of debt of $2.4 billion, on a capital base of under $500 million.

However, Novelis offered several strategic strengths. Novelis had a leading 19 percent global market share in foil products, 25 percent in construction and industrial products, and 43 percent in beverage cans. Novelis's business model was fairly straightforward: it bought primary aluminum for processing into rolled aluminum for the manufacture of finished products, such as cans and automobile parts. Also, Novelis's facilities were among the most modern in the industry, and the company was widely known for technological innovation in processed aluminum. Further, a widespread global presence and core competence in the efficient production of high-quality finished products created a global customer base in diverse high-value markets. Key customers included major brands such as Alcan, Anheuser-Busch, Coca-Cola, Ford, General Motors, Kodak, Tetra Pak, and Thyssen-Krupp. Birla also emphasized the strategic value of the acquisition: "Novelis is the result of a strategic thrust rather than waking up one morning and saying, 'Let's go global, it's fashionable, everybody's talking about it . . . let's spend $6 billion today.'"

On the strength of Novelis's technological expertise, global manufacturing footprint, and access to global customers, on February 10, 2007, Hindalco entered into an agreement to acquire Novelis in an all-cash transaction that valued Novelis at approximately $6 billion, including debt. Under the terms of the agreement, Novelis shareholders received a 17 percent premium over the closing price.

Hindalco raised $3.5 billion to finance the deal. Of that total amount, $3.03 billion was financed by UBS, ABN Amro, and Bank of America, and $450 million came from Hindalco reserves. The debt on the Novelis books of around $2.4 billion at the time of acquisition was refinanced due to change of ownership. The refinancing was completed in early July 2007 and included an asset-backed loan on Novelis's stocks and receivables. This gave Novelis the flexibility to draw a higher amount in case raw material prices increased.

Hindalco's stock fell by 13 percent and took a hit of more than $600 million in market capitalization the day after the acquisition was announced.[3] In response to criticism of the deal, Kumar Mangalam Birla maintained he had offered a "fair price" for Novelis. "When you are acquiring a world leader, you will have to pay a premium," he said.

Despite the strategic fit of the deal, some industry watchers remained skeptical regarding the price Hindalco paid to acquire a company that was accumulating losses. The overall value of the deal rested on three major factors: an increase in Hindalco's metal production, higher backward-related synergies, and above all (and beyond control), an increase in aluminum prices to ensure healthy revenue flows to Hindalco.

Other risks included the fact that although Novelis was a global leader, it did not have much pricing power, as it faced fierce competition from a handful of strong industry players who controlled over half the market. A substantial portion of Novelis's problems stemmed from a wrong call by the management on aluminum prices. To win more business from soft-drink manufacturers, it promised four customers that it would not increase product prices even if aluminum prices rose beyond a certain level. Unfortunately, aluminum prices shot up 39 percent between 2005 and 2006. To these four customers, Novelis was forced to sell its products at prices that were lower than the raw material costs. As these four accounted for 20 percent of Novelis's $9 billion revenues, this contributed to the large losses in financial year 2006. The last of these contracts will not expire until the end of 2009.[4]

As with any acquisition, merging a subsidiary would take significant resources, and there was no guarantee that the hoped-for synergies would materialize. Moreover, it would be expensive to merge operations of such scope and scale. But it was the structure of the (all-cash) deal that was of concern to many analysts. Birla readily acknowledged the adverse financial repercussions to the parent company in the short to medium term in his statement in the Hindalco 2006–2007 Annual Report. He asked his shareholders to remain "patient," writing: "I do realize that in the short-term the acquisition will cause strain on Hindalco's balance sheet. However, if you look at the bigger picture, this is one of the most striking acquisitions and over the long-term will undeniably create enormous shareholder value."[5]

The Merger Integration Process

Hindalco's experience with acquisitions prior to the Novelis deal had taught its leadership that a merger required four types of integration—financial, organizational and cultural, business processes, and market integration. Achieving successful financial integration was "pretty clear," according to Bhattacharya; "everybody needs to understand what the role of cost reduction is." The financial reporting systems and procedures have to be aligned.

Bhattacharya explained that the key success factor behind successful cultural integration is in the organizational structure. "We not only bought the assets, but the talent," he said, referring to many of the senior Novelis executives as "institutions" in their specific areas of excellence. Hindalco leadership realized that at a conceptual level what worked in past acquisitions would work again, but the actions would be different. The key concept that had guided previous integration efforts at Hindalco, according to Bhattacharya, was that "the best person should do the job. Do not disturb the management structure unnecessarily, just to prove a point." The leadership at Novelis was left untouched.

The value of the strong relationships with key clients was firmly appreciated because of the competitive advantage that solid codevelopment relationships could add in value-added downstream businesses. According to Bhattacharya:

> *I have personally met the major customers. I consistently saw that Novelis executives had developed fantastic relationships with each of them. Take Jaguar, in Birmingham, for example. I spent the day talking about the business, touring the factory, meeting people. At the end of the day, I shook the hand and said, "Nice to meet you. I hope to see you again here at Jaguar" to a particularly active and insightful participant of the team I'd spent the day with. His reply? "I'm not with Jaguar; I'm from Novelis." I was shocked . . . their relationship was so seamless.*

Although many Novelis executives remained in place, some significant changes were made. There was always a firm rationale behind a new Hindalco appointment. For example, the "best risk management guy," based on his expertise at Hindalco's copper division, was brought into Novelis to institutionalize this process. Hindalco also installed senior executives in logistics. Bhattacharya explained the rationale behind the appointments: "Given Novelis's global reach, logistics plays an important role in managing the costs as well as timely deliveries. Logistic management requires an enormous amount of coordination, expertise, not to mention the fire in the belly to do it. Logistics is key because managing inventory in a cash-starved company is vital. Subsequently, each one has earned enormous respect within Novelis."

These Hindalco appointments had two beneficial effects. First, they helped achieve business process integration between the two companies with respect to supply chain and logistics. Putting Hindalco's best person in this area in charge of manufacturing excellence in Europe was expected to improve the stock turns. Second, these initial top-notch appointments created value at the acquired firm. This helped turn around the attitude of the people at the acquired firm. Instead of causing employees to be wary that the Indians were coming to take over en masse, it created respect and demand at the acquired firm for more Hindalco experts. On the other hand, in areas where Hindalco realized that Novelis was superior, such as the planning process, Hindalco relied on Novelis expertise. The last process, one Hindalco launched in 2008, was market integration, seeding some products from Novelis factories into the Indian market. For example, demand for beverage cans required by Coke and United Breweries in India, was insufficient to produce them in India in economic scale, nor did India have the competence to manufacture them to world-class standards. But Novelis was a world leader in these products, and thus they could be introduced to the Indian market.

In the coming years, domestic production will be essential as many finished products need to be produced close to market. For example, importing aluminum cans is like importing air. According to Bhattacharya:

> Novelis was a great opportunity for developing the Indian market. Domestic annual per capita consumption of aluminum is about 1 kilo. In China, that figure is about 9 kilos, and in a developed market, the U.S., for example, it's 30 kilos. So even if we create half the per capita demand in China over the next five years, that would be 4.5 kilos for 1.1 billion people, representing domestic market demand of 6 billion kilos, up from the current 1.5 billion kilos. Half of Novelis's output could be potentially absorbed in India alone. This is particularly important because the European market is growing slowly. This is the business logic behind the acquisition.

Unwavering Commitment to a Strategic Vision

Despite the controversy over the deal, Birla remained squarely focused on its long-term vision for Hindalco. The acquisition launched Hindalco into the *Fortune* 500 list. With the Novelis subsidiary, Hindalco could expect to triple its turnover, to $15 billion in 2007. Strategically, the acquisition immediately created a global integrated aluminum producer with low-cost aluminum production facilities (Hindalco) and high-end aluminum rolled-product capabilities (Novelis). Bhattacharya summarized:

> *Our vision is to be a premium metals major, global in size and reach. The complementary assets and expertise of the team provides a strong platform for growth and success at this level.*
>
> *Thus, Novelis makes a perfect fit for Hindalco. There are enormous geographical market and product synergies. The Novelis acquisition gives Hindalco an instant leg up with its technologically sophisticated rolled-aluminum products capability, along with its scale and global footprint.*

In mid-2007, Hindalco announced a further expansion of its operations, with a view to increasing capacity to 1.5 million metric tons by 2011–2012. This would make Hindalco the world's fifth-largest producer, up from its 2007 position as thirteenth largest. With an unwavering focus on increasing production volumes from brownfield expansions in India, and with growth through the controversial acquisition of Novelis, Birla's vision to transform Hindalco from a low-cost Indian aluminum producer to a leading global integrated aluminum company is becoming a reality.

SEVEN

Mahindra & Mahindra

Leveraging India's Size for Global Scale in Tractors

When we Indians hit our pillows at night, our dreams about India's
future are not just colorful, but steroidal. All of us are finally
beginning to believe that the sandcastles we build in our minds are
not going to be simply washed away by the morning tide.

Anand Mahindra, Vice Chairman and Managing Director,
Mahindra & Mahindra

BORN IN 1945, as India was gaining independence, Mahindra
& Mahindra identifies closely with its Indian home base and
views itself as a microcosm of India, marching confidently onto the
global stage.[1] The company was founded at a meeting between K. C.
Mahindra and Barney Roos, inventor of the "general all-purpose
vehicle" known as the Jeep. Mahindra thought the Jeep would be
perfect for handling the rugged Indian terrain, so he hooked up with
partner Ghulam Mohammed to form a company called Mahindra &
Mohammed to assemble Jeeps under a franchise agreement with
Willys of the United States.

Two years later, India was born as an independent nation. The
country was divided into secular India and Muslim Pakistan.
Mohammed moved to Pakistan to become that country's first finance
minister; with his departure, Mahindra & Mahindra (M&M) was
formed. The company initially traded in steel, then in 1949 began
assembling Jeeps from kits imported from the United States, gradually
migrating to more and more indigenous content under licensing
arrangements with Kaiser Jeep and, later, American Motors. Mahindra

MAHINDRA & MAHINDRA SNAPSHOT

- Mahindra & Mahindra is among the top three tractor manufacturers in the world, with plants in Australia, China, India, and the United States.

- It is among the top five tractor brands in the world with a goal to become the world's largest tractor company by 2009 and make the Mahindra brand the largest selling single brand of tractors in the world.

- The market leader in multiutility vehicles in India, the company now exports to Asia, Africa, Europe, and Latin America.

- In 2006, M&M was on *Forbes* list of the two hundred most respected companies in the world.

- M&M has over fifty thousand employees throughout six continents.

---

produced a right-handed Jeep model for the domestic market to which specialized bodies could be added to make pickup trucks, ambulances, or minibuses.

Over time, M&M built on the twin platforms of steel and transportation to expand into agricultural tractors and commercial vehicles. Today, it is a multifaceted business with a global presence in eight key sectors and global revenue in 2008 of $6.7 billion. The eight sectors and the share of M&M's revenues from each sector are: automotive (30 percent), farm equipment (24 percent), information technology (15 percent), financial services (11 percent), automotive components (8 percent), hospitality (5 percent), steel processing and trading (4 percent), and infrastructure development (3 percent).

Of these, the focus of this chapter is on M&M's two largest businesses—automotive and farm equipment. M&M has been the market leader in utility vehicles in India since inception and currently accounts for about half of India's market for utility vehicles. The automotive sector exports to countries in Europe, Africa, South America, South Asia, and the Middle East. In farm equipment, M&M is among the top five tractor brands in the world. It has a global presence across six continents, with plants in India, the United States, China, and Australia and a worldwide network of eight hundred dealers. It is the largest producer of tractors in India and has been the market leader for over twenty-five years.

With the increase in the depth and scope of its business activities, going global became inevitable. As Anand Mahindra, vice chairman and managing director of Mahindra & Mahindra, noted: "We looked at the dynamics of the business we were in where we were already the largest tractor maker in India and India was the largest tractor market in the world. India has scale. We said, if you are not trying to become a global force, you are actually doing India a disservice."

But the path to going global did not always feel so smooth. As Mahindra noted, there were a few missteps along the way, the most notable of which was M&M's first international foray into Greece. Mahindra later called this the chapter on how *not* to do it.

Global Lessons Learned—the Hard Way

Initially, going global at M&M meant bidding on international tenders. The Reserve Bank of India (RBI) had very stringent rules about foreign currency, so tendering was a simple way of making currency transactions transparent. Greece represented a departure from global tendering as it involved setting up an assembly plant. The Greek M&M plant began operations in the mid-1980s; its claim to infamy was that it was regularly at the bottom of the list of the most respected multinationals in Greece.

When Mahindra asked in the early 1990s what M&M was doing in Greece, an unlikely country from the perspective of competitive advantage and market proximity, he was told that Greece was considered a reasonable market in which to sell 4x4 vehicles. But M&M's distributor in Greece became bankrupt and could not return the money it owed. This created a crisis for M&M because going to the RBI and explaining the situation would immediately arouse suspicion regarding possible illegal transfer of funds. Most Indian companies built contingency funds to deal with such crises, but M&M had no such capability. Mahindra finished the story:

> *So what we did was we told the guy the money you owe us is now equity! So we ended up with a partner who really wasn't worth partnering; we ended up with an assembly plant in the wrong part of the*

world and with no logic, no strategic intent at all. And it just languished; it just did worse and worse; there was no real commitment behind it. Just as you have the accidental tourist, you have the accidental MNC in Greece. I kept going back to the Reserve Bank and we finally worked out a package where we just closed the company.

Today, Mahindra notes, the situation with the RBI is entirely different, and Indian companies are permitted to accumulate significant capital outside the country provided there is market justification. The RBI has relaxed its attitude toward Indian companies investing abroad and will grant permission to send money to fund advertising. There is also an understanding that businesspeople are building markets and consequently there will be write-offs.

In its initial entry into America, M&M found it had set up an ad hoc distribution network for its tractors. This was another example of the company exploring international markets impetuously. A request for ten tractors in Texas resulted in a legal tussle between M&M and a distributor in Texas that culminated with the CFO of M&M, Bharat Doshi, being served a writ by a six-foot-four Texas marshal. As Mahindra put it: "We learned the lessons the hard way that when you go abroad, it's for the long haul. Your legal nose has to be clean and you need to have all your contingency plans in place."

Figure 7.1 charts M&M's expansion milestones.

Using a Strategic Road Map for Globalization

Though Greece was unsustainable, opportunities abounded in the United States, the largest tractor market in the world by revenues, for a company that was the largest tractor manufacturer in India. Clearly, a different, more systematic approach was required.

After the encounter with the U.S. marshal, M&M could have packed up and gone back home to India. Instead, it regrouped and began a rigorous strategic review of assets and competitive advantage with the purpose of uncovering how best to exploit key opportunities in the American market. Goals for market share were set according to target market. All the fundamentals of good business were put in

FIGURE 7-1

Mahindra & Mahindra's international growth milestones

1945	Mahindra & Mohammed established.
1948	Renamed Mahindra & Mahindra Limited.
1949	Jeep assembly commenced.
1956	Entered joint venture with Dr. Beck & Company, Germany.
1957	Established Mahindra Owen, a joint venture with Rubery Owen & Company, United Kingdom.
1963	Established the International Tractor Company of India, a joint venture with International Harvester Company, United States.
1965	Commenced manufacture of light commercial vehicles.
1969	Entered the world market with export of utility vehicles and spare parts.
1982	Launched Mahindra brand of tractors.
1984	Established Mahindra Hellenic Auto Industries S.A., a joint venture in Greece to assemble and market utility vehicles in Europe.
1996	Established Mahindra Ford India Limited, a joint venture with Ford Motor Company, United States, to manufacture passenger cars.
2003	Second tractor assembly plant set up in the United States.
2004	Launched Bolero and Scorpio in Latin America, Middle East, and South Africa.
2005	Acquired 80% stake in the joint venture with Jiangling Motors (that is, in Mahindra [China] Tractor Company).
2006	Held global launch of the Scorpio Pik-Up range in South Africa, an indication of the strategic importance of Mahindra South Africa's operations in the company's global growth plans.
	Announced plan for Mahindra to enter the United States with a sports utility vehicle and pickup by signing a distribution agreement with Global Vehicles USA Inc.
	Scorpio and the Bolero marched into Kenya as part of Mahindra & Mahindra's globalization drive.
2007	Mahindra International Engines Ltd. entered majority joint venture with Warrenville, U.S.–based Navistar, North America's largest combined commercial truck, school bus, and midrange diesel engine producer.
	Scorpio launched in Australia, Chile, the United States, and Morocco.

Source: Adapted from company information.

place. Then M&M ensured its best human resources were put in place to oversee implementation of the business plan. The mind-set of the past—"If it happens, it happens"—became "Let's make it happen." M&M was committed to winning in the world's largest free market.

This strategic overlay period began in 1991. Government reforms designed to make India more competitive were happening concomitantly, so a lot of work needed to be done, beginning with basic reengineering of the shop floor to restructuring of the labor force. Huge productivity gains had to be made. It was what Mahindra called "the General Electrification" of the business, the wholesale implementation of best practice across all sectors of the business and the quest for market leadership in every market in which M&M competed. Part of emulating GE was recognizing that in order to reduce risk, the firm had to go global.

The business "fitness regimen" was more than a physical exercise for Indian companies to enable them to thrive within the global climate. More than process improvement or asset rejuvenation, a sea change in attitude had to accompany the reforms. It took some time, ten years by Mahindra's estimation, but eventually M&M had the confidence to be world-beaters. As Mahindra explained:

> If your manufacturing is world-class, it doesn't mean anything—you can be a contract manufacturer. You can be a great marketer in India, but that could serve to market somebody else's product. You have the confidence to be multinational only if your product development engine is something that delivers confidence to you and you say, "I have the capability to create a sustainable pipeline of products/services that can pass muster around the world."

A pipeline of products and services, if successful, would lead to a "tipping point," a point at which physical and mental capabilities mesh to create a product or service that is world-ready. For M&M, the tipping point occurred in 2002 with the launch of the Scorpio.

The Scorpio

The Scorpio was a strategic, psychological, and symbolic turning point for Mahindra & Mahindra. And symbolism plays an important role in the transformation of a company. The launch of the Scorpio on June 19, 2002, marks the day M&M became a twenty-first-century company with global ambitions. Within the company it became a symbol of pride and, above all, a symbol of what Anand Mahindra considers to be M&M's unique source of competitive advantage: the ability to produce quality goods at the lowest price per unit of innovation.

The Scorpio was developed for $120 million—the largest product investment the company had ever made, yet roughly a fifth of what it would have cost in Detroit. With an engine from Renault, its axle from Dana Corporation, and metal coatings from Visteon Corporation, the Scorpio utilized the expertise of several world class suppliers. Furthermore, by enticing such suppliers to do the designing and testing, Mahindra cut the product development costs for the Scorpio. It was an investment that paid off handsomely. It gave M&M a leadership position in the Indian urban SUV market, alongside Tata Motors and Toyota. The Scorpio was also launched in parts of Europe and the Middle East as well as South Africa, where dozens of foreign and domestic brands battled for market share. The Scorpio represented the export-worthy manifestation of an Indian dream and was a significant confidence booster for M&M.

The Most Multinational of M&M's Businesses: Tractors

Of the company's eight key business areas, Mahindra considered tractors to be the most multinational based on that sector's strength as the longstanding market leader in India and the experience of building a global brand in the United States, the world's most difficult market. In 1963 M&M entered the tractor market through a joint venture with International Harvester to produce tractors for India. By 1983, M&M was the market leader in India, a position it has held ever since. Today Mahindra is among the top three tractor brands in the world. Key competitors are John Deere, ACCO, and New Holland. In 2006, M&M had a 32 percent share of the Indian market.

From the standpoint of "if you can succeed in America, you can succeed anywhere," M&M learned how to compete in the toughest rough-and-tumble free market in the world. However, nobody realized what a huge franchise M&M had built in the United States until *BusinessWeek* wrote a cover story in July 2006.[2] It was about a farmer in Mississippi who purchased a Mahindra tractor to clean up after the devastating destruction along the Gulf Coast from Hurricane Katrina. In the article, the farmer praised the Mahindra tractor. The farmer's credibility was enhanced by a photo of him and his two young kids sitting atop a shiny red Mahindra 5500. He was quoted as saying, "I've been around farm equipment all my life, and for $27,000, the 5500 is by far the best for the money . . . When you lock it into 4WD, you can move 3,000 pounds like it's nothing. The thing's an animal."

Confidence in M&M's quality and value greatly aided the company's strategy to become the market leader in the tractor segment through inorganic growth by leading the consolidation of capacity. In 2005, M&M started producing tractors in China through the majority acquisition of Jiangling Tractors. This was made easier because the Chinese were impressed with M&M's market share in the United States. Mahindra used to say he wanted M&M to be the world leader in terms of units of sale. However, now the goal was to become the world leader in terms of brand. This represented a significant shift in mind-set, and one rooted in the company's confidence. According to Mahindra, "We are so confident in our brand umbrella that we can buy anything, put it through our channel, and ramp it up."

In the American market, 40 percent of M&M sales come from selling tractors not manufactured by M&M. M&M sells Tomyang and Mitsubishi tractors under its brand name because these companies acknowledged that M&M's market position was better and they would benefit from association with the M&M brand.

Mahindra has a solid brand profile in the United States, particularly in the South, where the Mahindra jingle and billboards are ubiquitous. Although pleased with this unprecedented success with an Indian brand, Mahindra is not content. Consumers are much less familiar with the Mahindra brand than farmers, something Anand Mahindra, exposed to great global brands, is determined to change.

M&M's Automotive Businesses:
Winning Market Share

Niche businesses with global potential are, as Mahindra put it, "Like having an arrow with a pointed edge rather than a blunt instrument." M&M's goal is to replace Land Rover with the Mahindra brand. "When someone thinks off-road and four-wheel drive," Mahindra stated, "I want them to think Mahindra."

Although tractors are the foundation on which M&M's global presence was built, its Jeeps get the press because they are glamorous, sexy, and urban—and the business world thinks urban. Brand awareness built on the tractor franchise will be dwarfed if Mahindra gets a foothold in the United States, where consumer awareness of Mahindra SUVs is anticipated to trump tractors. According to Anand Mahindra, "SUVs will be what gets us known as a global brand." In 2006, M&M held 44 percent of the Indian MUV (multiutility vehicle) segment.

Mahindra's focus is not so much on volume but share of mind, the ultimate measure of brand might. Unlike the tractor sector, where inorganic growth makes sense, in the automotive business there is significant outsourcing so the focus can be entirely on building a brand. The tractor and automotive businesses do share an obsession with brand building; however, in the tractor business the goal is also to become the world's largest seller. Therefore, when M&M takes over a unit, weak brands become Mahindra, middling brands are cobranded, and strong brands are kept. In the automotive sector, the focus is entirely on building the Mahindra brand.

If the goal is to become the next Land Rover, then the acquisition of capacity is counterintuitive. As Mahindra put it, "You have to have the right product and you have to go and sell it." Finding distribution channels, whether organic or inorganic, makes strategic sense, but having the right product is paramount.

According to Mahindra, cultivating a sense of "customer co-ownership" is how M&M will build the right product that will create a global brand: "We want to be recognized as the most customer-centric corporation in the world. We feel that this is a mountain that hasn't been climbed by anybody in India yet. We have coined a new phrase. We say we want to create co-ownership. That's the Holy Grail. If you can get there, then your referral and all your customer loyalty come in."

When M&M launched its first car for the Indian market, a joint venture with Renault called the Mahindra Renault Logan, Mahindra noted how the car was specifically tailored for the Indian market. For example, Indian consumers don't just want an air conditioner that cools—they want one that freezes. So to please the Indian consumer, the entire air conditioning system was reengineered along with the steering system to accommodate right-handed driving at a localized cost 10 percent less than anywhere in the Renault world. And the Scorpio introduced in 2006 was redesigned to incorporate customer feedback obtained through a variety of orthodox (focus groups) and unorthodox (negative feedback) channels.

The Next Chapter: Breaking Invisible Shackles

Looking to the future, Mahindra concedes that Indian companies face challenges to be successful—RBI restrictions, infrastructure limitations, regulations—but these are niggling nuisances compared to what he calls the "invisible" shackles of a mind-set stuck in the past. Mahindra recounts how his high school ceremoniously placed examination papers in a locked box to be sent to England for correction. Today some English exam boards outsource correction of their papers to India! How things have changed.

For Anand Mahindra, globalization is not a panacea to be approached with giddy abandon. It is a mindful, profitable expansion into international markets where each acquisition is a puzzle piece that fits strategically into the whole: "We are looking at acquisitions in the auto component space to complete our design-to-delivery promise. We are looking for channels of distribution, so globalization is certainly going to be a growth driver. But it is based on strategy, so if you are a company that is focused on domestic economy only, that doesn't mean you are not going to get growth. You just better make sure that your strategic map is complete."

Celebrating sixty years of Indian independence, Mahindra quoted William Wordsworth describing the French Revolution in *The Prelude*—"Bliss was it in that dawn to be alive/But to be young was very heaven." If one were to substitute *Indian* for *young*, Mahindra said, one could describe his optimism about the future of his country and his company and their expanding global presence.

EIGHT

Hidesign, Marico, Godrej, VIP, and UB

Seeking Global Consumer Brands from India

Why haven't we had Indian brands going global . . . In the past we were not competitive or productive and our production processes and quality of output were developed to meet the demand in the domestic economy. But at last India is becoming a competitive economy. Our economic environment is now more conducive to international trade. We are in the process of gaining valuable knowledge in international management practices, including brand building and ways of doing business. Of course, we can also leverage Indian-specific core competencies—being producers of high-quality products at a low cost—to build a global brand.

Dilip G. Piramal, Chairman, VIP Industries

WITHIN INDIA, there is no shortage of blockbuster brands that have succeeded in establishing relevance, personality, and an emotional connection—key goals of any brand.[1] Yet not one Indian brand is found on a popular 2007 list, the Top 100 Global Brands.[2] That exalted club is dominated by U.S. brands, representing eight of the top ten. India's paucity of international brands is understandable: economic liberation began only in 1991, and Indian companies going global is even a more recent phenomenon. It took decades for Japanese brands Toyota (sixth) and Honda (nineteenth) and the South Korean brand Samsung (twenty-first) to make the list. These countries were once associated with poor quality and inefficiency, the perceptual hurdle that India currently faces. However, Indian consumer brands are entering an exciting new phase.

The Indian IT services sector has transformed the country's reputation, proving that India is capable of delivering world-class high-tech services. Infosys, TCS, and Wipro are jockeying with the likes of IBM and HP around the world. As Nandan Nilekani of Infosys put it, having a strong global brand is not a nicety, but a strategic imperative: "For us it is important to have a strong brand because our clients are global companies, and they want to see you as a long-term partner who is not risky. So you must be a known brand."

At the 2006 World Economic Forum in Davos, Switzerland, a concerted, coordinated effort was made to sell Brand India to international corporate and political elites with the theme "India Everywhere." It included a Bollywood gala, Indian food, and a large Indian contingent talking up attendees. The same year, the Frankfurt Book Fair featured Indian literature and culture. The spillover effect of media reports from these events, according to Nilekani, was worth "$1 billion in branding" not only for the country, but also for Indian brands, creating a perception of India as a leading-edge nation, culturally intriguing and worthy of international attention.

Yet, in contrast to building a brand with corporate customers or global elites, developing a global consumer brand is notoriously slow. Despite the success of Taj or Oberoi Hotels and Jet Airways, Indian consumer brands have yet to register on the global brand radar screen. Nevertheless, many companies are trying. We examine five companies who are adopting three different approaches to managing global consumer brands out of India. Hidesign, with its affordable luxury leather products, is building a global consumer brand but keeping the costs reasonable by focusing on a niche. Godrej and Marico accept that the product competencies developed for an Indian market are relevant only to similar emerging markets, and therefore focus their Indian brands toward such markets. Finally, United Breweries and VIP Industries accept the premise of the previous strategy, but through acquisition add Western established brands in order to have a multibrand portfolio that can target both emerging and developed markets.

Hidesign—Building a Global Consumer Brand

The boldest approach for an Indian brand with global aspirations is perhaps the strategy adopted by Hidesign. Instead of acquiring strong international brands, Hidesign has chosen to globally promote its own corporate brand. But how does a small Indian company build a global consumer brand if it doesn't want to wait decades or doesn't have millions to invest in doing so? It focuses on a niche—in Hidesign's case, the so-called mass luxury segment, with leather products proudly handcrafted in India. Instead of disassociating the brand from India, a country more famous for worshipping cows than making products from their hides, Hidesign is embracing its "Indianness."

Hidesign has an expansive portfolio of leather products, including bags for work and travel, accessories, and belts. It began in Pondicherry as a one-man workshop for tanned leather bags and jackets, and still remains true to its artisan roots by tanning the leather in the traditional way. Hides are soaked for forty days in vegetable extracts—bark seeds from Africa and India to make them supple. The leather is then hand rubbed with dyes (similar to staining wood) to add unique finishes. Once dyed, products are glued, stitched, and finished by hand. Even the buckles are handmade—dozens of workers sand-cast each buckle from fine river sand, then polish them by hand in eight stages. It is by virtue of its large pool of skilled labor that Hidesign can continue with traditional methods of production long abandoned by its Italian peers. The brand essence is captured in its tag line: "Real leather, crafted the forgotten way."

Hidesign products are positioned as "mass luxury"—stylish, yet affordable. According to Dilip Kapur, president:

Compared to Europe, we have the capability to create a product which is very individualistic but does not have to be sold at the high price levels that Europe needs for profitable sales. So I think we have a special space which we will call affordable luxury, or "mass luxury," where we belong. That is the niche. Our products each have individuality. They are very unique; without that you cannot call

yourself "luxury." And you cannot be affordable unless you have
cost advantage. So putting those two together is where we felt we
had a specific advantage.

The key target market, Kapur notes, is composed of "upwardly
mobile, independent, young-at-heart consumers between twenty and
fifty who travel frequently and internationally, who want to look
casually fashionable but never gaudy, and have a commitment to
ecology." Thirty-eight corporate stores in India and fifteen overseas
sell Hidesign products. Retail distribution is augmented by agreements with dozens of independent retailers around the globe, in Australia, Greece, Hong Kong, New Zealand, Russia, Scandinavia,
Slovakia, South Africa, the United Kingdom, and the United States.[3]
Instead of advertising, they use their retail stores to build brand
image. Hidesign stores and merchandise can be found in the duty-
free shopping areas of international airports such as Hong Kong in
the British Airways duty-free shop, as well as prestigious shopping
areas like a store in Carmel, California, located right next to Coach
and Louis Vuitton.

Domestic turnover is estimated to be growing at 15 to 20 percent
annually, to Rs. 100 crores in 2007 with international markets
adding an additional Rs. 200 crores.[4] But perhaps the biggest boost
to Hidesign as a brand came when global fashion icon Louis Vuitton
(seventeenth on the list of top global brands) acquired 20 percent of
the company, lending not only prestige, but also expertise in building
a strong global brand image.[5]

Extending Brands to Similar Markets

Marico and Godrej, both household names in India, were unknown
internationally until expansion into similar markets gradually made
them international players.

Marico's Parachute

Marico is a leading Indian consumer packaged goods company, and
Parachute is its flagship brand. Parachute operates in the specialized

category of coconut-based hair oils, hair creams, and gels. Known as the "original" coconut oil, it was a market leader in India for many years. Marico was unable to export Parachute until the early 1990s because the government saw vegetable oils as an essential commodity, always in short supply. However, the company observed that the product was being smuggled into markets such as the Middle East that had large Indian expatriate populations.

In the mid-nineties, to capitalize on the lifting of the export ban and the demand for Parachute among nonresident Indians, Marico started exporting to neighboring markets, where the populations were open to coconut-based hair products. From a small export business, Marico made its first serious push into international markets with its late 1990s entry into Bangladesh. It set up a manufacturing plant there to serve a population whose consumption patterns were very similar to those in India. Within a decade, Parachute had garnered a 70 percent-plus market share. In 2008, it was ranked as the sixth-most-trusted brand in Bangladesh by Bangladesh Brand Forum, ahead of global brands such as Coke, Pepsi, Sony, and Samsung!

Several product and packaging innovations were launched, including hair creams, gels, moisturizers, and treatments as well as new bottles and individual-use packets. But Marico realized that to successfully penetrate markets beyond South Asia, the company had to move from an India-centric approach to innovation to one that served the needs of the local markets. For example, Marico learned that Arab customers did not like the smell of coconut oil, preferred less stickiness, and used the product in an environment with high water chlorination, which damaged the hair. In response, the company launched a reformulation of the product that counteracted the harmful effects of chlorine. As a result of many such efforts, Marico's share of hair creams in the Arab Mideast markets has grown from 2 percent in 2002 to more than 20 percent in 2008. For its efforts, Marico received the outstanding marketing award from the *Gulf Marketing Review* forum.

Today, Parachute is the world's largest packaged coconut oil brand—a far cry from being a commodity player with a 1 percent market share. In 2007, Marico was included on *BusinessWeek*'s list of one hundred Asian hot growth companies and the *Standard & Poor's* list of global challengers.[6] Marico is present in over twenty-five countries with a substantial presence in Bangladesh, the Gulf, South Africa, and Egypt. After acquiring Fiancee and Haircode brands in Egypt, one out of six Egyptians is a Marico consumer. In the markets that it operates, the Parachute brand successfully competes against global brands like Sunsilk from Unilever and Brylcreem from Sara Lee. When asked how, Harsh Mariwala, chairman and managing director, observed, "We compete in categories which are peripheral for the major multinationals. They don't focus on them but for us, this is the main category and receives our best management attention and innovation."

Godrej Consumer Products

Founded in 1897, Godrej Group is one of India's oldest and largest consumer products and engineering companies, with a turnover in 2007 of over $2 billion and close to ten thousand employees. Godrej is a household name in India. Name it and Godrej probably makes it—from locks, safes, and other security steel equipment to soaps to typewriters. India's first prime minister, Jawaharlal Nehru, after accepting a bouquet from Sohrab Godrej, remarked, "Don't tell me you manufacture flowers also!"[7]

Although over one hundred years later the Godrej portfolio appears impossibly diverse, it grew organically and opportunistically from the first experiments with locks and soap. Godrej Consumer Products Ltd. (GCPL) is a strong domestic player in the personal care, hair care, and fabric care categories. Godrej's hair color division is a high-margin business, contributing 35 percent of GCPL's revenues and 65 percent of profits.

Godrej is the world's largest manufacturer of powder hair dye for gray coverage, sold in packets that are inexpensive, economical, and easy to use. In India, 400 million people use Godrej products every day, but the brand is virtually unknown elsewhere. "This is a huge challenge," acknowledged Adi Godrej, chairman and managing director, adding, "It will be a must for companies that operate in a field where brand is important to build their brands, because without a strong brand to promote, a great expansion to outside India will not be possible."

In 2006 Godrej set its sights on the developing world and acquired the leading South African company Rapidol, which had hair color market leadership in South Africa, Lesotho, Swaziland, Namibia, Zimbabwe, Angola, Mozambique, Congo, and Botswana. With the acquisition, Godrej gained not only a strong regional brand—Rapidol controlled 80 percent of the share of the fast-growing South African ethnic hair color market—but also well-established distribution channels on which it could piggyback to gain access for a select number of the company's Indian brands.[8]

Godrej planned to aggressively market its own brands in Africa, reflecting the company's confidence that it had entered a new market with an ethnic segment where it could compete comfortably. It now had a strong local brand and wide distribution channels to complement the company's core competence in marketing to the low-end segment of developing economies. Also, Godrej had adjusted its research and product development to cater to the unique hair of the African market as well as the Indian market. This confidence might spur other international acquisitions, including in China, the Philippines, Vietnam, Egypt, Nigeria, Brazil, and Mexico.

Godrej's acquisition of personal care Keyline Brands Ltd. in 2005 marked a strategic turning point for the company—Keyline Brands operated in developed markets, including the United Kingdom, Australia, and Canada. Though ownership of strong local brands was a key driver behind the acquisition, even more compelling in this particular acquisition were Keyline's well-established distribution channels, especially those with supermarket chains such as Sainsbury, Tesco, and Boots in the United Kingdom. According to Godrej, "Supermarkets have long-term relationships with local companies in developed markets. Without this, it is difficult to penetrate markets such as the U.K." Godrej will market its powder hair color in the lower end and creams at the higher end of the U.K. hair care market, catering to a large British Afro-Asian population.

Learning how to deal with developed country markets was another key aspect of the Keyline acquisition. Indian managers were sent to the United Kingdom so they could bring home knowledge of marketing consumer products in developed countries. But that's not all that was transferred to India from the United Kingdom—Godrej is planning to introduce Keyline Brands in India.

Partitioning Domestic and International Brands

In contrast to building its domestic brands overseas, VIP Industries and United Breweries developed multibrand portfolios by acquiring established Western brands. With strong international as well as domestic brands, they could successfully target both emerging and developed markets.

VIP Industries

Since VIP's creation in 1971, over 60 million pieces have rolled off its production lines, including suitcases, briefcases, and backpacks. It was by far the dominant domestic player by volume with brands such as VIP, Alfa, Footloose, and Buddy.

The luggage industry is divided into soft (fabric, leather) luggage and the much smaller hard (molded plastic) luggage segments. VIP, a leader in the soft luggage market domestically, dominated the hard luggage niche globally. Given its strong brand position in the Indian market, VIP also performed well in markets with a large expatriate Indian population, such as the Middle East and Singapore. VIP sold through 1,300 retail outlets in twenty-seven countries. Export turnover surpassed $8 million in 2004–2005, representing an increase of 145 percent over 2003–2004. As a result, VIP had developed into the second-largest manufacturer of luggage in the world, behind global giant Samsonite.

According to Dilip Piramal, chairman of VIP Industries, "VIP has always harbored international ambitions." In 2004 the opportunity arose to acquire Carlton, a thirty-year-old British family-run business that had gone bankrupt—but which was also the number four luggage brand in the United Kingdom. Around 80 percent of Carlton's business was in soft-sided luggage, with manufacturing subcontracted to China, just like every other luggage company. Even VIP outsourced all its soft-sided manufacturing to China. However, Carlton also owned hard-luggage manufacturing facilities in the United Kingdom, and these were transferred to India, where VIP expertise would build the niche hard-luggage Carlton brand alongside its own hard-luggage brands. Piramal explained the rationale behind the acquisition: "Successful acquisition of a well-known international brand offers significant synergies as well as a much-desired gateway to the world market. As London is the hub for the world market, successful presence in the U.K. market is very critical in achieving VIP's global aspirations. We believe we are off to a good start with successful acquisition of Carlton, but the long journey has just begun."

Carlton became an independent subsidiary of VIP with a new CEO, E. P. Suresh Menon, at the helm. The structure was designed to preserve Carlton's brand integrity by maintaining two very separate organizations, distinct from VIP in every way, from location to personnel to letterhead. As Menon put it: "The idea was to keep Carlton's U.K. heritage. And in the branded space, it was the first time an Indian company was planning to run a brand and sell that brand globally. This was a brand reaching out directly to European customers and understanding their tastes."

Carlton's distribution, design capability, and intellectual property rights gave VIP an entrée into the lucrative, more sophisticated European market. Carlton could go places where the VIP brand could not. Thus, VIP remained the Indian brand and Carlton would be the international brand—despite the fact that both were made in China. Piramal explained:

> *When you say Carlton of London or Delsey of Paris—high-fashion capitals of the world—the brand association is different than it would be for "VIP of India" . . . on our Carlton guarantee cards we write, "Designed and developed in the U.K." Manufactured in China, but designed in the U.K.*
>
> *We do this for marketing. In reality, I don't think it really matters to the consumer if the brand is coming from India or if it's manufactured in China. The product has to be good on its own merits. Whether it's an American, Indian, or British brand, it can be given an upscale image. The background of Indian manufacturing has nothing to do with India, so why link it to the brand? The only thing Indian is the intellectual ability.*

Piramal believed that the cachet of a British brand gave VIP a strong foundation upon which to grow globally. It was a powerful one-two punch—Carlton had the brand name and the heritage; VIP had the manufacturing muscle and hard-side design capability.

United Breweries

United Breweries began as a trading company importing fine liquors and cigars. With the death of his father in 1983, Vijay Mallya became chairman at the age of twenty-seven. He took charge of a liquor company that produced fewer than 3 million cases a year and grew it into the world's third-largest spirits company, with 2008 sales reaching 73 million cases. United Spirits Limited (USL), the beverage subsidiary of United Breweries Group, is now the dominant player in India with a 55 percent market share in value terms. USL's 140 brands cover a wide array of price points, and several are among the top domestic sellers in their category. For example, its Kingfisher beer is the domestic leader and is sold in sixty countries around the world.

The British Raj brought whiskey to India, and the country eventually developed into the world's largest whiskey market by far. Domestic brands, which are molasses based and distilled in India, still control about 90 percent of the Indian whiskey market. Historically, imported Scotch whiskey—premium blends manufactured from wheat, barley, and originating from Scotland—comprised only about 1 percent of the Indian market, as a result of tariffs of 550 percent.[9] But the 2007 reduction in import duties to 150 percent increased whiskey imports to India.[10] For a burgeoning Indian middle class who perceived drinking Scotch as part of a lifestyle choice along with iPods, American fashion labels, and imported consumer goods, premium spirits were a hyper growth segment. Despite its strong presence in the domestic market, USL lacked a premium Scotch whiskey to meet the demands of this market segment. Mallya looked to an acquisition outside of India to fill the gap.

After protracted negotiations, in May 2007, USL acquired Whyte & McKay (W&M), the fourth-largest producer of premium Scotch, for $1.2 billion. W&M brands include Dalmore and Isle of Jura single-malt labels, two prestigious brands. A bottle of sixty-four-year-old Dalmore recently sold for $100,000, making it among the world's most expensive single malts. W&M brands also include several economy whiskey brands (Mackinlays, Fettercairn, John Barr, Cluny, and Claymore) as well as Vladivar vodka and Glayva liqueur. With the acquisition of W&M, USL is jockeying to overtake Pernod-Ricard SA of France as the second-largest liquor company in the world, behind the U.K.-based Diageo PLC.

W&M became a wholly owned subsidiary of USL. However, in contrast to other firms discussed in this chapter, W&M brands were immediately integrated into United Spirit's domestic business. The W&M acquisition would fill the gap in USL's brand portfolio, which lacked premium Scotch whiskies. USL's well-entrenched distribution channels would expedite market penetration of W&M brands in India. The potential to dominate the fast-growing domestic market segment for premium Scotch became an immediate reality for USL with the stroke of Mallya's pen on the W&M deal. International sales also received a boost with the addition of more brands and expanded international distribution channels abroad. Brands, inventories, and distribution channels that accompanied the W&M acquisition would have taken decades for USL to create, if even possible, through organic growth.

But the billion-dollar-plus acquisition provided additional value, namely, ensuring a reliable supply of raw material. Prior to the acquisition, USL sourced bulk Scotch from its key competitors—including Diageo and Pernod-Ricard—as well as W&M and blended it with its domestic whiskey to make a more premium product. But with the acquisition of W&M's massive stockpiles of aging Scotch, USL was ensured a perennial supply to meet growing requirements for premium Scotch whiskey in India and its other key markets, including the fast-growing markets in China, Russia, Eastern Europe, and the Gulf states.

The rising economic tide bodes well for the fortunes of Indian consumer brands as a whole. Much like earlier brands from other developing countries, some Indian consumer brands are likely to become global contenders. It will be a while before India has a global brand with the name recognition of Sony or Samsung. Perhaps this will come to pass before the next batch of Dalmore forty-year-old single malt ages to perfection. But however long it takes, the outcome will no doubt taste as smooth and sweet.

NINE

Suzlon

Conceiving the Global Wind Energy Industry

We have a business model that's completely counterintuitive. The
concepts and design come from the Netherlands, the engineering
from Germany, the commercialization from Denmark. And the
large-scale application comes from India. Only an Indian brain
could dream up such a thing.

Tulsi Tanti,
Chairman and Managing Director, Suzlon Energy Limited

EVER SEE A propeller-like wind turbine and wonder how
renewable energy is literally changing the landscape?[1] Imagine a
windmill almost fifty stories high—the largest in Asia—towering
above the tiny hamlet of Sankaneri on the southern tip of the sub-
continent. It is a creation of Suzlon.[2]

The story of Suzlon's rise to global prominence has unfolded in
lockstep with the greening of the planet. In an extraordinarily short
time frame, Suzlon has gone from small textile manufacturer to lead-
ing-edge producer of wind turbines. How is this possible? As much
as, or perhaps more than, any Indian company that has gone global,
Suzlon aggressively leveraged global expertise.

SUZLON SNAPSHOT

- Suzlon is the fifth-ranked wind turbine manufacturer in the world, with a 10 percent global market share.
- Suzlon operates in twenty countries, across five continents.
- Global management headquarters is in the Netherlands, marketing headquarters is in Denmark, and the engineering center is headquartered in Pune.
- Suzlon employs over fourteen thousand people worldwide.[3]

Tanti: An Entrepreneur Responding to Indian-Specific Challenges

Tulsi Tanti jokes that "wind power was my seventeenth attempt at business."[4] The Suzlon story began in 1992 as a textile company with only twenty employees, and struggling with soaring energy costs and erratic availability of power to run its business. Tanti's line of polyester yarns was doing well, but India's shaky power grid and the rising cost of electricity was increasingly offsetting any profits. Tanti's highest cost after raw materials was electricity. As Tanti put it, "We were constantly innovating but we weren't able to control the price of power."

Tanti looked for alternatives, and after some study, settled on wind power as a solution to the ongoing problem in his main business. At that time, wind energy was not economically viable despite government subsidies because of the high interest rates on the large capital investment required to generate wind power. Yet Tanti took a bet that interest rates would come down and power costs would continue to go up. With a capital expenditure that exceeded the value of his textile business, Tanti obtained two small-capacity wind turbine generators. He continued to explain the genesis of Suzlon:

I said to myself, "I've got to find a way to contain power costs over the long term, so it won't affect our bottom line and will allow us consistent production." So we invested in the infrastructure for wind power, and within two years, the operation was commercially viable.

It was a great investment because it involved a one-time capital investment with small variable costs, which could be easily forecast. So I succeeded in predicting our costs for the decades to come, which hedged a large percentage of my costs in the textile business.

Tanti recognized at the time that, unintentionally, he had succeeded in creating a unique business model. This sparked a thought: Why not reexplore this concept and do it on a larger scale? Thus, back in 1995, Tanti set up Suzlon Energy Limited—India's first home-grown wind technology company.

An important success factor was that Suzlon's textile business itself was a client of the wind power generation, and thus, before offering the service to any external customer, Tanti had implemented it. This gave Suzlon first-hand knowledge of what customers would be looking for. The key to the development of the successful business model was Tanti's insight that "all I cared about as a customer was getting reliable power at a controlled price to hedge my primary operation."

Tanti realized that despite the incredible potential for wind power as a commercial opportunity, customers in India did not know anything about this technology or how to operate it. Furthermore, both internally generated funding and bank financing would not be available for customers because of the relatively large capital expenditure in wind technology relative to the size of the customer. The existing global wind turbine providers at that time, being equipment suppliers, restricted themselves primarily to simply selling wind turbines, leaving the rest for the customer to figure out.

After extensive research, Suzlon began with an entirely unique approach that Tanti referred to as "concept to commissioning." It meant that Suzlon became both provider and custodian of wind power generation for its clients. Tanti explained:

Our approach provides comfort for our customers. We do everything for our clients. We identify the sites, conduct the wind measurement study, the budgeting, build the substation and grid connections; then we take the responsibility for twenty years of operating maintenance. This is a real source of sustainable competitive advantage. This

*allows our customers to focus on their main business, while ensuring
a reliable, cost-efficient source of power.*

Suzlon also adopted an innovative approach to arranging the
financing for potential clients' investments in wind power infrastructure. Specifically, Suzlon's customers were responsible for 25 percent
of the up-front capital investment, and Suzlon helped arrange for the
remaining 75 percent. Suzlon executives would accompany potential
customers to their banks and educate the loan managers on how the
investment made sound strategic sense. At first glance, banks were
uncomfortable financing investments in wind power, as the investment often was the equivalent of the company's total assets. Suzlon
representatives would explain that the investment was critical to support the overall business, because without a reliable energy source at
a capped price, the main business was not sustainable. This strategy
was very successful—whereas initially, just one or two banks
financed wind power projects, by 2008, forty to fifty Indian banks
were financing wind power generation projects for Suzlon's clients.

By 1999, the company achieved market leadership in India. It has
consistently maintained over 50 percent market share in its home
country, installing over 3,000 megawatts of wind turbine capacity
and developing and implementing several large-scale wind farms
throughout India. In Vankusavade, Maharashtra, Suzlon's wind farm
employs 566 turbines with installed capacity of over 205 megawatts.
In Sanganeri, Tamil Nadu, Suzlon has developed a wind farm with a
planned capacity of over 500 megawatts, and in Dhulia, Maharashtra, Suzlon developed one of the world's largest wind farms with a
planned capacity of over 1,000 megawatts.

In September 2005, the company went public with an IPO that
launched Suzlon into the top twenty-five Indian corporations in market capitalization. But what Tanti was particularly proud of was the
fact that Suzlon had created the market for wind power in India,
increasing the country's energy supply, which in turn would increase
productivity and raise living standards. This was particularly important as all Suzlon's projects are located in rural India, where rising
living standards through increased productivity has dramatic consequences. The environmentally friendly nature of wind power was a
further source of pride to Tanti.

The Wind Power Industry: Growing at Gale Force

In 2007, over 19 gigawatts of new wind power capacity was added globally, with the United States, China, Spain, and India leading the way. Control of the global wind power market has remained up in the air, with major players, primarily from Europe, vying with American and Asian upstarts. The leading global players, Denmark's Vestas Wind Systems and Spain's Gamesa, have been stalwarts in the European market, with wind power in their respective home countries hovering around 10 and 20 percent of total power generation, compared with a total of 1 percent worldwide.[5] But the growth of wind power—fed by financial incentives and fueled by environmental concerns about fossil fuels—attracted the mainstream interest of such well-established and resource-rich companies as General Electric, which picked up Enron Wind in 2002 for a song, and Siemens, which acquired Danish Bonus Energy in 2004.

The top four players—Vestas (23 percent), Gamesa (15 percent), Enercon (14 percent), and GE Wind (17 percent)—still represented almost three-quarters of global supply, but their market position, given anticipated growth dynamics strongly favoring China and the United States, was far from secure.[6] Interestingly, the United States and China had two of the lowest percentages of installed turbines made by a domestic company (see table 9-1), an opportunity that was not lost on Suzlon as it customized its strategy to maximize its global reach.

The government has actively supported the wind industry in India. Suzlon has benefited from government intervention that set targets for power generation from renewable sources, provided financial incentives for installation, and developed certification standards. Tanti lobbied the state government of Maharashtra to institute a tax break that allowed companies to offset their windmill costs with a credit on their sales tax bill. For customers like Indian motorcycle manufacturer Bajaj Auto, this was important. Its chairman, Rahul Bajaj, said that while impressed by the Suzlon business model, had it not been for the tax break, "I am not sure whether we would have gone ahead."[7]

India responded to the favorable climate its government provided and by 2007, India had the world's fourth-largest wind power capacity, behind Germany, Spain, and the United States. Much of India's

TABLE 9-1

Largest wind markets and domestic wind companies

Country (installed capacity, 2006)	Percentage of Installed Turbines Made by Domestic Companies (2006)
Denmark (3,101 MW)	100% Vestas
Spain (11,614 MW)	76% Gamesa, Ecotecnia, EHN/Ingetur
Germany (20,652 MW)	55% Enercon, REpower, Nordex, Fuhrlander, Siemens (formerly Bonus)
India (6,228 MW)	**52% Suzlon**
China (2,588 MW)	39% Goldwind
United States (11,575 MW)	37% GE Wind

Source: Adapted from Joanna I. Lewis, "A Comparison of Wind Power Industry Development Strategies in Spain, India and China," prepared for the Center for Resource Solutions, San Francisco, July 19, 2007, and Global Wind Energy Council.

success in overachieving its wind power target is attributable to the success of Suzlon in its home market. Suzlon's 52 percent market share is more than double that of its closest rivals in India, Enercon (24 percent) and Vestas (22 percent).[8] A crucial and growing market, India is the linchpin of Suzlon's strategy, which includes developing key regional markets such as North America, China, Europe, and Australia.

Suzlon's Global Strategy: Best of All Worlds

Suzlon's strategy to be successful in the wind power industry was based on three critical factors: going global, acquiring technology to offer a complete portfolio, and marrying Europe's expertise with India's low costs. As a result of this strategy, Suzlon has the highest margins and the highest growth in the global wind power industry.

Going Global

With his textile exports background, Tanti recognized from the beginning that wind energy was a global opportunity. Tanti realized that since wind power generation was capital intensive and required sustained investment in technology, Suzlon would have to go global if it were to recover its investment. Back in 1995, Tanti focused on the domestic market, feeling that Suzlon was not ready to enter the world stage. Nonetheless, given that India represented a fraction of the global market (8–10 percent), going global was always a strategic imperative.

By 2003, Suzlon had a 50 percent market share, and it was then that Tanti felt Suzlon was ready to move onto the global stage. The first international foray was into the United States, with a sale to John Deere. This was one of the first significant sales of wind power technology from the third world to the developed world! China, Europe, Australia, and then Brazil followed in quick succession.

By 2008, 70 percent of Suzlon's revenue was generated from international sales. Looking for growth, Suzlon looked past traditional markets for wind energy, and entered new and emerging high-growth markets. Suzlon had successfully navigated the transition from a local player operating in a nascent industry to a company poised to become as global as the wind.

Acquiring World-Class Technology to Offer a Complete Portfolio

Suzlon's "concept to commissioning" mantra required full vertical integration of the supply chain (see figure 9-1). Given the huge and growing demand for wind power technologies, Suzlon understood that the only way it could be competitive would be to manufacture as

FIGURE 9-1

Suzlon: Concept to commissioning

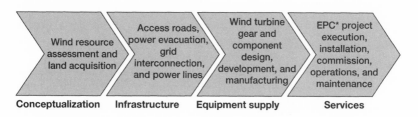

*Energy performance contract.

Source: Adapted from Suzlon Energy Limited investor presentation, September 2008 (www.suzlon.com).

many components as possible to ensure both supply and quality, accelerate delivery, and keep prices low. In addition, a comprehensive portfolio would enable Suzlon to seamlessly integrate its product line with existing turbine technology R&D efforts. Over time, Suzlon developed comprehensive manufacturing capabilities for all critical components in wind turbines.

Accessing world-class technology was a key impetus for Suzlon's early global ambitions. Making technology development a central objective, Suzlon developed an internationalized business model that leveraged Europe's traditional leadership, talent, and experience in wind energy technology right from inception.

Suzlon did not evolve from turbine technology and therefore had to develop expertise cooperatively through a series of agreements with foreign companies. The first of these was Sudwind GmbH Windkraft-tanlagen, a second-tier German company that shared technical know-how in exchange for royalty payments.[9] When Sudwind went bust in the late 1990s, Suzlon hired its engineers and set up an R&D center for turbines in Germany. Similarly, buying AE-Rotor Technick BV, a bankrupt Dutch company, enabled Suzlon to design and manufacture rotor blades.[10] Gradually, Suzlon accumulated expertise that it was able to supplement with its own R&D, with the ultimate goal being the design, development, and upgrade of the entire supply chain.

Suzlon strategically selected regional markets for cultivation with research and development in the Netherlands (rotor blades), Belgium (gearboxes), and Germany (wind turbines); with market subsidiaries in the United States and Australia; and with manufacturing facilities in Tianjin, China, and Minnesota. In 2004, Suzlon established international headquarters in Denmark. Denmark was not only a world leader in the integration of wind power, but was also a strategic location, since Vestas and NEG Micon had just merged and a pool of laid-off talent was readily available.[11] International research centers, presence, and acquisitions brought world-class technology as well as access to the important European markets.

Taking integration forward, Suzlon acquired Hansen Transmissions of Belgium in 2006. It was the second-largest foreign takeover by an Indian company in any industry and cemented Suzlon's position, both strategically and symbolically, as a top-tier global manufacturer.

Most importantly, purchasing Hansen plugged a critical gap in Suzlon's supply chain. The acquisition of the world's second leading gearbox maker gave Suzlon manufacturing and technology development capability for wind gearboxes, enabling an integrated R&D approach to designing ever more efficient wind turbines.

The Hansen acquisition was a result of a comprehensive mapping of the industry to assess who had the best technology in each area. On the strength of Suzlon's potential sales, post acquisition, Hansen was able to increase its scale by around four to five times. This Belgian arm of Suzlon was then listed on the London Stock Exchange in late 2007. The result was that the $565 million purchase in 2006 now had a market capitalization of $3 billion!

Typically, Indian and Chinese manufacturers, being smaller companies with a limited range of products, produce turbines smaller than those of their larger global competitors. Therefore, through the 2007 acquisition of REpower, Suzlon augmented existing expertise by introducing the Suzlon ecosystem to larger turbines in the 1.5 to 5.0 megawatt range. The significance of this addition cannot be

FIGURE 9-2

Suzlon international growth milestones

1995	Formed Suzlon Energy.
2001	Established AE Rotor Holding BV in the Netherlands, focusing on blade technologies.
2001	Formed Suzlon Energy GmBH in Germany for design and development of wind turbine generators.
2001	Commenced marketing operations at Suzlon Wind Energy, United States.
2003	Set up office in Beijing.
2004	Formed Suzlon Energy A/S Denmark, international marketing headquarters for Europe.
2006	Acquired Hansen Transmissions International NV, Belgium, one of the world's largest gearbox manufacturers.
2006	Established a manufacturing facility producing blades and nose cones in Pipestone, Minnesota.
2007	Acquired REpower with a market share of 3 percent worldwide and a complementary portfolio.

Source: Adapted from http://www.suzlon.com/Milestone.aspx?cp=1_5.

underestimated since trends worldwide were toward larger, presumably more efficient turbines that save money on installation costs. The acquisition also enabled Suzlon to enter the large European markets—Germany (where REpower had a 10 percent share), the United Kingdom, and France—and complement its product portfolio through presence in the offshore wind energy segment. Further, Suzlon and REpower planned a new Global Technology Center in Hamburg, Germany, that would coordinate Suzlon's global R&D efforts.

Figure 9-2 provides a summary of Suzlon's growth.

Marry Europe's Expertise with India's Low Costs

Suzlon's goal was and always will be to reduce the cost of wind power to make it ever more competitive with older technologies, thus helping customers get the best internal rate of return (IRR) from their investment in wind energy. Research, local market knowledge, and technological expertise from abroad was synergized with a strong engineering backbone in India, bringing together the expertise of different centers of excellence to build "best of all worlds" solutions.

Expanding internationally while maintaining the majority of its manufacturing in India gave Suzlon access to capital as well as low manufacturing and labor costs. Although 70 percent of sales were international, ten thousand of Suzlon's almost fourteen thousand employees were located in India. This helped build a competitive advantage over European rivals who operated in higher-cost regions.[12] Moreover, this meant Suzlon's turbines cost 20 percent less than their U.S. and European counterparts.[13] Manufacturing presence in other countries such as the United States and China was established strategically to increase accessibility to key markets.

Components made in India fed global demand for wind power and were in turn nourished by enhancements developed at Suzlon R&D centers in Europe. Suzlon's global network was thus built to optimize itself in a spiral of continuous innovation. The REpower acquisition combined with the decision to locate Suzlon's headquarters in Denmark—renowned for its large, technologically advanced turbines—addressed a significant product span issue and positioned Suzlon for a future of supplying large volumes across the world. Running REpower products through Suzlon's supply chain helped

FIGURE 9-3

Suzlon's product mix mapped to key markets

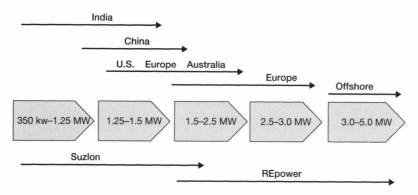

Source: Adapted from Suzlon Energy Limited investor presentation, September 2008 (www.suzlon.com).

REpower to improve its margins and, consistent with previous global moves, enabled Suzlon to capitalize on REpower's expertise and brand equity. Figure 9-3 illustrates how Suzlon's acquisition of REpower helped map the product mix to key markets.

Tanti explained that Suzlon focused on providing value to its customers while ensuring the highest margins for Suzlon. The REpower acquisition fit into this strategy:

> *Acquisitions play a key part of this strategy. We follow a path of identifying the best players in the industry to acquire based on their technology, such as REpower, the Dutch company we acquired. REpower is the leader in offshore technology and they have a commercialized product already in the market. Thus, we targeted them specifically for our portfolio. If you cannot integrate technology, you cannot get the highest margin. But REpower was fully integrated, and a leader in technology. This expanded our capacity from 3,600 megawatts to 15,000 megawatts, reaping significant economies-of-scale benefits.*

Future Challenges

Suzlon is currently the fifth-largest wind company in the global market, but in Tanti's mind, global ranking was not as important as remaining a high-growth, high-margin player. According to Tanti, Suzlon achieved the highest gross margins in the industry from 1998 to 2007. Thus, his first challenge is maintaining this financial performance.

His second challenge is managing cultural diversity. Suzlon operated in twenty countries in 2008, but Tanti's goal is to expand to over forty countries within five years. The challenge will be in integrating so many cultures—having them perform as one team, with one uniting organizational culture, toward one corporate mission. Tanti expects that increasingly more of his time will be invested in people management in the coming years. However, Tanti's efforts will not be directed toward controlling people, but rather in encouraging "a free hand" in their management while providing a "a very clear direction for Suzlon's vision."

Tanti's third challenge is to ensure growth of 20 to 25 percent annually through efficient supply chain management. Suzlon has the capacity to expand due to its unique business model. Tanti explains: "We are fortunate that in 2003 we took the decision to fully vertically integrate our operations. Today, Suzlon is the only company in the sector that manufactures their own key components."

By 2012, it is anticipated that electricity produced by wind power will represent 3 percent of global electricity consumption (up from 1 percent in 2007). The impressive growth of wind-powered electricity in the United States and China over the last few years is expected to continue. Suzlon's response to global developments has been to increase the pace of globalization and focus even more diligently on R&D. As of 2007, 81 percent of Suzlon's employees were engaged in technical functions. The company's goal moving forward is technical leadership in wind energy and a top-three ranking in all key global markets. And as Tanti explains, it rests on the back of a unique strategy:

> Our unique strategy that I call "concept to commissioning" has proven to be a real source of sustainable competitive advantage, first in India, and then throughout both the developing and the developed world. Further, various centers of excellence have allowed us to build the "best of all worlds" products when combined with the engineering expertise within India. These strategies have pushed Suzlon's growth from $300,000 in our first year to $2.8 billion in 2008, just one decade later.

Tata Group

Driving for Multi-industry Global Leadership

> One hundred years from now, I expect Tata to be much bigger than
> it is now. More importantly, I hope the group comes to be regarded
> as being the best in India—best in the manner in which we operate,
> best in the products we deliver, and best in our value systems and
> ethics. Having said that, I hope that a hundred years from now we
> will spread our wings far beyond India.
>
> *Ratan N. Tata, Chairman, Tata Group*

CHANCES ARE, if you had never heard of an Indian company or
thought about India as anything but an outsourcing destination, you found news of Tata Motors and its revolutionary 100,000
rupee car at least somewhat shocking. Making headlines the world
over, the Nano or "People's Car" cast Tata Group and Indian innovation into the global spotlight like never before.[1] How did a company that began operation in the late nineteenth century with a
textile mill get from there to here? The Tata Group presents us with a
textbook case of a well-managed $63 billion company choosing
strategically advantageous avenues to global success.[2] Throughout
India, the Tata brand is ubiquitous, associated with a vast array of
products—credit cards, telephones, salt, tea, coffee, clothing, jewelry,
cars, and trucks.

But Tata also presents us with a story about not only prosperity,
but just as important, philanthropy. The Tata Group is a source

- Tata is India's largest business group, with 2008 revenues of $63 billion.

- Tata Group comprises ninety-eight companies in seven business sectors—engineering (most notably Tata Motors), materials (Tata Steel), information technology (Tata Consultancy Services), consumer products (Tata Tea), energy (Tata Power), chemicals (Tata Chemicals), and services (Taj Hotels).

- Global sales for the financial year ending March 2008 (prior to the consolidation of Jaguar and Land Rover) represent 61 percent of Tata Group. It operates in over eighty countries and exports to eighty-five.

- As of 2008, 350,000 employees, of whom 30 percent are outside India.

of Indian pride, a hugely successful global company run on ethical business principles. It is a company that has never been tainted by bribes. Its trusts provide substantive philanthropic projects in the alleviation of poverty, disaster relief, and the creation of Indian scientific and cultural institutions. The group's holding company, Tata Sons, is two-thirds owned by charitable trusts, and as a result two-thirds of the dividends goes to philanthropy. In the words of Alan Rosling, the executive spearheading Tata's internationalization, "We're making money so our shareholders can give it away."

It is an ethos with deep roots.

Tata History

In a free enterprise the community is not just another stakeholder in the business, but is in fact the very reason for its existence.

Jamsetji Tata, founder of the Tata Group (1839–1904)

Tata Group's history has always been as much a part of the company as its physical structure. The founder's legacy remains so prevalent, it seems to take on a corporeal presence that continues as a defining principle of management decision making.

Tata Group's founder Jamsetji Tata had a vision of a grand, audacious future for himself, his company, and for India at large. In 1868, at the age of twenty-nine, he set up the trading company that was the foundation of Tata Group. The economic development of India through industrialization was at the root of his philosophy. Jamsetji traveled to England, where he became convinced that an Indian company could and should compete with the British in the textile industry. In 1874 he established a textile company, and inaugurated The Empress Mill in 1877.

With his business successfully established, Jamsetji provided the foundation for what would become a lasting legacy—setting up Asia's first iron and steel company, generating hydroelectric power with India's first private sector power utility, and creating the Indian Institute of Science—all realized after his death. It was rumored that when he took two British men to lunch to a hotel and was denied entry because he was Indian, Jamsetji resolved to set up the world's finest hotel. Tata's Taj Hotel, the flagship hotel of India's first luxury chain, opened in 1904 with its own post office, laundry, and electroplating plant and was the first building in Bombay to be lit by electricity.

Jamsetji's philanthropic principles were rooted in the belief that for India to emerge from poverty the finest minds had to be identified— regardless of caste or creed—and harnessed and directed toward the service of nation building. He offered his workers shorter working hours, well-ventilated workplaces, and many other progressive work practices that were faithfully emulated by his successors. Thus, Jamsetji set the tone for Tata Group, pioneering the philosophy of combining far-reaching industrial ambition and deep compassion.

> May I appeal to all who live in this land to work in harmony
> and cooperation for its development.
>
> *Sir Dorab Tata, Chairman (1904–1932)*

Jamsetji's eldest son Dorab took up his father's vision and established an integrated steel plant that was the largest single unit in the British Empire. An incredulous Sir Frederick Upcott, the chief commissioner of the Great Indian Peninsular Railway, promised to "eat every pound of steel rail [the Tatas] succeed in making" but was nowhere to be seen when the first ingot rolled off the line in 1912.

Dorab's additional contributions to Tata included three hydro-electric power companies, a soap and cooking oil company, two cement companies, and an aviation unit pioneered by J. R. D. Tata. He also was committed to research and development, and oversaw the establishment of the Indian Institute of Science in Bangalore.

Sir Dorab financed the Indian contingent to the Paris Olympiad in 1924, but his crowning achievement was to put all his wealth, including a 245-carat Jubilee diamond, into a trust for the advancement of learning and research, the relief of distress, and other charitable purposes. This was the beginning of the Sir Dorabji Tata Trust and the expression of the philanthropic spirit first expressed by his father. In 2006–2007, it disbursed the equivalent of more than $20 million to NGOs, individuals, and trust-promoted institutions.

> The wealth gathered by Jamsetji Tata and his sons in a half century
> of industrial pioneering formed but a minute fraction of the
> amount by which they enriched the nation. What came from the
> people has gone back to the people many times over.
>
> *J. R. D. Tata, Chairman (1938–1991)*

Born in Paris in 1904 to R. D. Tata, a business partner and relative of Jamsetji Tata, and his French wife Sooni, J. R. D. Tata (hereinafter referred to as JRD) was educated in France, Japan, and England before he joined Tata as an unpaid apprentice in December 1925.

The first of JRD's adventures in business was born of his childhood passion for flying. In 1929 JRD became one of the first Indians to be granted a commercial pilot's license and the key figure in the establishment of Tata Aviation Service, the airmail service that was the forerunner to Tata Airlines and Air India. The first flight in the history of Indian aviation lifted off from Drigh Road in Karachi with JRD at the controls. JRD nourished and nurtured his airline until it became a world-class carrier. In 1953, the government of India's first prime minister, Jawaharlal Nehru, nationalized Air India, a decision JRD fiercely resisted because although he and Nehru were friends, they differed on matters of economic policy. JRD believed in economic liberalization long before India embraced it.

With JRD at the helm, Tata began developing a rock-solid reputation for not engaging in the practices common at many Indian companies—creating posts for relatives and dispensing favors for financial or personal gain. JRD pushed to bring in professionals. The "License Raj" era created a difficult, if not hostile, environment for ethical entrepreneurship and a distrust of capitalism that ran counter to the Tata ethos. At one point, Nehru famously said to JRD, "Don't talk to me of profit; it is a dirty word." Nonetheless, over the fifty-plus years of JRD's stewardship, the group expanded into many new businesses, including chemicals, automobiles, tea, and information technology.

The Global Turning Point: Ratan Tata

Tata insiders often point to the ascension of Ratan Tata to chairman as a turning point for the company. As R. Gopalakrishnan, executive director of Tata Sons, put it: "In 1991 when Ratan Tata became chairman, he said you must shape up, you are all flabby . . . and he had to do this without criticizing the past."

Protected by the insular policies of the Indian government, many Tata Group companies had become comfortable. For example, neither Tata Steel nor Tata Motors had been tested against a formidable global competitor on its domestic turf. Ratan Tata had studied at Cornell, worked in Australia, and had enough international experience to perceive just how flabby and uncompetitive Tata had become. Therefore his first task would be to get Tata in competitive shape. His second task would be to take Tata global.

The fitness regimen, as all fitness regimens are, was both painful and rewarding. Between 1991 and 2002 Ratan Tata's shaping-up process had several dimensions including cost reduction, productivity, process, and quality improvements, acquiring technology, portfolio restructuring, investment in training, innovation, and action.

As would be expected, the group companies went through the usual phases, from denial to acceptance. Eventually, a strong foundation was established in India that would serve as a platform global expansion.

Admittedly, Ratan Tata's early years as chairman were tumultuous, but an extensive review of the business, including a study of China versus India, convinced him an audacious Chinese approach was the way to go: "Whether they built a port or a highway, they did it big, the kind of scale that caused skeptics to say, 'My God, this is over the top,' but China always grew into it."[3] India, he concluded, should also think big—and so should the Tata Group. The strategy was to expand aggressively, using a combination of acquisitions and organic growth, to reach global status.

As Alan Rosling, director of Tata Sons, explained:

The starting point of the globalization process was an appreciation that many, though not all, of Tata businesses were exposed to global markets driven by the opening of markets and technological changes. Therefore, it was a strategic imperative for many of our businesses to internationalize or they would struggle to remain competitive. In essence what we have done is taken the bigger businesses of the group and begun a process to try to gain a stronger competitive position in their industries on a global basis. Frankly we are still early in this process.

Some businesses, like TCS, grew organically almost entirely, by investing overseas in greenfield projects. Others have used acquisitions to help with globalization. From the mid-1990s to 2003, Tata acquired on average one company per year. In 2004, it acquired five. In 2005, it acquired twelve and in 2006, more than twenty. And the scale of acquisitions grew over time as well, with Tetley Tea in 2000, Corus Steel in 2007, and, perhaps most famously, Jaguar–Land Rover in 2008 (see table 10-1). Overall, Tata has conducted thirty-seven cross border acquisitions valued at $18 billion. The result of this organic growth and acquisitions has been truly remarkable. In 2008, the Tata Group generated $38 billion in international revenues.

TABLE 10-1

Tata Group's select acquisitions

	Tata Company	Acquired Company	Country	Stake Acquired	Value
2000	Tata Tea	Tetley Group	United Kingdom	100%	$407 million
2004	Tata Motors	Daewoo Commercial Vehicle Company	South Korea	100%	$102 million
	Tata Communications	Tyco Global Network			$135 million
2005	Tata Steel	NatSteel Asia Pte. Ltd.	Singapore	100%	$468.10 million
	Tata Motors	Hispano Carrocera	Spain	21%	€12 million
	Tata Chemicals	Indo Maroc Phosphore S.A.	Morocco	Equal partner	$38 million
	Indian Hotels	The Pierre	United States	Property lease	$45 million
	Tata Communications	Teleglobe International	Canada		$239 million
	Tata Tea	Good Earth Corporation	United States	100%	$32 million
	Indian Hotels	Starwood Group (W Hotel)	Australia	100%	$29 million
2006	Tata Steel	Millennium Steel	Thailand	67.11%	$404 million
	Tata Coffee	Eight O'Clock Coffee Company		100%	$220 million
2007	Tata Steel	Corus	United Kingdom	100%	$12.1 billion
	Indian Hotels	Campton Place Hotel	United States		$58 million
	Tata Power	PT Kaltim Prima Coal and PT Arutmin	Indonesia	30% equity	$1.1 billion
2008	Tata Motors	Jaguar and Land Rover	United Kingdom		$2.3 billion

Source: Adapted from Tata Web site (www.tata.com).

Tata's Global Strategy: Cajoling

An overarching global strategy delivered autocratically from the top and rigorously monitored is definitely not Tata's style. When Ratan Tata determined that a redefinition of the company from domestic to global was required, he did not deliver an edict. Rather, he "cajoled" Tata companies to make global thinking a part of their business plans.

This "cajoling" approach to top-down leadership is a function of Tata's structure and corporate philosophy. Tata has an unusual corporate structure (see figure 10-1) with Tata Sons and Tata Industries, the privately held parents, holding controlling stakes in dozens of publicly held companies, and through them hundreds of subsidiaries.

The parent–adult child metaphor is one R. Gopalakrishnan uses when he describes how Tata operates:

> *The way we run our companies is this: each company is an adult son, an individual citizen with his own board of directors who direct that company and its strategies. And he's supposed to take*

FIGURE 10-1

Tata holding structure

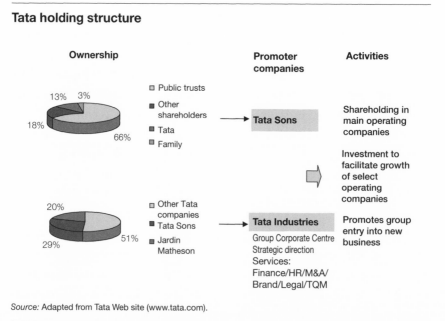

Source: Adapted from Tata Web site (www.tata.com).

care of himself. We therefore treat them like adults, and with adults there will be occasional differences of opinion, but if the board of directors blesses it, then that adult is free to do what he wants to do. The only way we will exercise our role as parent is if they do something that is violently different from what we want to do. In that situation, we would behave like an investor and cash out.

Rarely does Tata cash out, but it has happened. If a Tata company decided to do something that is on Tata's list of taboos—for example, invest in tobacco, alcohol, newspapers, or film—then Tata would revoke the company's rights to the Tata name, change management, and ultimately cash out. Similarly, if the Tata parent decided that something was in the interest of the group, all Tata offspring would be expected to fall into line unless compliance would adversely affect shareholder interests. Noncompliance with ethical or moral standards constitutes grounds for breaking ties.

According to Tata's governance model, the parent has three key functions: to provide vision, guidance, and perspective, or what Gopalakrishnan calls "centering" or "a sense of destiny"; to control the Tata brand; and to allocate resources including funding deals. Globalization was one such destiny that had significant implications for the Tata brand and for resource allocation.

As Gopalakrishnan describes it, "Globalization was an idea planted by Ratan Tata in the same way a firecracker is ignited . . . People saw sparks and said, 'Can I be a part of this?' And each company CEO, once engaged, returned to their units and discussed it with their top team and started to get intellectually and emotionally committed."

Once a Tata company decides to expand globally, the Tata parent is there to help provide financial support and intellectual rigor. Alan Rosling's responsibility is internationalization from the corporate center: "My function as the group executive director responsible for internationalization is to make sure that, first and foremost, every group company has thought this through. And the answer will be different for different industries. There is no single strategy, although at group level we have set some indicative targets and have prioritized geographies. But if Tata Motors says, 'I want to go to Korea,' no one stops them just because it's not on the list of priority countries."

Thus Rosling ensures that a workable plan for globalization is in place and that the company is fit to go global. He also helps clear the way for Tata companies going global with a team on the ground in key geographies—the United States, United Kingdom, China, Bangladesh, and South Africa. The overseas offices assist Tata operating companies with business development, external relations, and creating group synergies.

Ratan Tata has asserted at many employee forums that the philosophy Tata is trying to adopt is to go global locally, to become a contributing part of those countries into which it expands, and to enjoy the same degree of trust that Tata does in India. In other words, Tata wants to be seen as a local company rather than an Indian company. As Ravi Kant, director of Tata Motors, put it: "The Tata philosophy is to be seen as a local company. Hence, we keep mostly local management and work to augment and support them. We connect ourselves with the society and environment in which we operate, both politically, with ties to government, or culturally, through taking part in various activities like having an Indian food festival or a music program. We want to experience the pains and ecstasies of the community."

A large part of the Tata parent's job is to maintain the integrity of the family brand name. One of the conditions for a company to get the Tata name is that it must embrace the Tata Business Excellence Model and Tata Quality Management. At the Tata Management Training Center (TMTC), Tata calls in people from all over the world, including employees from the companies it is acquiring. As Dr. J. J. Irani, director of Tata Sons, described TMTC: "It's a residential program where we bring in people for about two weeks. We don't talk to them about steel or motors or anything like that. We talk to them about good ethics, good business principles, and things like that."

Everybody working in a Tata company must sign a code of conduct (see the box, "Tata Group Code of Conduct"). Over two hundred thousand people have signed it. Gopalakrishnan refers to it as a "bible" and adds that it contains "all the dilemmas and questions of conduct that have come up—we are clergy that go around and say, 'What troubles you in your heart?'" Part of the vetting process in any Tata acquisition is a comfort level with the ethics and culture of the

Tata Group Code of Conduct

Integrity: We must conduct our business fairly, with honesty and transparency. Everything we do must stand the test of public scrutiny.

Understanding: We must be caring, show respect, compassion and humanity for our colleagues and customers around the world, and always work for the benefit of the communities we serve.

Excellence: We must constantly strive to achieve the highest possible standards in our day-to-day work and in the quality of the goods and services we provide.

Unity: We must work cohesively with our colleagues across the Group and with our customers and partners around the world, building strong relationships based on tolerance, understanding and mutual cooperation.

Responsibility: We must continue to be responsible, sensitive to the countries, communities and environments in which we work, always ensuring that what comes from the people goes back to the people many times over.

Source: http://www.tata.com/article.aspx?artid=CKdRrD5ZDV4=.

potential acquisition target. If congruence in culture is not there, Tata will not proceed with the purchase.

The strong corporate social responsibility commitment has helped Tata in its global strategy, especially with regard to acquisitions. According to a popular story, former British prime minister Tony Blair's comments during Tata's attempted takeover of Jaguar and Land Rover illustrate this. He reportedly said that it was the best thing for Britain, because Tata comes with a track record of managing people and managing communities, they have been welcomed to other countries, and people respect them.[4]

This does not mean to imply that Tata does not struggle at times. In December 2007, Tata hit a snag when it sought to increase its stake in Orient-Express Hotels, a luxury hotels, trains, and cruises group. Paul White, CEO of Orient-Express, wrote a scathing letter to Tata that he posted on his company's Web site and copied to the Securities and Exchange Commission in which he rejected a tie to Taj, stating, "Any association of our luxury brands and properties with your brands and properties would result in a reduction in the value of our brands." Tata demanded an apology, but White had raised a thorny image issue associated with Indian ownership and brand image.

Ratan Tata, as the charismatic global ambassador of Tata Group, has been instrumental in putting potential takeover targets at ease. Internally, he has backed acquisitions by Tata companies with funds. As R. Gopalakrishnan puts it, "When papa can bankroll you, it shows that the son is a son; it's not like he's separated." In many ways, he has been the engine driving Tata's globalization.

The result has been a dramatic enhancement in the group's international revenues, from 20 to 60 percent in five years. As figure 10-2 indicates, some of the more global businesses are Tata Tea, Tata Steel, and Tata Motors. We will take up each of these three to show the differing global strategies adopted by the individual companies. (Tata Consultancy Services is discussed in chapter 3.)

Tata Tea: Acquiring a Global Brand

Tata Tea was the first Tata company to make an audacious acquisition, seven years before Tata Steel and its Corus deal. It acquired Tetley Tea, the venerable British tea manufacturer and second-largest tea brand in the world, in a leveraged buyout. R. K. Krishna Kumar, director of Tata Sons and vice chairman of Tata Tea, describes why Tata Tea was successful in its bid for Tetley in 2000 and did not succeed in a previous effort in 1995: "In 1995 we did not succeed because we did not want to go into a high-risk situation. By 2000 we had become less risk averse. Tetley was three times the size of Tata Tea. In a sense, on paper the risk looked too big, but if you looked beyond the financial and technical to the managerial capability—the real due diligence—it was highly doable. You have to look at it as a partnership, not to see it as two entities, but to see the new reality as one entity."

FIGURE 10-2

Tata Group international revenue

FY2007 Domestic/global splits:

Tea	28/72
Motors	86/14
Hotels	72/28
Steel	21/79
Consulting	10/90

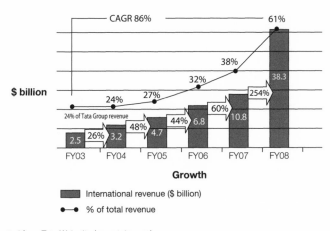

Source: Adapted from Tata Web site (www.tata.com).

And so Tata Tea and Tetley combined global forces under the Tetley brand umbrella, making one plus one considerably more than two. Tetley expanded both brand and geography, moving far beyond black tea into the beverage category with a significant presence in the fruit and herbal tea business.

In the newly merged company, what mattered most was not country of origin, but what Kumar calls a "global mind-set." As he put it, "How many senior managers at Tetley have a world view is the key question. Tetley has acquired other companies—they were so charged after the merger. The overall quality of the Tetley organization was enhanced by this acquisition and the focus on the global mind-set. They are seeing new opportunities. This is important." And so the Tata connection enabled Tetley to reinvent itself, incubate new ideas, and break out of the black tea paradigm.

Tata Steel: Building a Competitive Launch Pad for Globalization

In the 1980s Tata Steel, protected by government tariffs and the fact that it was one of only two choices in India for steel, was outdated, uneconomical, and uncompetitive. A liberalization program was on the horizon—everybody was talking about it—and Tata Steel had to make itself competitive. In 1994, Tata Steel was ranked in the fifties among eighty members of the International Steel Institute. It set a ten-year goal of being among the most cost-effective steel producers in the world. Within six years, Tata Steel had catapulted to the top five, where it has remained ever since.

But the modernization process was not without pain. Tata invested $2.5 billion in capital upgrades and reduced manpower from seventy-eight thousand to thirty-eight thousand in Bihar, a place where jobs were not plentiful. As J. J. Irani describes those times:

> People used to say, "For shoes there's Bata and for jobs there's Tata." But we had a very humane system. Out of the culled jobs, ten thousand went through natural retirement processes, not normal attrition. At least thirty thousand went through voluntary retirement schemes. It wasn't an open scheme where people volunteer. We had a system where we picked employees for retirement based on age, disabilities, or lack of education. It was a very generous scheme where everybody benefited.

Even though Tata Steel cut its labor force in half, there was no labor unrest. This is a testament to the generosity of Tata's retirement program and the goodwill built up over the years between Tata and its employees, and a response to those who might say corporate responsibility is laudable, but does not pay dividends.

Once Tata Steel had established itself domestically as an economically efficient producer, it was in a good position to go global. Corus Steel, an Anglo-Dutch company previously known as British Steel, was looking for suitors, and Ratan Tata wasted no time in taking advantage of this serendipity. Some at Tata Steel were intimidated by the sheer size of the acquisition, but Ratan Tata instilled confidence. He was convinced Corus was a good fit for Tata Steel, and he liked what he saw and heard from Corus management. He knew they would be friends whether the deal went forward or not, always a good sign for the ethically minded Tata.[5]

When the $12 billion plus deal went through in April 2007, after many months of negotiations getting to know each other, Tata gained access to the European market, a complementary product portfolio, and 19 million metric tons of capacity. With its low-cost production, Tata was the perfect feeder partner for Corus and its finished-products expertise. And Corus had a very good research establishment that would help Tata advance its own technology.

Not bad for a company whose steel output Sir Frederick Upcott offered to eat. Somewhere Jamsetji Tata must have been smiling.

Tata Motors: Global De-Risking

When India liberalized its economy, Tata Motors was focused on commercial vehicles, which tends to be a rather cyclical business. Liberalization allowed Tata Motors in 1998 to diversify into passenger cars and reduce its exposure to the commercial vehicles market. Still, Tata Motors was hit hard in 2000–2001 as the commercial vehicles market shrank by almost 40 percent. Going global became an imperative to offset not only the structural changes in the market that accompanied liberalization, but also the cyclicality of the business. As Ravi Kant, managing director of Tata Motors, put it, "Although commercial vehicles are cyclical in any economy, in any country, it's not the same cycle." Therefore, while some economies are expanding, others are contracting. Kant knew that he could de-risk with a portfolio that balanced highly cyclical medium and heavy trucks with the moderately cyclical commercial vehicles, and the least cyclical buses. He could further de-risk the business model by going global.

Kant also knew that Tata was reaching the saturation point in India. It had a 55 percent share in commercial vehicles to which it was adding 1 to 2 percent per year. There had to be an upper limit. To grow, therefore, Tata Motors had to look elsewhere. The third reason to go global was that it would improve Tata's competitive fitness inside India, since global exposure inevitably means exposure to fierce global competition.

With a case for globalization made, the strategy development process stratified geographical markets according to their stage in market evolution, from stages 1 to 4 as follows: stage 1 consisted of less-developed countries such as Africa (where India was a decade ago); stage 2 markets were countries like China (where India is heading); stage 3 included countries such as Brazil and Korea; and stage 4 countries were fully developed markets like western Europe and the United States.[6] Ravi Kant describes the strategy this way:

We chose those countries which would be receptive to our kind of product—stage 1, stage 2, and partly stage 3 countries—and expanded organically. We also did one more study: we segmented customers in India and found there are four segments—price sensitive on one end and performance oriented on the other—with two segments in between. We found that these four segments exist not only in India, but other geographies, although the mix varies. We targeted price and what we call the quick-payback segment and found success this way. We didn't try to go to the top.

The strategy of starting at the bottom of the price pyramid and gradually moving up was the same one that Japan followed with much success. Tata knew it could not compete indefinitely in the price-sensitive low end of the market, nor would it want to compete exclusively where room to maneuver is limited and profit margins are small.

Organic growth targeting stage 1 and 2 countries with Tata's existing portfolio was one-half of the globalization strategy. South Asia, South Africa, West Africa, and Latin America fit the profile. Getting into more developed markets where the Tata brand name was not known and distribution channels did not exist would be trickier. An inorganic growth strategy would be required for developed stage 3 and stage 4 markets.

Acquisition of a truck plant in Korea and a stake in a bus company in Spain not only exploited a market opportunity, but filled out Tata's product portfolio, thus de-risking the business by geography and product breadth. In addition, Tata entered a joint venture with Marco Polo, the largest independent bus manufacturer in the world, to set up the world's largest bus-manufacturing facility in India. And a series of alliances with Fiat gave Tata access to a range of technologies. As Ravi Kant describes it: "Fiat has products like ours and we found that at the very top, the chairman/CEO level, there was a genuine, honest, transparent desire to work with Tata Motors. It started with a relationship between Mr. Agnelli [president and chairman of Fiat] and JRD Tata, who have known each other for many years, but the relationship between Tata and Fiat has grown closer in the last couple of years. At the moment, we are looking at cooperation in Latin America and other geographies."

Once again, Tata forged a business relationship from a personal relationship built on complementary objectives. In 2004, Tata Motors acquired Daewoo Commercial Vehicle Co. for $102 million. Daewoo presented an opportunity to get into Korea, a fairly advanced stage 3 market, and there were synergies between the two companies in terms of product strategy, international marketing, and R&D.

Tata Motors was one of ten bidders for Daewoo, including Chinese and European companies. Initially, it faced some difficulty in being accepted as a serious bidder, but Ratan Tata suggested that Tata should see itself as a Korean company, not as an Indian company in Korea. Tata connected itself to everything Korean—the society, the environment, and the government. As much as possible, it became Korean in thought and outlook. This philosophy meant Tata would retain the Korean management, and assist them by sending some Indian Tata people to Korea. As Ravi Kant described it, "The operation would be run basically by Koreans. That would give them a sense of pride. When you bid with this kind of attitude, you put out a signal that you are not just buying assets, but a running company which you want to grow. It has worked beautifully so far."

Tata Motors had been working on a world truck for India and international markets and Daewoo provided the base to build it, rather than starting from ground zero. The merger made it possible to enter the market two to three years early. Business risk was reduced when Tata gained access to Daewoo's experience, and Tata's international scope protected Daewoo. When the Korean market shrank by 40 percent, Tata exported 50 percent of production, insulating the company from disaster.

The Nano Project

The next major global initiative was directed to the domestic market with the paradigm-shifting Nano, the "People's Car." Ratan Tata had always had an unconscious urge to do something for the people of India, and transportation was of particular interest. Two-wheelers—with the father driving, the elder child standing in front, and the wife behind holding a baby—were very much the norm in India, but a relatively unsafe mode of transporting a family. The two-wheeler image is what got Tata thinking about safer and affordable forms of transport.

His first doodle was to rebuild cars around the scooter, but over time, with the success of Tata's entry car, Indica, Tata's thinking gravitated to something more carlike and revolutionary, as well as global. It was never meant to be a Rs.1-lakh ($2,500) car—that happened when, off-the-cuff, Tata was asked for a target price in an interview at the Geneva Car Show. Nonetheless, Ratan Tata took one lakh back to India and presented it as the target price. His people were aghast, but they delivered by questioning every element, from door handles to engine placement to location of the instrument cluster. And they did it without placing a quality stigma on the car. The price was achieved by developing an innovative distribution model that will sell the auto in kits to entrepreneurs who will assemble them for buyers.

The final product, the Nano, represented a seemingly perfect marriage of philanthropic and commercial interests. It catapulted the group into sixth place on *Business Week*'s list of the world's most innovative companies (see table 10-2). As *Business Week* explained: "The Mumbai-based conglomerate jumps onto our list for the first time, fueled by its paradigm-busting $2,500 'Nano' car for the masses."[7]

The way Tata envisions it, the Nano is akin to the Swatch, a product introduced at a disruptively low price that dominated its niche, but did not undermine the market. The Nano is aimed at cannibalizing

TABLE 10-2

World's most innovative companies according to *BusinessWeek*

Rank	Company	Country
1	Apple	United States
2	Google	United States
3	Toyota Motor	Japan
4	General Electric	United States
5	Microsoft	United States
6	Tata Group	India
7	Nintendo	Japan
8	Procter & Gamble	United States
9	Sony	Japan
10	Nokia	Finland
11	Amazon.com	United States
12	IBM	United States
13	Research in Motion	Canada
14	BMW	Germany
15	Hewlett-Packard	United States

Source: Adapted from "The World's 50 Most Innovative Companies," *BusinessWeek*, April 28, 2008, http://bwnt.businessweek.com/interactive_reports/innovative_companies/.

some of the lower-end car market and some of the higher-end motor-cycle and scooter market. It will eat into both of those markets but will also create a market of its own. In India, the Nano will offer trans-portation of a quality that many millions of people thought was beyond their reach. In more developed countries, perhaps it will appeal to an expanding appetite for small cars and an upgraded Nano for western Europe may take Nano global.

From the Rs.1-lakh car to the $2.3 billion Jaguar–Land Rover deal, Tata has significant investments at both ends of the market spec-trum. With the addition of Jaguar–Land Rover, Tata's acquisition of the champions of British industry that began with Tetley Tea in 2000 and continued with Corus Steel in 2007 prompted one New Delhi consultant to joke: "The Tata's headquarters will be in London soon!"[8] Alan Rosling conceded that these acquisitions represented "a big shock for our traditional mind-set because India obviously is where our businesses are based," but added that the impact would be blunted because Tata has a century-long history with the United Kingdom, and India has a natural affiliation with the United Kingdom based on historic ties, a common language, and similar legal system.

Cultural affinities aside, many commentators voiced concern about the Tata Motors takeover of Jaguar–Land Rover based on Tata's newness to the car industry and focus on the low end of the market where, though admittedly masterful, it lacked experience managing a luxury brand. Objectively the larger challenge will be the turnaround of two companies that have struggled to make profits for their previous owners. In addition, there is the integration of Corus, a company that has historically had among the lowest profit margins in the industry. And this has to be accomplished in the face of a liquidity crisis.

The acquisition of Jaguar–Land Rover, the creation of the Nano, and numerous other acquisitions and innovations have proven that Tata has embraced China's "think big" approach and taken it places India has never seen before, all the while remaining in touch with the core philanthropic values upon which the company was built. As Tata grows further afield and a new generation of management assumes the mantle of leadership, staying true to those values, as Ratan Tata readily admits, will be a constant challenge.

> We have two guiding arrows—one points overseas, where we want to expand markets for our existing products. The other points right here to India, where we want to explore the large mass market that is emerging—not by following but by breaking ground in product development and seeing how we can do something that hasn't been done before.
>
> *Ratan Tata*

ELEVEN

Dual Identity

Indians as Customers, Competitors, and Collaborators

E VER SINCE THE rise of the British in India over 250 years ago, Indians have devoted considerable energy to understanding the West. Indians had little choice but to develop an insight into the English mind-set, as the British were the rulers and, like all invaders, confident of their cultural superiority.[1] Preindependence, children of the Indian elite often had an English governess followed by a university education in England. For example, India's first prime minister, Jawaharlal Nehru, the son of a wealthy barrister, had a series of English governesses and tutors, and was later sent to study at the hallowed portals of Harrow and Cambridge University.

In the 1960s, the focus shifted from England, as Indian university students and immigrants increasingly headed to the United States. Today, about ninety-four thousand Indians are enrolled at U.S. colleges and universities, constituting the largest group of foreign students in the country.[2] Even those upper- and middle-class Indians who choose to remain in India are exposed to a significant amount of Western culture. India accounts for the largest sales of English literature "classics" as U.K. and U.S. educators ditch them in an effort to modernize and politically balance the curriculum. Business schools in India frequently use American books, case studies, and examples. All of this helps provide the educated Indian a certain level of understanding of Western business practices and culture.

In contrast, Westerners do not seek to understand Indian business to a similar degree. Even in comparison to the other two Asian powers, China and Japan, there is substantially less business literature on India. A quick check on Amazon for books on "Japanese business practices," "Chinese business practices," and "Indian business practices" brought up 783 for Japan, 440 for China, and only 195 for India. Furthermore, unlike the dedicated books on China and Japan, the books that came up for India were rarely dedicated to India, but instead were more general titles that merely mentioned India.

There is a subtle reason why it never occurs to most people to view Indian business practices as being as unique as those of China or Japan, and therefore worthy of careful study. Indians are proficient in adopting dual identities. When Indians encounter foreigners, especially Westerners, they adopt markers of global identity in dress, food, and even consumption of cultural products. Yet their Indian identity is never abandoned. When they return to interacting with other Indians and at home, they revert to their own dress, eat Indian food, and use local cultural products. Consider these facts: 96 percent of all music consumed in India is domestically produced, Hollywood movies can barely get an audience against Bollywood, and women overwhelmingly dress in Indian fashions.

The Duality of Indians

This concept of duality has a long history in India. The industrial revolution brought to India by the British moved people to the factories in urban centers, forcing them to work alongside members of other castes. At the factories, different castes mixed relatively freely, ate at the same cafeterias, traveled in the same buses, and attended political rallies with one another. Brahmins and upper castes had even taken to working in jobs considered highly polluting—for example, the tanning of skins and hides. There was no conflict in the work of upper castes in industry and their obligations as good Hindus. The factory and home environments were separate spheres and had different standards of conduct and behavior. For example, Indians used Western dress, spoke English, and followed Western customs in the workplace, while at home they used Indian dress, spoke the local language, and conducted themselves as good Hindus. This is what Singer called compartmentalization.[3] It allows Indians to be highly adaptable by sometimes "wearing their castes" and at other times "wearing their shirts."

This adaptability has ancient roots and may grow from a uniquely Indian ability to separate between what in Hinduism is known as "karma," or work, and "tatva," or essence, one's own individuality. It allowed Indian workers to adapt from the caste-oriented village life to the relatively caste-blind factory floor. It allows them today to thrive in all kinds of unfamiliar professional global environments even as they reconstruct and preserve the Indian microcosm culturally and socially. Most Indians can comfortably exist with seemingly contradictory worlds and ideas at the same time. Perhaps it even gives them a competitive advantage to live and flourish in a world of religious, cultural, and ethnic diversity.

Foreigners need to be careful as Indians are very good at adopting a dual identity. The Indian executives or businesspeople whom foreigners encounter seem, at least relative to Chinese or Japanese executives, almost Western in their outlook. The fluency with which Indians speak English combined with their familiarity with Western concepts and the West, often having studied there, can lull the Westerner into believing that Indians are quite like them. But Indians, despite their apparent Western business outlook, do have some distinct tendencies in how they approach business.

Given the rise of India as a market and the Indian global companies featured in this book, non-Indians will increasingly face Indians as customers, competitors, and collaborators. In this chapter, we examine how Indian companies play each of these roles. While the traits we present are general Indian tendencies, one must of course remember that the answers are complex, with many differences in a country inhabited by more than a billion people. It is often said: "Whatever you say about India is true; and so is its opposite." For example, India is one of the poorest countries in the world when measured by GDP per capita or on various health and literacy metrics. Yet *Forbes* magazine's 2008 list of billionaires included fifty-three Indians, more than any other country except the United States, Russia, and Germany![4]

Indians as Customers

Indians have a long tradition as buyers and sellers with foreign countries, having traded for centuries with their neighbors in the Middle East and Southeast Asia. Since the fifteenth century, this trade also included Europe, though trade with the Romans has been documented as early as the first century. This has led Indians engaged in business to have a "trader" mentality, with both its positive and negative connotations. Positively, this makes them highly entrepreneurial, always looking for opportunities to do business. Perhaps negatively, especially from the supplier's perspective, this makes them inordinately price sensitive in their purchasing. In other words, Indians are tough negotiators and love bargaining. Any foreigner desiring to sell to an Indian firm should be prepared for this.

Indian procurement officers like to be knowledgeable buyers and drive a hard bargain. For example, R. C. Bhargava, former purchase director of Suzuki India, used his knowledge of costs almost cold-bloodedly in purchase negotiations. Car tires have always been sold as proprietary products. Nowhere in the world was their price negotiated on a cost-plus basis. Yet, Bhargava stunned the tire industry in India by declaring: "You show me your cost structure and I will give you a remunerative margin."[5] Indians use their knowledge of zero-based costing remarkably well in buying situations.

Indians are not shy of using their relationships in business. For example, Shiv Shivram, a veteran buyer of forty years with Imperial Tobacco and Dunlop, is friendly with salespersons at all levels. When the general sales manager of a vendor comes to negotiate a contract, one of the vendor's salesmen he is friendly with will whisper the bottom price in Shivram's ear. Thus when Shivram negotiates, he knows the price below which he cannot go as it would hurt the seller. The strategy is to use long-standing relationships to get the best deal while giving a fair return, but not to squeeze the last dollar out of the seller.

When major purchases, big-ticket items, or capital equipment are at stake, the negotiations can be frustrating to non-Indians. Westerners are often heard complaining that the discussions take forever and the specifications keep changing. Consider, for example, the current rush by foreign vendors to sell arms to India. Reflecting on the experience, Rear Admiral Rees Ward, head of the United Kingdom's defense manufacturers' trade association, said: "It is a rapidly growing market of a potential superpower . . . however, the procurement processes often cause delays and cancellations and therefore overseas companies need to understand that they have to commit to the long haul if they are going to win contracts."[6]

After months of tough negotiations have brought a handshake agreement and the deal is ready to be signed the next morning, be prepared for a surprise. It is too soon to start celebrating. At the eleventh hour, after the lowest price has been negotiated, it will be length of credit that will determine who gets the order. There will be a new negotiation about the payment terms because Indian companies, usually strapped for cash, like long credit cycles.

The negotiations are conducted by the professional managers in the company. However, with any significant purchase, the promoter or owner will be brought in to bless the deal at the final stage. The professional managers of family-owned companies are usually unwilling to stick their necks out and complete the transaction without involving the promoter. Doing so may leave the professional manager open to the accusation of having received a kickback from the supplier.

Peter Smith, retired senior executive of General Electric, who for thirty years sold power plants to many Indian companies, remarked: "After the negotiations are over and the draft purchase order has been seen by the seller, the real decision maker arrives. Usually the promoter stands in the background till the end. Then the final negotiations begin!" The seller must remember to hold something back because the promoter, to "keep face," must be able to demonstrate to his managers that he managed to negotiate a little bit more.

With liberalization, the supplier practice of giving bribes to the managers of private companies has mostly died out. However, the vendor may still give the promoter something he or she likes as a gift. Usually, one of the customer's professional managers will let the vendor know that the boss has a particular soft spot for, say, a watch, which is then dutifully presented to the promoter at this final meeting. However, these gifts are not always one way, as Indian buyers will also give gifts to their foreign suppliers. They will invest in building relationships with the suppliers' key executives because they understand that in future deals, these executives have the power to reduce prices or extend credit terms.

In meeting the demanding price of Indian companies, foreign companies should bear a few things in mind. First, the price consciousness of Indians is often about the "fair" price rather than the lowest price. Indians hate to hear that someone else managed to purchase the same item for less, and price information is transmitted remarkably efficiently in India. Thus, when dealing with multiple Indian firms, it is best to maintain price integrity.

Second, while quality is important for Indian companies, it is not the most important factor when placing an order. Often to obtain a better price from the vendor, Indian firms are willing to compromise on quality and specifications. Rarely do they need, and are willing to pay for, all the bells and whistles.

Third, with major capital equipment purchases, vendor financing is often important to Indian companies. They will frequently be willing to make concessions on price in order to obtain financing for the deal. For example, Bharti, India's leading telecom operator, built its entire network using vendor financing from the likes of Ericsson and IBM. There was no way the company could have funded the massive network expansion from its own pockets.

Sometimes, Indian companies may even ask for vendor financing of the promoter's equity. For example, the vendor agrees to take a stake of, say, $50 million in equity, which will later be sold back to the promoter for a predetermined price. This gives the promoter the funds to operate the business as well as place the orders for the capital equipment needed. To some extent this is changing in India, as capital markets are developing and financing is available. As a result, Indian companies do not need to rely as much on their traditional sources of funding, like family and their own resources. Still, even today, their ambition is frequently beyond the financial resources available.

Indians as Competitors

Most Indian companies—the cases presented in this book are exceptions—do not have a well-thought-out strategy for global markets. Therefore, they are forced into relying on price as their single biggest competitive tool. They are fierce price competitors, displaying a high propensity to use an entry pricing strategy in global markets, at times pricing even below marginal costs. Beyond the lack of a clear nonprice competitive strategy, there are some good reasons why Indian companies rely heavily on price to compete in global markets.

The lack of an upscale country image means that brands from India desiring to go global, like their Asian predecessors from Japan, Korea, and China, have little option but to use price as the dominant lever. For example, when Mahindra & Mahindra introduced its sports utility vehicle in the United Kingdom, it was by far the cheapest seven-seater 4x4 in the U.K. market. Selling at £13,000, it was cheaper by about £8,000 compared to the next-lowest-priced vehicle. Pawan Goenka, president of Mahindra's automotive sector, explained: "The price is our USP [unique selling point] . . . we have the lowest-priced comparable vehicle in all the markets we're in, and hopefully we give good value to the customer."[7]

India is fortunate to have one of the lower-cost economies, which means that Indian companies are willing and able to survive using price as a competitive lever. Furthermore, because the Indian domestic market is highly price conscious, Indian firms are comfortable playing the price game. As Ratan Tata remarked: "Being in this market, contrary to what everyone believes, you always need to be more competitive than what you have to be outside, because the buying power in this country is so low. So you're always thinking of how to address that segment of the market."[8]

What makes Indians rather aggressive, and some would say not very disciplined, price competitors is that they hate to lose. Often they are too eager to get the business. Pradip Kamat, chief executive of Indus International, a U.S.-based business that facilitates supply links between the two countries, observed about Indian companies: "[They] are reluctant to say no . . . Some [potential partners from India] are not sufficiently assertive in pushing back against what the U.S. companies are asking them to do."[9] Indian firms are not as flexible as the Chinese, but this desire to "win" at any cost not surprisingly results in some detrimental follow-on effects.

To obtain the orders, salespeople routinely overcommit the firm, and at times forget to inform the delivery team. Sometimes they agree to delivery schedules that the company cannot meet.[10] At other times, the vendor realizes that the order was secured at an unreasonably low price. To be able to turn a profit, the Indian supplier may be forced to retrofit (lower) the specifications. Furthermore, small Indian exporters have limited working capital resources to execute large global orders. As one U.S. executive who had experience with Indian suppliers was quoted in the *Financial Times*: "The easiest way to kill some of them off is to give them a large order which they find difficult to fulfill."[11] All of this causes considerable customer dissatisfaction— and Indian suppliers tend to be sales rather than marketing oriented.

The lack of a sound competitive strategy also leads many Indian companies to overrely on the quality of their salespeople. The fact that they are competing on price combined with their lack of experience in global markets leads them to favor having an Indian salesforce. Unfortunately, this rarely works, especially in countries where English is not the language of business. Indian companies are only now learning that customer-facing units must reflect the culture of the customer. The more successful Indian global companies have had a steep learning curve on this dimension.

Indian companies in global markets do not seem to have patience for long hauls. The customer lifetime value concept is less developed in Indian firms. As Allan Scott, vice president of business development in the United States for an Indian Tier 2 IT services company, remarked: "If the lead time to an order is anything more than six months, my Indian bosses want my time redeployed to other prospects."[12]

Indian business executives and owners are very effective at getting information from competitors using their personal relationships. Given the strong heritage of the family business culture in India, they do not hesitate to leverage friendships and family relationships to help their business. Unlike many Western executives, who would see it as inappropriate to pressure one's friends for business purposes, Narayana Murthy, chief mentor of Infosys Technologies and India's best-known professional entrepreneur, observed that to compete successfully one needs to use one's personal and professional relationships equally and not avoid doing so.

Indians as Collaborators

Indians as collaborators play two roles vis-à-vis foreign companies. In the past, given the strict restrictions on foreign ownership, a joint venture with an Indian partner was mandatory for any foreign company seeking to do business in India. Thus there is a long history and rich experience on which to draw conclusions about how Indian companies behave with their foreign joint venture partners. The more recent collaborative phenomenon is how Indians behave when they acquire foreign companies. In the next two sections we distinguish between these two roles.

Indians as Joint Venture Partners

While international companies from Wal-Mart Stores to Fiat are rushing to India through joint ventures with Indian firms, India can safely be regarded as the joint venture graveyard of the world based on evidence of the past two decades. One of the largest business houses of India, who at one time boasted about managing fifteen joint ventures with *Fortune* 1000 companies, now has no surviving joint venture. A McKinsey study found that of the twenty-five major joint ventures between foreign and Indian companies established from 1993 to 2003, only three still survived in 2005.[13] For example, consider Modicorp, which during the 1990s had lined up alliances with Motorola, Walt Disney, and Xerox.[14] As a result, Modicorp's chairman, B. K. Modi, was popularly referred to as "Mr. JV." Since then about a dozen of his joint ventures, including those with the three American companies, have dissolved.

Why have Indians failed as collaborators in joint ventures with foreign partners in India? The problem was that before 1991, joint ventures were mandatory for foreign companies seeking to enter India. Even today, after liberalization, many of the large and fast-growing sectors of the economy, such as retailing, consumer banking, telecommunications, and media, require an Indian partner.[15] Thus the foreign partners enter into these joint ventures without really desiring an Indian partner, but are forced to have one for market access. Often the Indian partner has few industry-specific competencies to contribute beyond local knowledge, as was the case with Tesco's and Wal-Mart's retailing alliances with the Tata Group and Bharti, respectively. In contrast, the Indian partners believe they have substantive contributions to make to the joint ventures, high expectations of contributions from the foreign partners, and disproportionate power in the relationship because the local laws have tipped the scales in their favor. The result is a significant mismatch in expectations between the two partners, and as would be anticipated, a subsequent falling out between the partners.

Unlike in neighboring regions like the Middle East or Southeast Asia, Indian partners are not interested in playing passive roles as portfolio investors in their joint ventures. They prefer to have at least 50 percent holding and in most cases controlling interest. In addition, their expectations of the major multinational corporations that are usually their foreign partners are high. Specifically, foreign partners should:

- Be relatively noninterfering.

- Freely share their distinctive and superior expertise with respect to processes, systems, and technology.

- Be willing to train the Indian joint venture executives, and accept that sometimes after this training, these executives may be transferred to other companies that are wholly owned by the Indian partner.

- Provide a strong reference if and when the Indian partner may need to raise funds for other ventures.

- Direct business to the joint venture company from their operations in other countries and, if possible, from their customers as well.

While one can argue about how reasonable these expectations are, the problem is usually not in these expectations. The McKinsey study referred to earlier argued that most of the joint ventures ran into trouble because the Indian partners were unable to invest enough to expand the business quickly and match the ambitions of the foreign companies. This is not a uniquely Indian problem, as it occurs frequently in the developing world in joint ventures between large multinational corporations and relatively small local investors. One solution may be to allow the foreign partner to increase its stake in the joint venture in return for disproportionately funding the growth. Yet this is often a problem because the Indian investor is either unable to dilute its share for legal reasons (it may be required by law to maintain a minimum equity participation) or unwilling to do so.

Since the economic liberalization of the early 1990s, the Indian government has gradually allowed foreign companies to operate alone or increase their stake in many industries. As a result, a large number of the Indian joint ventures have lost their reason to exist from the foreign partners' perspective. They either wish to buy out the Indian partner or set up an independent unit separate from the existing joint venture. This part of the joint venture story in India has been rather unpleasant. Almost always, the foreign partner is in a hurry to exit, and the Indian partner finds itself with an exceptionally good negotiating hand. Valuation of exit pricing on a scale of 1:5 is not unusual, depending upon whether the foreign partner desires to sell (receives twenty cents on the dollar) or buy (pays several times market value).

For example, when the Indian government eased restrictions for foreign companies in investment banking, both Goldman Sachs and Merrill Lynch looked to exit their existing joint ventures with Indian partners. Goldman Sachs sold its stake in its successful joint venture with Kotak Mahindra Bank Ltd. for about $75 million, while Merrill Lynch bought most of its stake in DSP Merrill Lynch for about $500 million.[16]

If instead of exiting, the foreign firm wants to set up an independent unit in the same business as the joint venture, the Indian government requires the foreign company to first obtain a "no-objection" certificate from its local partner. As one can imagine, "same business" is open to multiple interpretations and often leads to considerable conflict between partners. For example, in 2006, Danone faced resistance from the Wadia Group, its Indian joint venture partner in the cookie maker Britannia Industries Ltd. Britannia is 25 percent owned by the Wadia family and 25 percent owned by the Danone Group, with the rest publicly held. Danone wanted to exit the joint venture and set up its own wholly owned operations in order to pursue larger dairy and water opportunities. The Wadia Group took Danone to court in order to stop Danone from investing in another Indian company. Although Danone had a no-objection certificate from the Wadias in 1996, the government felt that it was too old and asked Danone to obtain a new one. After acrimonious negotiations and lawsuits between the two parties, in 2008 Danone agreed to sell its stake to the Wadias.[17]

Given the poor track record of partnerships, some foreign companies are reluctant to invest in India. One India-based financial consultant was quoted in the *Wall Street Journal*: "Anyone who gets into a joint venture in India should assume it will fail and be comfortable with the terms of what happens when it does fail."[18] As a result, the recent foreign entrants, who because of restrictive government policies still have to pursue India through joint ventures, realize that these marriages are not made in heaven. Detailed separation clauses are now part of the joint venture agreement.

Overall, India is rapidly moving away from the era of joint ventures. Bayer, Gillette, Goodyear, Datacraft, EMI, Sprint, Suzuki, Merrill Lynch, Xerox, Vodafone, and many more have exited their Indian joint ventures with the sole purpose of reappearing with 100 percent owned companies. While the days of joint ventures in India may be mostly over, the era of Indian companies forming joint ventures outside India is just starting. However, it is still too early to draw any conclusions about Indians as collaborators on this front.

Indians as Acquirers

There are two major differences in the storyline for Indians as acquirers of foreign companies compared to Indians as joint venture partners. First, foreign acquisitions by Indian firms are still a relatively recent phenomenon. Indian companies have been doing deals outside their borders in any significant manner only since 2000. In contrast, Indians have been playing the role of joint venture partners of multinational companies since India's independence in 1947. Thus the conclusions drawn here about Indians as acquirers will be more tentative.

Second, despite the short history, our research indicates that Indians as acquirers is a very positive story overall. Unlike their record as joint venture partners, Indians have been rather skillful with their acquisitions. Despite some Western fears (especially prominent in the Arcelor takeover and Tata's battle with Orient-Express Hotels) about Indians as the "barbarians at the gate," Indian companies for the most part have not sought to destabilize acquired companies unnecessarily, both in the acquisition process and the integration process.

Perhaps one reason for the success of Indian firms in acquisitions is that Indian executives and companies learn to operate in a challenging business environment as well as to negotiate within a diverse, democratic society. Managing a business in Maharashtra, with its relatively business-friendly state government, is rather different from managing a business in West Bengal, with the Communist Party of India Marxist (CPIM) in power, versus managing a business in Bihar, India's most lawless state with a relatively greater proportion of convicted criminals represented in the state legislature. Every large Indian company conducts business in all of these states, so executives become masters at managing the context. The lessons learned in India hold them in good stead when acquiring foreign companies.

Given that laws in India are not sympathetic to hostile takeovers, Indian firms until now have sought to make global acquisitions in a soft manner, after obtaining the buy-in of the potential target firm's management. Whether this will continue as Indian companies grow more ambitious is hard to speculate, but the Arcelor-Mittal deal indicates that some hostile takeovers will be necessary despite Indian firms' predisposition to eschew aggressive takeover tactics. However, probably to smooth over the ruffled feathers, the company is now called ArcelorMittal.

One very visible change in Indian firms is their transformation from low-price bidders for distressed assets to buyers that pay competitive global market prices for top-quality, strategically complementary foreign assets. Indian companies, relative to their size, are willing and able to make large acquisitions. Consider Tata Tea's acquisition of Tetley, a company three times its size; Tata Steel's takeover of the larger Corus; or Hindalco's purchase of Novelis after taking on significant debt. Indians are very entrepreneurial and demonstrate enormous risk appetite. Furthermore, the conglomerate model of the large Indian business houses allows them to use the assets of the entire family of companies within the group rather than be restricted to the resources or leverage of any individual company.

Some clear patterns are visible with respect to the types of acquisitions that Indian firms seem to gravitate to in foreign markets. With the significant exception of Mittal Steel's emerging market strategy, most Indian companies are seeking foreign acquisitions that bring complementary competencies. The foreign acquisitions help obtain brands that resonate with Western consumers (e.g., Carlton luggage by VIP or Tetley by Tata Tea), obtain access to foreign distribution networks or customers (e.g., Dana's U.K. operation by Bharat Forge, or various European acquisitions by Ranbaxy), extend the product portfolio to higher-priced and more sophisticated products (e.g., Arcelor by Mittal or Novelis by Hindalco), or add significant R&D capabilities (e.g., Hansen and REpower by Suzlon).

In terms of the integration process, Indian companies know from their domestic operations about the importance of other stakeholders, especially the government and trade unions. India has strong unions as well as influential politicians and bureaucrats. While wailing against them may be a particular sport among Indian executives, they do realize that these stakeholders play a crucial role in the success of any business. Thus Indian companies tend to have a nonconfrontational approach toward local governments and trade unions.

Indians often complain that the foreign companies in India sometimes use expatriates who do not understand the local context. We saw repeatedly in our case studies that when Indian firms make acquisitions, they are aware of the superior local knowledge of the management talent and tend to retain them in the acquired venture. Only with Mittal Steel's acquisitions in emerging markets of previously state-owned plants do we see a significant ferrying of technical staff and top management from India to their newly acquired steel companies. Mittal did so to address the significant competence gaps in these countries with respect to the management of steel plants. But Mittal did not follow this practice in its Arcelor acquisition.

Some observers, such as S. Mahalingam, CFO of TCS, believe that because Indian companies lack significant experience with global acquisitions, they have taken a rather "tentative view" on how to deal with the acquired organization.[19] The philosophy seems to be, "Don't rock the boat till you are sure." TCS during the last three years has acquired some twenty small and midsize IT services and consulting companies in the United Kingdom, Continental Europe, United States, and Australia. TCS has apparently followed a strategy similar to that of most Indian companies in that they have left the senior executives and management structure intact. They have used Indian managers with significant global exposure to work as an "organizational and cultural bridge" between TCS and the acquired companies.

Santrupt Misra, director of human resources at Aditya Birla Group, believes that the management of companies acquired by Indians have been left in place primarily for three reasons.[20] First is "unfamiliarity" with local regulatory environment, local politicians, and cultural nuances. Second, these foreign acquisitions have come at a time when India is booming, and getting top Indian executives to move to developed countries is difficult as they perceive their standard of living would decline with the expatriate assignment! Third, companies need to demonstrate cultural diversity. Since the top management in India is usually Indian, leaving the acquired foreign firm's top executives in place enhances the diversity ratio.

In the future, the practice of leaving top management in place may change. One factor driving this is that Indian firms have paid dearly for their acquisitions in developed markets and need to recover this investment by imposing higher growth targets on the acquired firms. Unfortunately, managers whose experience is in the developed world are used to performing, and being satisfied with, annual growth targets of 2 to 5 percent. It is hard to convince them to accept more ambitious goals. In contrast, Indian executives have regularly responded with double-digit growth over the past decade, given the boom in the economy. As a result, as Santrupt Misra observed: "You start thinking, should I struggle to convince the local manager to accept the higher growth target, or send one of my Indian managers."[21]

The preceding discussion of course highlights the challenges of costly acquisitions at the top of the business cycle, which are primarily debt. The acquirers can be tempted to put unrealistically high targets on the acquired firm. When the 2008 liquidity crisis is added to this mix, it portends a challenging time ahead for Indian firms that have completed large acquisitions between 2006 and 2007.

Indian companies have been slower in incorporating top management from the acquired companies into their own structures in India. Tata is further ahead in this process than other Indian companies. Seven years after the Tetley acquisition, the head of Tetley sits on the board of Tata Tea, and Tata Tea's R&D center head in India is a Tetley scientist. More than half of the boards of TCS and Tata Steel are non-Indians.

Conclusion

The chapter has outlined the different ways in which Indians behave as customers, competitors, and collaborators. Most of the patterns are well developed with the exception of Indian companies as acquirers. The Indian experience here is recent and still evolving. Regardless of which role the Indian company is playing, the soft relationship factors and symbolic gestures are important to Indians, especially when negotiating with Westerners. As a former colonized power, Indians need to feel that they are getting adequate respect and being treated as equals. Indians are sometimes too quick to take offense in their dealings with foreigners, and Westerners are well advised to remember this. Indians have a thin skin.

Challenges for Indian Multinationals

India today is in the mainstream of global consciousness. There is
a newfound sense of self-assuredness. The entrepreneurship and
dynamism its corporate houses have shown over the last five years
have been and continue to be quite remarkable. However, while the
age of the Indian multinational is undoubtedly here, we in India
Inc. have a long way to go.

Kumar Mangalam Birla, Chairman, Aditya Birla Group

THE COMPANIES PROFILED in this book have made remarkable progress in the past fifteen years. They have transformed
themselves from being tentative, small, primarily domestic players
into confident global corporations that seek to take on the world. Yet
this is an evolving story. Despite the bullish sentiment in India and
the high level of confidence among Indian executives in their ability
to manage multinational corporations, one must not forget that the
"Indian multinational" is still in an embryonic stage.

As the experience of the more recent Japanese and Korean multinationals like Toyota and Samsung demonstrate, it takes decades
before national champions, relatively unknown outside their domestic markets, become multinational corporations with world-leading
positions within their industry. There is no reason to expect that the
process of building the Indian global powerhouses, capable of operating seamlessly across the world, will be substantially faster. This
chapter discusses the four challenges that India's multinationals face
on this journey.

The India Challenge—Goading the Elephant
Toward Modernization

Companies are products of their environments, and India's global powerhouses must therefore grapple with both the advantages and the disadvantages of operating out of India. The advantages have been repeatedly enumerated in this book. Yet many foreigners, especially Westerners visiting India for the first time, are amazed at how Indians can function effectively in what they view as the challenging Indian business environment.

Bureaucratic Restraints

The bureaucratic machinery of India, as reflected in its 10-million-strong civil service army, equaling the population of countries such as Belgium and the Czech Republic, is corroded with apathy and corruption.[1] The time it takes to obtain a business license in India ranges from 159 days in Bhubaneshwar to 522 days in Ranchi.[2] On average, it takes 225 days to obtain a building permit. The Four Seasons Hotel that Shiv Jatia opened in Mumbai in 2008 required 165 government permits, including a special license for the vegetable-weighing scale in the kitchen and one for each of the bathroom scales put in the guest rooms![3]

No wonder that the 2009 World Bank report on the "ease of doing business" in different countries ranked India at 122![4] For Indian companies and their executives, conducting business in India requires finding creative solutions to the problems that one invariably encounters. While one can only admire their ingenuity in overcoming bureaucratic hurdles, there is little doubt that it places additional transactional costs on global companies operating out of India.

Part of the reason behind the unfriendly business environment is the reflexive ambivalence toward the West, multinational corporations, and entrepreneurs built deep into the Indian psyche because of its colonial history. Many Indians regard multinationals as modern incarnations of the British East India Company, which came to India to trade and stayed to rule.[5] Therefore, there is substantial resistance to allowing multinationals to freely enter and prosper in India. One sees this currently in the protests surrounding the entry of multinational companies like Wal-Mart into the Indian retail sector, which is still 96 percent independent mom and pop stores.

Entrepreneurs are seen as throwbacks to the landed gentry, called *zamindars*, who often brutally exploited the peasantry during British rule. Thus protests, such as those against the new Tata plant to build the Nano car in West Bengal, find substantial support among the deprived segments of society. The government is supposed to play the role of being the last and only protector of the common man. It is a losing proposition for politicians to defend free trade, multinational corporations, or businesspeople in a democracy where the large majority of citizens are still poor. Despite the reforms of 1991, few Indian governments have made an effort to reach out and educate the citizens on the advantages of the global economy and free trade. There is a consensus among the ruling elites that liberalization must continue to proceed. However, political leaders prefer to pursue modernization and liberalization by stealth.

To restrain business and "profiteering" while increasing ethical practices and good governance in companies, the government frequently increases regulations. Unfortunately, too often it seems to be trying to mandate by law behaviors that are best encouraged through development of values. The result is that many of the new regulations become a source of revenues for corrupt administrators and extra costs for business, without actually producing the intended benefits in terms of behavior change. While the ease of doing business does differ across states, at its worst, in states like Bihar, 5 to 10 percent of the project costs of setting up a new plant must be set aside for side-payments to local mafia, politicians, and bureaucrats.

Despite the loosening hands of the government and bureaucrats on the Indian economy, one must still be realistic as to how free, open, and transparent the market is. India is not as yet the United States or United Kingdom in its business environment. The truth is that like in China, the Middle East, and Russia, governments still matter, and their ability to affect the fortunes of a company or business group must not be underestimated. Any Indian entrepreneur instinctively understands this.

As an illustration of the power of politicians, consider the following two stories about Lakshmi Mittal at parties in England and India, respectively. At both parties, the guests were mostly Indian executives, entrepreneurs, and politicians. At the English party, he stood in a corner while a long line of guests formed, with each person coming forward to shake his hand. At the party in India, guests did stop by now and then, but there was no crowd around him. Instead, long lines formed around a few chief ministers of Indian states in attendance. Indian businesspeople know the power of politicians and the ability of the latter to bestow largesse and remove obstacles. Cozying up to politicians and bureaucrats in India has always been part of the skill set of any businessman for survival and success.

Infrastructure Failures

The most common complaint by business is that the government has failed to deliver adequate infrastructure. The lack of national policy in crucial areas, poor transportation infrastructure, woefully inadequate power generation capacity, and a slow legal system are all hampering the growth of more global powerhouses out of India.

The autonomy of state governments adds to the confusion and detracts from the scale advantages that should accrue to businesses located in a country of more than a billion people. Unlike America, India has yet to create a single internal market.[6] Each state imposes its own inspection requirements, duties, and regulations on shipments that cross its borders, even en route to another state. For example, in the United States a trucker can haul a load a thousand miles in about twenty hours. In India, the equivalent journey takes four to five days, and that is after a round of reforms—five years ago, it took twelve days.[7]

An Indian subsidiary of a French multinational exporting to Korea from Chennai in South India did an analysis of its transportation costs. It cost more to transport the company's products from its factory near Chennai to the Chennai port, a distance of forty kilometers, than it cost to transport them the five thousand kilometers from the Chennai port to Korea! In addition, the average time to clear exports through customs in India is nearly sixteen days, in contrast to only six days in China or the OECD (Organisation for Economic Co-operation and Development) countries.[8]

Improvements, when planned and executed, fall woefully short of meeting the demand. It seems that Indian governments are always planning for the present rather than the future. For example, the new Bangalore airport is being built by a private consortium that includes the developers of the Zurich airport. Yet in the three years since construction began, air traffic has doubled. Most of the road and rail links to the airport that the government promised have been delayed or scrapped altogether, partly because of the mountain of lawsuits over acquiring the land and partly because they involve thirty-two government agencies, which do not always cooperate with one another.[9] The IT sector famously housed in Bangalore has been vocal in its criticism of the failure of the local government to provide adequate infrastructure for the city. Yet, the IT sector has also successfully lobbied to get itself exempt from paying any taxes on its export income.

Acute power shortages have forced companies into the power generation business in order to run their operations in an uninterrupted manner. New factory construction is delayed as suppliers of power equipment are overwhelmed with orders. Having to build a power source increases both the capital outlays and subsequent operating costs for industrial plants. Captive power costs 50 to 100 percent more than that from the grid. Unreliable power supply and power outages are estimated to cost Indian business 7 percent of sales, six times that in China.[10] A 2008 study indicated that India needs to add the equivalent of half the electricity-generating capacity of the United Kingdom each year if it is to maintain its present rapid rate of economic growth.[11]

The World Bank ranked India 173 out of 175 countries for contract enforcement in 2006, ahead of only Bangladesh and Timor-Leste.[12] The number of unresolved cases at the Supreme Court stood at 43,580 in June 2007, up from 19,806 in 1998.[13] It takes an average of four years to enforce a contract, compared with less than ten months in China.[14] Costs eat up 40 percent of a claim's value. In April 2008, the prime minister, Manmohan Singh, while inaugurating the annual conference of chief ministers and chief justices, stated that "corruption is another challenge we face both in the government and the judiciary."[15] But since a quarter of the members of parliament in Delhi have criminal charges against them, they have little interest in reforms that might expedite their own trials! The weak legal framework lowers the willingness of many foreign firms to invest in India.

Businesses operating in India cannot escape these challenges. However, as Indian companies become truly multinational, they will embrace a global mind-set. This will lead them to examine options, and some will choose to move their headquarters, or at least a significant part of their operations, to more business-friendly environments. Already the headquarters of "Indian" global powerhouses like ArcelorMittal, Suzlon, and Vedanta are located in Luxembourg, Denmark, and London, respectively, rather than India.

Alan Rosling, executive director of Tata Sons, observed: "You go overseas for reasons that are to do with your business, and then you can find that doing business in other countries can be easier."[16] As a result, Tata increasingly looks overseas for growth. However, the challenging Indian business environment has one beneficial effect. It teaches Indian managers to succeed in imperfect market conditions. Thus, when they encounter other challenging environments in emerging markets, managers from companies like ArcelorMittal are able to operate quite effectively. And when they are sent to the more friendly and transparent business regimes of developed countries, it is relatively easy for them to thrive.

The Brand India Challenge—More Than Fakirs and Call Centers

Brand India is currently receiving a lot of positive press. Yet Brand India is weak in many ways. In the minds of most citizens of developed countries, India still conjures up images of exotic lands and customs, or the mass poor. Not surprisingly, this a source of much frustration to Indians, who would prefer that Brand India be associated with the more modern India, resplendent with world-class businesses, skyscrapers, and malls. Why does this image of "old India" still persist in Western media?

Brand India Constraints

In branding, it is what is different or unique vis-à-vis other brands that gets attention. Modern India, while new to Indians, is not unique compared to other, more advanced countries. In fact, if anything, it is still lagging. The unique India from a global perspective is still largely the "historical India," the "poor India," and the "exotic India." Given this branding principle, it is to be expected that the IT sector, where India is uniquely claiming to be the back office of the world, is the only part of "modern India" that receives significant global press coverage.

The Duke of Edinburgh, in one of his many gaffes, once remarked that a shoddily installed fuse box in an Edinburgh factory he was visiting looked "like it was put in by an Indian."[17] Countries go through an evolution with respect to brand image as they develop economically. The initial market entry strategy for a company from a developing country is usually based on offering cheaper products of acceptable (sometimes barely acceptable) quality. We have seen this before with Japan, Korea, and now China. Because consumers in developed countries are unfamiliar with the developing country, they can be persuaded to buy products made in that country only on the basis of price.

Over time, as the country develops and some of its companies take global leadership positions with regard to quality—as determined via objective product performance tests conducted in developed countries—the country brand image starts climbing. Consistent with the higher brand image, prices can begin to rise and may even sustain premium positioning, as Sony, Toyota, and Samsung have demonstrated. Yet brand image always lags behind the rise in quality enhancements.

The shackles of Brand India, where even sophisticated people outside India see it as associated with call centers and software engineers, are not consistent with creating and managing sexy consumer products. There are important exceptions in certain niche specialist areas, where the stereotypical image of India may have a beneficial effect. For example, "exotic India" has a positive impact if one is selling ayurvedic medicines, spas, exotic foods, or fabrics. The general country of origin effects described above apply primarily to consumer products. In business marketing, the country brand image has smaller, though still significant, effects as firms are dealing with a few knowledgeable buyers.

Confronting Brand India

Brand building, besides being an expensive, long-term effort, has to be funded through internally generated cash. Not content to be toiling away at the bottom of the global brand pyramids for decades, impatient companies from India realize that it is easier to buy existing global brands and raise the funds for these acquisitions through external sources. Yet as Mittal's experience with Arcelor and Tata demonstrates, country of origin brand image does have spillover effects when attempting to acquire global brands. It was also responsible for the resistance that Tata faced in buying the global luxury brands like Orient-Express, Land Rover, and Jaguar. The U.S. dealers of Jaguar objected to Tata as a potential owner of the brand. Ken Gorin, Jaguar Business Operations Council's chairman, said the American customers were not "ready for ownership out of India of a luxury car brand such as Jaguar."[18]

Kumar Birla noted that Indian companies would "take some time to move up the ladder of brand recognition."[19] His firm's experience was consistent with the hard work that it takes to overcome the initial negative perceptions of Brand India. He observed:

In the 1960s, when my father, fettered by the Licence Raj, looked beyond the Indian shores, it was truly a visionary act. We take great pride in the fact of our group being the first truly Indian MNC, having established major companies in the Southeast Asia. But in this region, it has taken us years of sustained performance—following best employment practices and being a good corporate citizen—to earn brand recognition . . . Let me give you another example—how we built our brand in Canada. We acquired a pulp mill that had been closed. We had to convince diverse constituencies, ranging from the union to the provincial government and politicians. This took long, but our candor, sincerity and commitment paid off. Today, many employees in the mill feel that they are better off as part of an Indian MNC rather than with a local company that presided over its closure.[20]

Brand India is also complex. Undoubtedly, in terms of hard power (cash and armaments) India is poor, especially compared to China, its Asian competitor on the global stage. However, when it comes to soft power (ideas and values), Brand India—because of its history, large private sector, functioning democracy, and free press as well as the relatively peaceful coexistence of its multicultural, multireligious population—has a positive image. Thus, when confronted by a takeover, many Western companies and their managements would prefer an Indian company as an acquirer compared to a potential Chinese, Russian, or Middle Eastern suitor. Furthermore, over time, perceptions of India as being associated with the Third World will become weaker. As Sir Martin Sorrell, chief executive of advertising agency WPP, remarked, "India and China might have been on the wrong side of history for the past 200 years but for the next 200 years they will be on the right side of it."[21]

The Cross-Border Acquisition Challenge— Matching Ambition and Capabilities

In their hurry to become global powerhouses, Indian companies often prefer the acquisition route, as the many prominent foreign acquisitions mentioned in this book demonstrate. Under the radar, numerous smaller deals are also taking place—for example, DLF, a leading Indian property developer, bought the luxury Aman resorts; Dr. Reddy's acquired Germany's Betapharm; Vijay Mallya, India's liquor baron, bought the Spyker Formula One team and renamed it Force India; and Videocon purchased Thomson's picture tubes business.

Containing Ambition

Some of the reasons for the spurt in foreign acquisitions, such as the desire to compete on the world stage and the need to grow beyond the scale possible in India, are solid. The favorable Indian economic environment, fat profits, higher valuations, and weakening of government regulations on overseas acquisitions have all helped in successful takeovers. However, the recent spate of high-profile acquisitions by Indian companies has led to a national euphoria. For example, "The

Empire Strikes Back" was a common headline in Indian press coverage of the purchase of the iconic British brands, Land Rover and Jaguar, by Tata Motors.

This national pride means that Indians have also been quick to take offense when they have encountered resistance by target companies such as Arcelor, Jaguar, or Orient-Express. The Indian newspapers have been full of reports of perceived racism, and high-profile Indian politicians have weighed in on the issue. More reflective Indians may have noted that hostile takeovers of Indian companies by foreign companies are almost impossible within the current regulatory framework in India.

The current nationalistic euphoria prevailing in India sometimes appears more like jingoism. It needs to be tempered as it can induce corporate overreach. The tribalistic rivalry between the large family-controlled groups that dominate Indian business (most recently observed when Mukesh Ambani foiled his brother Anil's bid to take over South Africa's mobile operator MTN) has the potential to turn into a race to win status by snapping up ever-larger trophy assets. In India's closely knit business community, it is almost becoming a kind of fashion statement for companies to make foreign acquisitions. The result may be that Indian companies embark on ever more audacious international megadeals, inspired by aggressive empire-building ambitions rather than by the solid commercial logic and careful appraisal of investment returns that have characterized past Indian acquisitions abroad.[22]

The impetus for many of the acquisitions in 2006–2007 was not that the Indian companies were particularly globally dominant in their industry or rich.[23] Rather, one of the primary facilitators was the easy liquidity prevailing in the markets. Big deals based on easy liquidity, however, tend to load a company with debt or dilute shareholders equity through the needed issuance of new stock. Both Tata Steel and Hindalco were put on a credit rating watch after they announced their foreign acquisitions. For both companies and for Suzlon, announcement of cross-border deals saw immediate drops in their stock price.

As a result of the financial crisis of 2008, one can safely say that for the foreseeable future, gone are the days when acquirers could use the assets, and sometimes even the cash flow, of the target company as collateral. We are back to the traditional conservative practices for now—when lending institutions will ask for the core assets of the acquiring company, at 50 to 90 percent of actual valuation, as the collateral. This will slow down the cross-border M&A activity that we have seen from Indian firms between 2001–2007.

The academic research is pretty unambiguous on the success of mergers and acquisitions. Approximately half of all M&A deals fail, and the casualty rate increases with the size of the deal as well as for cross-border deals versus domestic deals. The foreign acquisitions experience of other Asian countries, like Japan and China, also indicates a high failure rate. Therefore, there is no reason to believe that India's success rate will be significantly different.

Integrating Capabilities

Indian foreign acquisitions have typically sought access to technology (product innovation capabilities), brands, and distribution. However, product innovation and branding are creative functions, which have to be managed differently from the efficiency-driven manufacturing function. Indian firms are excellent at optimizing existing businesses by squeezing economies and managing costs. But innovation, and even branding to some extent, requires "waste" as it is hard to predict which idea will ultimately succeed. Several dead ends must be pursued in order to find one successful new product. Furthermore, unlike the quick payback one can obtain by pursuing efficiency gains, product innovation and branding have to be managed with much longer time horizons. These are finely tuned functions, and integrating them smoothly into existing businesses is hard enough even for experienced operators; doing so across borders is harder still.[24]

The short-term business culture combined with a typically top-down corporate model controlled by a single all-powerful leader still prevails too frequently in Indian companies. These attributes work well for serving the volatile local market, which requires speedy decision making, and for managing efficient manufacturing systems. But these are not the ideal attributes for firms seeking innovation with a creative workforce and inspirational processes. Nor are they appropriate for complex multinational organizations, staffed by a culturally diverse workforce with their own values and a perplexing habit of doing things their own way.[25]

Indian managements, never very deep, are becoming seriously stretched as they integrate complex acquisitions in different time zones while managing their businesses in a domestic market under attack from foreign competition.[26] Foreign acquisitions increase execution risk dramatically, especially since Indian companies lack experience in absorbing international businesses with different corporate cultures and employment rules. The hunger to become a global powerhouse may not always be matched by a company's current capabilities. In the case of both Japan and Korea, it took several decades to build the required capabilities. But sometimes, one wonders whether this patience exists in India.

The Talent Management Challenge—Creating Global Mind-set and Innovation

India's greatest resource is supposed to be its deep talent pool, its people. The entire outsourcing debate in the West has been framed in light of the large pool of relatively cheap technical and English-speaking talent that is available in India. The sad reality of India today is that despite access to more than a billion people, Indian business is running out of talent.

The Talent Crunch

While the absolute number of graduates in India is large, the quality is not very deep. One study estimated that if one considers technical skills, English fluency, teamwork, and presentation skills, only 25 percent of India's engineering graduates, 15 percent of its finance and accounting professionals, and 10 percent of professionals with any kind of degrees are adequately qualified for working in the outsourcing sector or with multinational companies.[27] Thus the available pool is much smaller than the raw numbers, such as four hundred thousand Indian engineering graduates per year, that are often touted. Creating more than one million jobs a year, corporate India requires a large influx of talent. The burgeoning demand for top executives means that the country needs at least three to four hundred CEOs and five thousand functional heads each year.

Predictably, the talent crunch has resulted in escalating salaries, which have been consistently bid up by 10 to 20 percent per year over the past decade, and attrition rates that currently run at 30 to 40 percent. Employees constantly switch employers for better pay, and salaries for senior staff are approaching Western levels.[28] Performing employees regularly bring counteroffers and ask them to be matched. Underperforming employees who are let go routinely resurface at other firms at twice their salary. As a consequence, Indian managers probably have the highest standard of living in the world with a plethora of perquisites, including free housing, club memberships, chauffer-driven cars, and generous expense accounts. My Indian friends may not like to hear this, but the reality in India is that people are getting overpaid (on a standard of living comparison) and overtitled, relative to their global competence.

Since the 1991 liberalization, Indian employees have seen only the positive side of free markets in terms of rising wages, opportunities, and living standards. In late 2008 companies started considering layoffs or reduction of benefits for the first time since liberalization. At companies like Jet Airways and SAP, where such actions were implemented, employees were rebellious. To some extent the slowdown will ease the talent crunch in the short run, as companies seek to tighten their belts. Historically, Indian companies and their managers have been excellent at squeezing efficiencies. Unfortunately, the rapid growth over the past decade has weakened cost discipline in many companies, especially among younger executives.

The talent crunch will require finding pools of talent that are relatively untapped, including expatriates, populations in smaller cities, and especially, increasing female participation in corporate India. The number of expatriates in India is currently about a hundred thousand and doubling every two years. The World Economic Forum annually ranks countries on gender equality by measuring discrepancies between men and women in education, economic participation, political empowerment, and health. India ranked 114 out of the 128 countries on the list, between Ethiopia and Bahrain.[29] Clearly, as the

Indian outsourcing sector has done, corporate India must do more to leverage this half of India's potential talent.

The Global Mind-set

For India's global powerhouses, the human resources problem is exacerbated by the combination of two additional factors. First, Indian firms are overwhelmingly Indian despite their global presence and ambitions. Azim Premji, chairman of Wipro, noted that 95 percent of Wipro employees are of Indian origin and the top management is more used to working with other Indians.[30] Similarly, Phaneesh Murthy, CEO of iGate Global Solutions, observed, "Less than 1 percent of our talent is today non-Indian. Even in the top two to three companies in the sector today, less than 5 percent of the talent pool is ethnically diverse [of other nationalities]. Everyone just seems to be very comfortable hiring Indians everywhere."[31] Yet R. Krishna Kumar, director of Tata Sons, noted that one of the fundamental competencies needed in managers is a global view, and finding managers with that mind-set is tough in India.

India, like the United States and other large countries, struggles to develop a global mind-set because there are so many domestic opportunities. For example, Indian fashion designers have set their sights on succeeding on the global stage. Yet their biggest and fastest-growing market by far is India. The 2008 Delhi Fashion Week is the premier event in the country to attract foreign interest in Indian designers. It attracted eighty-two designers and one hundred fifty buyers, of whom seventy were from abroad. Sounds successful, but 85 percent of the sales were to Indian buyers, who prefer the more traditional styles. As would be expected, this presents a significant dilemma for Indian designers and their financial backers in their pursuit of global opportunities.[32]

Indians, though admired for being hard working, suffer from being seen as hierarchical, individualistic, and arrogant in their attitudes. To build global powerhouses, Indian talent will have to become more team oriented, process oriented, and learning oriented. The experience of most Indians is growing up in a country of a billion people with limited opportunities. As a result, the competition from a young age is very intense—each person for himself or herself. The need to shine as an individual means that team orientation is poor. People want to score, not pass the ball. No wonder, despite having what are usually acknowledged as the best players in a team sport, like field hockey, India regularly loses to more team-oriented countries like the Netherlands. In global corporations, there is little that any individual can achieve without building teams. Teams, especially cross-national and cross-functional groups, are where most of the important work in multinational firms is done today.

The intense competition for resources in India also teaches Indians that following the process may result in being stuck at the back of the line. As a result, even children find that their parents constantly reinforce the ability to short-circuit processes and jump the queue. Successful Indians have learned how to be "entrepreneurial." However, to build large global organizations requires creating world-class processes, be they for important functions, such as annual planning and budgeting, or more mundane operations, like travel. Experience indicates that it is a challenge to get employees in India to follow a process because everyone believes that they personally should be exempt from it. But this is no way to run multinational corporations.

Unlike the Scandinavians, the Swiss, or the Thais, Indians have never been a humble lot. It is not in the Indian DNA. The recent economic success of India has unfortunately reinforced this lack of humility. As an example, consider the following comments that appeared in the British *Sunday Times* newspaper.[33] Pavan Varma, a former Indian diplomat and now head of the Indian Council for Cultural Relations in Delhi, was asked about India's success in acquiring English companies. He was quoted as saying, "When the first British envoy came to meet Emperor Jahangir in the seventeenth century, he was not allowed to sit in the royal presence, he had to stand . . . Then India controlled 24 percent of the world's gross domestic product and a quarter of international trade." He went on to say, "Now there's a sense of pride that the wheel of history is changing. The biggest success of colonialism was the colonization of our minds. It takes a great deal of time to reverse that, but there is a reversal . . . Indians take pride that the relationship is now one of equality, that India is an emerging power and Britain is a former power."[34] One would expect more of a diplomat! Success in global markets, however, requires the humility to learn from foreign partners and executives, who know more about their local markets.

In the final analysis, the fact is that there are just not enough Indian managers with a global mind-set to go around. Indian companies may prefer to have "Indians" posted to their global operations, but increasingly Indians from India are unwilling to accept foreign assignments. The number of Indian managers with the capabilities to lead global teams is small given the relatively recent phenomenon of Indian firms going global. Not surprisingly, the most dramatic escalation in compensation has been for those Indian managers who have demonstrated a global outlook. If globalization is to be carried on the backs of Indian managers, the global ambitions of Indian companies will be severely stunted. Reflecting on this, Adi Godrej of the Godrej Group observed: "Unfortunately, most globalization attempts by Indian companies tend to lead to Indian managers being sent . . . This is obviously very logical because Indian managers have the competency and the cost is reasonable. However, cultural differences are big, and I believe integrating various nationalities into the business is the way to go."[35]

Therefore, it is imperative that Indian companies and their promoters learn to speed up their processes to integrate and embrace a multicultural workforce. For India's global powerhouses, these challenges require, as Kumar Birla states:

[the need to] work constantly to open the organization's windows to the winds of new ideas and a multiethnic workforce . . . It is relatively simple to address cross-border issues pertaining to technology, finance, markets, and products, but extremely difficult to cope with challenges relating to the human dimension. Being a true-blue multinational is only partly about geographic spread. It is more about a mind-set that wants to leverage resources seamlessly, across geographic boundaries. It is a mind-set that is eager to build unique capabilities to transcend the barriers of language and cultures to create value. It's about being global in attitudes without letting go of your roots.[36]

Creating Innovation Capabilities

India is fast losing its low-cost position. In Mumbai, executive compensation levels for the financial sector are higher than in London, rental costs are above those in New York, and electricity is dearer than in Tokyo! Indian companies will need to evolve from their low-cost position. As Azim Premji, chairman of Wipro, mentioned, in the crucial IT sector, cost arbitrage is one entry point but the continued growth of the sector will have to be based on quality.[37]

Increasingly, Indian companies will have to do more with their intellectual resources. The software sector will have to aspire to be the poet, not just the scribe. Indian exports of its own software, or licensing of its own intellectual property (IP), amounted to only about $450 million in the year ending March 31, 2007.[38] This is a tiny fraction of India's IT service exports. India's IT sector, as is commonly noted, must go beyond "renting out IQ and start creating IP" if it is to compete in the face of ever-rising costs.

The challenge for Indian companies is to develop innovative products. The premium for innovation and branding in products is best demonstrated in a cost analysis of Apple's 30 GB iPod with video, which has a wholesale price of $224.[39] It is manufactured in China and consists of 424 parts, of which three hundred cost one cent or less. The most expensive component is the display module, worth about $20, which is made in Japan by Toshiba-Matsushita. China assembles and tests all of the parts, but this accounts for just $3.70! Apple claims the largest share of the price—about $80 in gross profit.

Closer to home, consider Infosys, perhaps India's best-known firm.[40] Microsoft and Infosys commenced commercial operations about five years apart, 1975 versus 1981. Yet Microsoft's fiscal year 2008 revenues were $60 billion, with profits of $22 billion, whereas Infosys barely managed to top $4 billion in revenues and $1 billion in profits. While Microsoft has incessantly focused on developing innovative products, Infosys has focused on services. It is not as if Microsoft's programmers are from another planet; on the contrary, a significant percentage of them are of Indian origin. The reality, harsh as it may seem, is that even iconic Indian firms like Infosys have still not completely overcome the mental block. The challenge is to move from "outsourced and made in India" to "imagined and owned in India."

The problem for Indian companies in developing innovative products is that it requires a heavy capital outlay up front, which may never be recouped if the product fails to find enough customers. In contrast, service revenues are labor intensive and more predictable. Even i-flex solutions, India's biggest software-product success, survived its early years by running a profitable services business on the side.

In Indian companies, imitation still crowds out invention. For example, the much-vaunted pharma sector in India is populated by generics companies such as Cipla, Dr. Reddy's, Nicholas Piramal, and Ranbaxy, all of which are relatively global. While they have small drug-discovery arms, few of them are willing to take the deep risks that new drug research entails. Most, like Nicholas Piramal and Ranbaxy, have spun off the new drug-discovery units because of the longer time horizon and higher risks. Invention may be a wonderful thing, but Indian companies still prefer that it be done on someone else's balance sheet.[41] So, though India is one of the world's largest producers of drugs, it copies almost all of the compounds. Similarly, Indians and Indian companies may write most of the world's software, but they rarely own the result.

Concluding Remarks

This book has introduced a new set of global competitors from India that are emerging on the world stage. For most of them, the evolving strategy is to marry low-cost operations in India with the high-margin markets of the West. The companies profiled in this book are already seeing significant international success, and in the future many more Indian companies are expected to spread their wings successfully across the globe.

In the transformation process, one has to contemplate, "What does 'Indian multinational' mean?" and "How does one turn from an Indian unilateralist into a global multilateralist?" Anand Mahindra, vice chairman and managing director of Mahindra & Mahindra, argues that to be a truly global organization, it is not the percentage of sales from overseas markets that matters, but outlook:

> *I say that it is a mind-set more than anything else. I realized you come to the point of being a multinational when your reflexes, your thought processes, and the processes in your company are global— when your processes reflexively are global. For example, when we are looking for a new head of R&D, we have a talent management process like large companies do and the database search throws up a list of internal talent. When I looked at this list I got two Chinese names and one German name. That to me is reflexive multinational thinking.*[42]

But as India's global powerhouses confront and overcome the global mind-set challenge, they may become like Sony, or at least Toyota or Samsung—considered more truly "multinational" than a company that is referred to as, say, a "Japanese multinational" or a "Korean multinational." True, strong values from the home country always linger at the heart of any multinational corporation, but in the brain, such companies are global in how they view their resources and opportunities.

To become a truly global corporation, a company has to transcend the home country advantage. In India, this is happening with the "born global" IT companies, such as Infosys, Wipro, and TCS, that are making their first steps toward this global future. The Japanese companies, like Toyota, learned to make cars in the United States and France without Japanese workers. Similarly, Indian software companies are learning to outsource without Indian workers as they set up operations in other countries where they can tap into pools of foreign workers in the face of talent constraints in India. They must clone their Indian back offices in unfamiliar nations and manage Canadian, Chinese, Filipino, Mexican, Polish, and Saudi workers to be more productive than their respective local outsourcing companies could make them.[43] This will become their future source of competitive advantage, not the cheap pool of Indian software engineers.

An American bank wanted a computer system to handle loans in Spanish for Hispanic customers. Given the unique needs of Hispanic clients, the bank thought it best to have a Mexican team develop such a system as it would have the right language skills as well as a grasp of the cultural nuances. But instead, Infosys, which had recently opened a facility in Monterrey, Mexico, was selected rather than a Mexican vendor or an American vendor with Mexican operations. The result is that a company in the United States is hiring an Indian firm seven thousand miles away to supply it with Mexican engineers working one hundred fifty miles south of the U.S. border.

This is how India's global powerhouses increasingly will operate— by bringing new capabilities to the world of business. Indian and Chinese companies will not be content, and in fact will not be able, to remain forever in the low-cost position. They will move up the value chain and adopt disciplines like innovation and branding. The Japanese and Koreans both started in this low-cost manner and their global companies have moved up over time. Why would this not be the right trajectory for India's global powerhouses? Therein lies the forthcoming challenge from India's global powerhouses to the multinationals from the developed world, who rule today. A change in leadership is coming, and the baton has to be handed over. Future lists of the five hundred largest global companies will increasingly have an Indian and Chinese presence. The world of business—and, more importantly, the world's customers—will be better for it.

NOTES

Introduction

1. Arun Prabhudesai, "Indian Mergers and Acquisitions: The Changing Face of Indian Business," August 16, 2007, http://trak.in/tags/business/2007/08/16/indian-mergers-acquisitions-changing-indian-business/.

2. Joe Leahy, "Deal Frenzy Shows Few Signs of Cooling Off," *Financial Times,* January 25, 2008, 5.

3. "Marauding Maharajahs," *Economist,* March 31, 2007, 85–86.

4. "Tested Mettle," *Economist,* July 28, 2007, 74.

5. Sudeshna Sen, "Indian Cos Rank No. 2 Among Foreign Employers in Britain," *Economic Times,* July 4, 2008, http://economictimes.indiatimes.com/articleshow/articleshow/3194776.cms.

6. Clay Chandler, "India's Global Reach," *Fortune* (Europe edition), October 29, 2007, 64.

7. The two observations of the developed world as having declining domestic markets and being high-margin markets may seem contradictory. But while there is very little growth in the developed markets, prices are still relatively high compared to the developing markets. Therefore, for companies from the developing world with their low costs, the developed world seems to have attractive, high-margin markets.

8. John Elliot, "Manufacturing Takes Off," *Fortune* (Europe edition), October 29, 2007, 77–83.

9. "Rise of the New Business Powers," *Financial Times Weekend,* June 28–29, 2008, 14.

10. C. K. Prahalad has made this point several times.

11. B. G. Shirsat, "Infy, TCS, Wipro: World's Top 3 IT Firms by Market Cap," October 3, 2006, http://inhome.rediff.com/money/2006/oct/03it.htm.

12. Joe Leahy, "Western IT Consultancies Take the Fight to India," *Financial Times,* June 5, 2007, 6.

13. Amy Yee, "Moving Up the Value Chain," *Financial Times,* January 24, 2008, 4.

14. Anand Giridharadas, "Outsourcing Moves to the Front Office," *International Herald Tribune,* April 4, 2007, 10.

15. Anil K. Gupta and Haiyan Wang, "How to Get China and India Right," *Sloan Management Review,* April 27, 2007, http://sloanreview.mit.edu/wsj/insight/global/2007/04/27/01/.

16. The Anglo-Dutch Unilever in early 2008 was headed by Frenchman Patrick Cescau, and he had no British or Dutch nationals on his multinational executive team.

17. Giridharadas, "Outsourcing Moves to the Front Office."

18. "Emerging Giants," *BusinessWeek,* July 31, 2006.

19. "What's Holding India Back," *Economist,* March 8, 2008, 11.

20. "Multinationals in Asia: All Mouth and No Trousers," *Economist,* March 31, 2007, 86.

21. Joe Leahy, "India Overtakes Japan in Turner's Asia Sales," *Financial Times,* April 14, 2008, 22.

22. Heather Timmons and Somini Sengupta, "Foreigners Scrambling to Sell India New Arms," *International Herald Tribune,* August 31, 2007, 1.

23. "Citigroup Finds the Brightest Star of a Bright Region," *Financial Times,* India and Globalisation insert, January 25, 2008, 4.

24. Yee, "Moving Up the Value Chain."

25. Adrian Michaels, "Luxury Producers Told Not to Neglect US," *Financial Times,* February 16, 2008, 9.

26. Andrew Parker, "Upwardly Mobile," *Financial Times,* February 11, 2008, 9.

27. Ibid.

28. Fareed Zakaria, *The Post-American World* (New York: W. W. Norton, 2008), makes the same point with illustrative newspaper headlines from the turn of the previous century.

29. Roger Cohen, "The Baton Passes to Asia," *International Herald Tribune,* March 31, 2008, 6.

30. "Taking Flight," *Economist,* September 8, 2007, 65.

31. Searched on Expedia, June 18, 2008, for direct flights departing London on June 21 and returning June 24.

32. Martin Fackler, "Japanese Look to India as Model in Education," *International Herald Tribune,* January 2, 2008, 11.

33. "Dutch Quell School Hours Protest," BBC News, November 27, 2007, http://news.bbc.co.uk/1/hi/world/europe/7115847.stm.

34. This poll was reported in Zakaria, *The Post-American World,* where a similar argument about the change in world power positions is articulated.

35. Peter Aspden, "French Film, Global Culture," *Financial Times,* July 12, 2008, Life & Arts insert, 12.

36. Nicolai Ouroussoff, "In Changing Face of Beijing, a Look at the New China," *New York Times,* July 13, 2008, 1.

37. Cohen, "The Baton Passes to Asia."

38. All quotes from these executives that are not explicitly referenced to a published source were gleaned from our interviews.

39. The majority of the interviews were conducted face to face with all three of us present. However, for logistical reasons, sometimes an interview had to be conducted by one or two of us. In exceptional cases (Harsh Mariwala, Tulsi Tanti, and a couple of TCS executives), the interviews were conducted over the telephone.

40. Ravi Ramamurti and Jitendra V. Singh also include ArcelorMittal with the following explanation: "Perhaps the best Indian example is Arcelor-Mittal, if because of Lakshmi Mittal's national origin, one can count it as Indian. At any rate, Arcelor-Mittal seems to have inspired Indian companies." Ravi Ramamurti and Jitendra V. Singh, "Generic Strategies of India's Emerging Multinationals," in *Emerging Multinationals from Emerging Markets,* eds. Ravi Ramamurti and Jitendra V. Singh (Cambridge, UK: Cambridge University Press, forthcoming 2009).

41. Ramamurti and Singh, "Generic Strategies of India's Emerging Multinationals."

Chapter One

1. Fareed Zakaria, *The Post-American World* (New York: W. W. Norton, 2008).

2. See Paul Kennedy, *The Rise and Fall of the Great Powers: Economic Change and Military Conflict 1500–2000* (New York: Random House, 1987).

3. See http://en.wikipedia.org/wiki/Thomas_Babbington_Macaulay.

4. Tarun Khanna and Yishay Yafeh, "Business Groups in Emerging Markets: Paragons or Parasites?" *Journal of Economic Literature* 45, no. 2 (2007): 331–372.

5. Ben L. Kedia, Debmalya Mukherjee, and Somnath Lahiri, "Indian Business

Groups: Evolution and Transformation," *Asia Pacific Journal of Management* 23, no. 4 (2006): 559–577.

6. This section describing the traditional business model is based on many conversations between the author and his late father. Given its sensitive nature, despite being widely known in upper echelons of Indian business circles, this model was never really documented in the press as far as we know. And, of course no one will go on record.

7. Khanna and Yafeh, "Business Groups in Emerging Markets: Paragons or Parasites?"

8. Pankaj Ghemawat and Tarun Khanna, "The Nature of Diversified Business Groups," *Journal of Industrial Economics* 46 (1998): 35–61.

9. Kedia, Mukherjee, and Lahiri, "Indian Business Groups: Evolution and Transformation."

10. See Kedia, Mukherjee, and Lahiri, "Indian Business Groups: Evolution and Transformation," and Khanna and Yafeh, "Business Groups in Emerging Markets: Paragons or Parasites?"

11. Kedia, Mukherjee, and Lahiri, "Indian Business Groups: Evolution and Transformation."

12. Jagdish N. Bhagwati and T. N. Srinivasan, *Foreign Trade Regimes and Economic Development: India* (New York: NBER, 1975).

13. B. Elango and Chinmay Pattnaik, "Building Capabilities for International Operations Through Networks: A Study of Indian Firms," *Journal of International Business Studies* 38, no. 4 (2007): 541–555.

14. Sanjaya Lall, "The Emergence of Third World Multinationals: Indian Joint Ventures Overseas," *World Development* 10, no. 2 (1982): 127–146.

15. All data from Lall, ibid.

16. Montek S. Ahluwalia, "Economic Reforms in India Since 1991: Has Gradualism Worked?" 2002, http://planningcommission.nic.in/aboutus/speech/spemsa/msa008.doc.

17. Eric D. Beinhocker, Diana Farrell, and Adil S. Zainulbhai, "Tracking the Growth of India's Middle Class," *McKinsey Quarterly,* August 2007, http://www.mckinseyquarterly.com/Economic_Studies/Country_Reports/Tracking_the_growth_of_Indias_middle_class_2032?gp=1.

18. Ibid.

19. Paromita Shastri, "319 Million Indians Live on Less Than a Dollar a Day: Report," http://www.livemint.com/2007/11/07000102/319-million-Indians-live-on-le.html.

20. J. Bradford DeLong, "Preliminary Thoughts on India's Economic Growth," April 2001, http://econ161.berkeley.edu/TotW/India.html.

21. Ibid.

22. John Elliot, "Manufacturing Takes Off," *Fortune* (Europe edition), October 29, 2007, 80.

23. "Face Value: Ram Drive," *Economist,* August 23, 2008, 59.

24. Anuradha Raghunathan, "Anand Mahindra's Great Global Dreams," *Forbes,* April 19, 2006, http://www.rediff.com/money/2006/apr/19forbes.htm.

25. Elliot, "Manufacturing Takes Off."

26. S. D. Naik, "Decade of Corporate Churning and Change," *Hindu Business Line,* July 31, 2001, http://www.thehindubusinessline.com/businessline/2001/07/31/stories/043120ma.htm.

27. Kedia, Mukherjee, and Lahiri, "Indian Business Groups: Evolution and Transformation."

28. Baba Kalyani of Bharat Forge, interview by authors, February 5, 2007.

29. Raghunathan, "Anand Mahindra's Great Global Dreams."

30. The Ranbaxy example comes from Christopher Bartlett and Sumantra Ghoshal, "Going Global," *Harvard Business Review,* March 2000, 132–141.

31. http://www.ranbaxy.com/aboutus/aboutus.aspx.

32. Anand Mahindra of Mahindra & Mahindra, interview by authors, February 7, 2007.

33. Megha Bahree, "Palatial Pieces," *Forbes,* July 5, 2007, http://www.forbes.com/business/global/2007/0507/026.html.

34. Ravi Ramamurti and Jitendra V. Singh, "Generic Strategies of India's Emerging Multinationals," in *Emerging Multinationals from Emerging Markets,* eds. Ravi Ramamurti and Jitendra V. Singh (Cambridge, UK: Cambridge University Press, forthcoming 2009).

35. Nandan Nilekani of Infosys, interview by authors, December 21, 2006.

36. Anand Mahindra of Mahindra & Mahindra, interview by authors, February 7, 2007.

37. Lall, "The Emergence of Third World Multinationals: Indian Joint Ventures Overseas."

38. Zakaria, *The Post-American World.*

Chapter Two

1. For this chapter we interviewed Aditya Mittal of ArcelorMittal.

2. "The World's Billionaires," *Forbes,* May 3, 2008, http://www.forbes.com/lists/2008/10/billionaires08_Lakshmi-Mittal_R0YG.html.

3. ArcelorMittal Corporate Page, http://www.arcelormittal.com.

4. Douglas Frantz, "Temirtau Journal; Steel Company Buys a Mill, Gets a Kazakh Town," *New York Times,* August 1, 2001, http://query.nytimes.com/gst/fullpage.html?res=9502EFDB1F3DF932A3575BC0A9679C8B63.

5. Malay Mukherjee currently sits on the board of directors of ArcelorMittal. http://www.forbes.com/finance/mktguideapps/personinfo/FromPersonIdPerson-Tearsheet.jhtml?passedPersonId=916697.

6. "How Mittal Steel Proved Its Mettle in a Tough Marketplace," November 30, 2005, http://knowledge.wharton.upenn.edu/article.cfm?articleid=1314.

7. Abhijit Sinha, "Mittal's Master Stroke: Building Global Empire Through Acquisitions," case study (ICFAI Business School, 2007).

8. ArcelorMittal company brochure.

9. Sinha, "Mittal's Master Stroke: Building Global Empire Through Acquisitions."

10. ArcelorMittal Corporate Page, http://www.arcelormittal.com.

11. See "History of Mittal Steel" at http://www.arcelormittal.com.

12. See ArcelorMittal Corporate Page, http://www.arcelormittal.com.

13. Sinha, "Mittal's Master Stroke: Building Global Empire Through Acquisitions."

14. Anne-Marie Cagna, "The Steel War: Mittal vs. Arcelor," case study (INSEAD, 2007).

15. "Arcelor Up in Arms," *Economist,* April 29, 2006.

16. Cagna, "The Steel War: Mittal vs. Arcelor."

17. Iron & Steel Statistics Bureau, 2008.

18. Ibid.

Chapter Three

1. For this chapter we interviewed Nandan Nilekani of Infosys; Rajesh Hukku of i-flex solutions; P. V. Kannan of 24/7; Azim Premji and Sundip Nandy of Wipro; Ganesh

Natarajan of NASSCOM; and S. Ramadorai, S. Mahalingam, N. Chandrasekaran, and S. Padmanabhan of TCS.

2. Latest figures (2008) from NASSCOM (National Association of Software and Services Companies), an Indian IT industry organization. NASSCOM was established in 1988 to facilitate business and trade across the country's software and services industries. The association has over 1,200 members, which include 250 global companies, www.nasscom.org.

3. Infosys, July 17, 2006, http://www.daijiworld.com/news/news_disp.asp?n_id=24129&n_tit=News+headlines.

4. Infosys, *Annual Report*, 2008.

5. Simon Robinson, "Meritocracy Is the Model," *Time*, December 13, 2007.

6. Justin Doebele, "The Softest Pillow," *Forbes*, February 9, 2002, http://www.forbes.com/global/2002/0902/036_print.html.

7. "Infosys' Long Journey to Success," *Indian Express*, July 29, 2006, http://www.expressindia.com/news/fullstory.php?newsid=71740#compstory.

8. NASSCOM, 2008.

9. "Understanding the New Grip of Vendor Polarization," Forrester Research report, June 2008.

10. Revenues for fiscal year ending March 31, 2008, press release, http://www.tcs.com/news_events/press_releases/Pages/TCSclocksRs22863cr57billioninrevenuesinFY08.aspx.

11. Revenues for fiscal year ending March 31, 2008, press release, http://www.wipro.com/analyst_report_mar_08/US_GAAP_Press_Release-Q4-FY08.pdf.

12. http://www.forbes.com/lists/2008/10/billionaires08_Azim-Premji_1UFS.html.

13. http://www.oracle.com/corporate/acquisition.html.

14. "i-flex Income at Rs 416 Crore," *Financial Express*, May 6, 2008, http://www.financialexpress.com/news/iflex-income-at-Rs-416-crore/306280/.

15. See the "FLEXCUBE Suite of Products" at http://www.iflexsolutions.com/iflex/company/Summary.aspx?mnu=p1s1.

16. "Rajesh Hukku," June 9, 2003, http://www.businessweek.com/magazine/content/03_23/b3836613.htm.

17. Tim Weber, "Earning IT Money the Indian Way," December 14, 2004, http://news.bbc.co.uk/1/hi/business/4071369.stm.

18. "Rajesh Hukku," http://www.time.com/time/2003/survivors/hukku.html.

19. Gartner Inc. The web address where the report is referenced: http://www.destinationcrm.com/Articles/CRM-News/Daily-News/Worldwide-Outsourcing-Market-to-Grow-8.1%-in-'08-47196.aspx.

20. Simon Crompton, "India's Rise in Medical Tourism," *Times* (London), August 14, 2007, http://travel.timesonline.co.uk/tol/life_and_style/travel/destinations/india/article2257994.ece.

21. V. M. Sundaram, "Pharma Industry in India," *Drugs News Perspect*, January–February 2008, http://www.ncbi.nlm.nih.gov/pubmed/18301810.

22. Neelam Verjee and Archna Shukla, "Finally, a Hollywood Movie Made in India," *Mint*, April 26, 2008, 1.

23. Nandini Lakshman, "Is India's Diamond Industry Losing Its Luster?" *BusinessWeek*, May 31, 2007, http://www.businessweek.com/globalbiz/content/may2007/gb20070531_362724.htm.

24. Jonathan Allen, "Mumbai Seeks a Role as Diamond Capital," *International Herald Tribune*, July 14, 2008, 18.

Chapter Four

1. For this chapter we interviewed Baba N. Kalyani of Bharat Forge.

2. For an account of this transformation, we are indebted to an excellent source provided by J. Ramachandran and Sourav Mukherji, Bharat Forge Limited, "Forging Leadership," case study (Indian Institute of Management, 2005).

3. This data from MOST-Inquire is reported in the case study by Ramachandran and Mukherji, "Forging Leadership."

4. This data from J. P. Morgan is reported in the case study by Ramachandran and Mukherji, "Forging Leadership."

Chapter Five

1. For this chapter we interviewed Ashok Goel and R. Chandrasekhar of Essel Propack.

Chapter Six

1. For this chapter we interviewed Kumar Mangalam Birla, Debu Bhattacharya, and Santrupt Misra of the Aditya Birla Group.

2. M. Anand, "Hindalco-Novelis: The (Scary) Untold Story," *Business World Magazine,* February 26, 2007.

3. $US 1 = approximately 41 INR in mid 2007.

4. Anand, "Hindalco-Novelis: The (Scary) Untold Story."

5. Hindalco, *Annual Report,* 2006–2007.

Chapter Seven

1. For this chapter we interviewed Anand Mahindra of Mahindra & Mahindra.

2. Peter Engardio, "Emerging Giants," *BusinessWeek,* July 31, 2006.

Chapter Eight

1. For this chapter, we interviewed Nandan Nilekani of Infosys; Dilip Kapur of Hidesign; Dilip G. Piramal, Sudhir Jatia, and Suresh Menon of VIP Industries; Adi Godrej of Godrej Group; and Harsh Mariwala of Marico.

2. No Chinese, African, or Middle Eastern brand appears on the list either. "The 100 Top Brands," *BusinessWeek*/Interbrand, August 6, 2007, http://www.businessweek.com/pdfs/2007/0732_globalbrands.pdf.

3. Hidesign is also a contract manufacturer for various brand names, including Armani, Marlboro, and Replay.

4. Company information.

5. "The 100 Top Brands."

6. http://www.livemint.com/2007/11/21133404/13-Indian-firms-in-Asia8217.html?d=1; and http://www2.standardandpoors.com/spf/pdf/index/050907_GlobalChallengers.pdf.

7. B. K. Karanjia, *Godrej: A Hundred Years 1897–1997,* Vol I. (New Delhi: Penguin Books India/Viking, 1997).

8. http://www.godrejconsumerproducts.net/investors/Q2%20FY2007-08%20Result%20Communication.pdf.

9. For simplicity, *Scotch* refers to whiskey from Scotland, originating from wheat, whereas *whiskey* refers to any blend of molasses-based spirits.

10. Indian Brand Equity Foundation, http://www.ibef.org/artdisplay.aspx?tdy=1&cat_id=60&art_id=18661.

Chapter Nine

1. For this chapter, we interviewed Tulsi Tanti of Suzlon.

2. Kushan Mitra, "Is Suzlon Built to Last?" *Business Today*, May 21, 2006, http://archives.digitaltoday.in/businesstoday/20060521/features1.html.

3. All snapshot information from "Suzlon Fact Sheet," http://www.suzlon.com/FactSheet.html?cp=1_4.

4. Alka Kshirsagar, *Hindu Business Line*, May 26, 2007, http://www.thehindubusinessline.com/2007/05/26/stories/2007052602200200.htm.

5. Alex Halperin, "A Shift in Wind Power?" *Business Week*, November 21, 2005.

6. From BTM Consult ApS, March 2008, as reported by Suzlon to investors.

7. Tom Wright, "India's Windmill Empire Begins to Show Cracks," *Wall Street Journal*, April 18, 2008, 1.

8. From BTM Consult ApS, March 2008, as reported by Suzlon to investors.

9. Halperin, "A Shift in Wind Power?"

10. Wright, "India's Windmill Empire Begins to Show Cracks."

11. Joanna I. Lewis, "A Comparison of Wind Power Industry Development Strategies in Spain, India and China," report prepared for the Center for Resource Solutions, San Francisco, July 19, 2007.

12. Ibid.

13. Wright, "India's Windmill Empire Begins to Show Cracks."

Chapter Ten

1. For this chapter, we interviewed Ravi Kant, R. Gopalakrishnan, J. J. Irani, Alan Rosling, and R. K. Krishna Kumar of Tata Group.

2. Tarun Khanna and Krishna G. Palepu, "Emerging Giants: Building World-class Companies in Developing Countries," *Harvard Business Review*, October 2006, 60–69.

3. Pete Engardio, "The Last Rajah," *Business Week*, August 2, 2007, http://www.businessweek.com/globalbiz/content/aug2007/gb2007082_325502.htm.

4. Quoted on Tata Steel centenary Web site, http://www.tatasteel100.com/people/index.asp.

5. Engardio, "The Last Rajah."

6. Khanna and Palepu, "Emerging Giants."

7. Jena McGregor, "The World's Most Innovative Companies," *Business Week*, April 28, 2008, 62.

8. Joe Leahy, "Tata Digests Rich Diet of English Takeaways," *Financial Times*, April 1, 2008.

Chapter Eleven

1. Of course, this was true primarily for the Indian elites, not the poor masses on subsistence as the latter rarely, if ever, came into contact with the British.

2. "New Record: 94,563 Indian Students in US," *Times of India*, November 8, 2008, 4.

3. Milton Singer, *When a Great Tradition Modernizes: An Anthropological Approach to Indian Civilization* (London: Pall Mall Press, 1972).

4. "Charting the Rich," *Forbes,* March 24, 2008, 128.

5. Personal anecdote.

6. Sylvia Pfeifer and Amy Yee, "Winning Contracts Is Only the First Battle," *Financial Times,* February 16, 2008, 9.

7. Emma Smith, "Moving In to Sting the SUV Big Boys," *Sunday Times,* InGear insert, December 23, 2007, 6–7.

8. Joe Leahy, "Unleashed: Why Indian Companies Are Setting Their Sights on Western Rivals," *Financial Times,* February 7, 2007, 13.

9. Peter Marsh, "The Next Workshop of the World," *Financial Times,* July 3, 2007, 13.

10. Ibid.

11. Ibid.

12. Personal communication.

13. Reported in Peter Wonacott and Eric Bellman, "India Proves to Be a Rocky Market for Foreign Joint Ventures," *Wall Street Journal*, February 1, 2007, 18.

14. Peter Wonacott and Eric Bellman, "India Proves to be a Rocky Market for Foreign Joint Ventures," *Wall Street Journal*, February 1, 2007, 18.

15. Ibid.

16. Ibid.

17. "Wadias to Acquire Danone's Stake in Britannia," *Iris News Digest,* October 15, 2008, http://myiris.com/newsCentre/storyShow.php?fileR=20081015075728043&dir=2008/10/15&secID=livenews&code1=&code=.

18. Wonacott and Bellman, "India Proves to be a Rocky Market for Foreign Joint Ventures."

19. S. Mahalingam, CFO and executive director, TCS, interview with authors, December 18, 2006.

20. Santrupt Misra, director of HR, Aditya Birla Group, interview with authors, April 23, 2008.

21. Ibid.

Conclusion

1. "What's Holding India Back," *Economist,* March 8, 2008, 11.

2. Eion Callan and Andrew England, "Egypt Leads in Cutting Red Tape," *Financial Times,* September 26, 2007, 12.

3. Joe Leahy, "Riches Rise from Poverty in Mumbai Slum Clearance," *Financial Times,* May 6, 2008, 6.

4. "Doing Business 2008: Five Years of Doing Business Reforms," http://www.doingbusiness.org/Features/Feature-2008-22.aspx.

5. This argument was made rather well by Sunanda K. Datta-Ray, "Burning Supermarkets: Why Indians Fight Modernization," *International Herald Tribune,* September 11, 2007, 8.

6. "Wal-Mart in India," *Wall Street Journal Europe,* August 13, 2007, 9.

7. Ibid.

8. Joe Leahy, "A Passage Through India," *Financial Times,* June 30, 2008, 11.

9. Somini Sengupta, "No Salve for Growing Pains in Bangalore," *International Herald Tribune,* May 22, 2008, 2.

10. Leahy, "A Passage Through India."

11. Joe Leahy, "India Warned on Power Capacity," *Financial Times*, June 4, 2008, 12.

12. Jo Johnson, "How Justice Is Delayed and Denied in India," *Financial Times*, September 6, 2007, 11.

13. Ibid.

14. Ibid.

15. "CJI Is Silent on PM's Corruption in Gov't Remark," *Times of India*, April 20, 2008, 8.

16. Anand Giridharadas, "Struggling at Home, Tata Succeeds Abroad," *International Herald Tribune*, September 5, 2008, 14.

17. Emma Smith, "Moving In to Sting the SUV Big Boys," *Sunday Times*, InGear insert, December 23, 2007, 6–7.

18. Jo Johnson, "Indian Anger at US Business Snub to Tata," *Financial Times*, December 14, 2007, 12. Subsequently, Mr. Gorin recanted his remarks, saying he was misquoted.

19. Kumar Mangalam Birla, "New Frontiers, New Thinking," *Outlook Business*, May 5, 2007.

20. Ibid.

21. Joe Leahy, Amy Yee, Mure Dickie, and Geoff Dyer, "Bidding for Brands: India and China Acquire a Taste for Luxury," *Financial Times*, January 11, 2008, 13.

22. Guy de Jonquières, "Asian Companies Should Not Rush to Go Global," *Financial Times*, November 9, 2006, 14.

23. Philip Bowring, "A Closer Look at India," *International Herald Tribune*, February 9, 2008, 12.

24. Jonquières, "Asian Companies Should Not Rush to Go Global."

25. Ibid.

26. Joe Leahy, "Deal Frenzy Shows Few Signs of Cooling Off," *Financial Times*, January 25, 2008, 5.

27. "Extending India's Global Leadership of IT and BPO industries," NASSCOM-McKinsey Report 2005, http://www.mckinsey.com/locations/india/mckinseyonindia/pdf/NASSCOM_McKinsey_Report_2005.pdf.

28. "Gravity's Pull," *Economist*, December 15, 2007, 75–76.

29. "Global Gender Gap," *Time*, November 26, 2007, 14–15.

30. Azim Premji, speech presented at Aditya Birla India Centre Distinguished Speaker Series (London: London Business School, November 3, 2006).

31. "India Inc. Facing Diversity Test," *Economic Times*, December 31, 2007.

32. "Stepping Out," *Economist*, April 5, 2008, 77.

33. Dean Nelson, "The Reverse Raj," *Sunday Times*, March 30, 2008, 14.

34. Ibid.

35. Adi Godrej, interview by authors, December 20, 2006.

36. Kumar Mangalam Birla, interview by authors, September 30, 2008.

37. Premji, speech.

38. "Leapfrogging or Piggybacking?" *Economist*, November 10, 2007, special report on technology in India and China, 5–9.

39. This analysis was reported in "Leapfrogging or Piggybacking?"

40. We are grateful to one of our reviewers for observing this.

41. "Transcending the Genre," *Economist*, November 10, 2007, special report on technology in India and China, 6.

42. Anand Mahindra, interview by authors, February 7, 2007.

43. Anand Giridharadas, "India Outsources Its Own Outsourcing," *International Herald Tribune*, September 25, 2007, 1.

INDEX

Note: Page numbers followed by "*f*" refer to figures; those followed by "*t*" refer to tables.

Nirmalya Kumar is Professor of Marketing, Director of the Centre for Marketing, and Co-Director of Aditya Birla India Centre at the London Business School.

Kumar has taught at Harvard Business School, IMD (Switzerland), and Northwestern University and has been the winner of several teaching honors over the years.

He has worked with more than fifty *Fortune* 500 companies in fifty different countries as a coach, seminar leader, and speaker on strategy and marketing. He has served on the board of directors of ACC, Ambuja Cements, Bata India, BP Ergo, Defaqto, and Zensar Technologies. He is frequently mentioned in the press, including *Business Week, Financial Times, International Herald Tribune,* and *Wall Street Journal,* and has appeared on the BBC, CNBC, and CNN.

A prolific writer, Kumar is the author of *Global Marketing* (BusinessWorld) as well as *Marketing as Strategy: Understanding the CEO's Agenda for Driving Growth and Innovation, Private Label Strategy: How to Meet the Store Brand Challenge* (with J.-B. Steenkamp), and *Value Merchants: Demonstrating and Documenting Superior Value in Business Markets* (with J. Anderson and J. Narus), all published by Harvard Business School Press.

Kumar has written more than forty cases and teaching notes, including on Amazon, Red Bull, Zara, and Wal-Mart, and has won three *Business Week*/ECCH awards for most adopted cases. In addition, he has published four articles for the *Harvard Business Review,* most recently "Strategies to Fight Low-Cost Rivals." Academic papers have appeared in *Academy of Management Journal, Journal of Marketing,* and *Journal of Marketing Research.* These articles have received more than fifteen hundred citations.

Pradipta K. Mohapatra is the Co-Founder and chairman of Executive & Business Coaching Foundation India Limited. His early career with the government and the multinational firm Dunlop gave him a enlightening ringside view of the oppressive socialist era. His long career on the board of India's $3 billion RPG Group put him at the center of an anxious and tentative India during early liberalization and a confident and globally emerging India thereafter. During the last decade his association on the boards of Indian joint ventures with EMI Music, Vodafone, Fujitsu, GlobalOne, and Jardines and their subsequent dissolution offered him some very unique experience in multicultural philosophies and styles of working. Mohapatra sits on the board of a number of companies around the world and undertakes significant public assignments at the national and regional level in organizations such as the Confederation of Indian Industries. His pioneering work in India's retailing and digital delivery industries has been documented in a number of case studies at IMD, Lausanne, and IIM, Ahmedabad.

Suj Chandrasekhar is President of Strategic Insights, a business strategy firm based in Washington, D.C. Chandrasekhar's main area of interest is the impact of globalization on organizational growth strategies as they relate to sales, marketing, and product development functions. She is a frequent speaker and presenter on these topics and has helped in the growth and restructuring of major corporations. Her interests also include leadership development and executive coaching.